Cuban Americans

FROM TRAUMA TO TRIUMPH

Twayne's Immigrant Heritage of America Series

Thomas J. Archdeacon, *General Editor*

Cuban Americans

FROM TRAUMA TO TRIUMPH

James S. Olson and Judith E. Olson

TWAYNE PUBLISHERS
An Imprint of Simon & Schuster Macmillan
New York

Prentice Hall International
London Mexico City New Delhi Singapore Sydney Toronto

Cuban Americans: From Trauma to Triumph
James S. Olson and Judith E. Olson

Copyright ©1995 by James S. Olson and Judith E. Olson

Twayne Publishers
An Imprint of Simon & Schuster Macmillan
866 Third Avenue
New York, New York 10022

Library of Congress Cataloging-in-Publication Data

Olson, James Stuart, 1946–
    Cuban Americans / James S. Olson and Judith E. Olson
        p.   cm.—(Twayne's immigrant heritage of America series)
    Includes bibliographical references and index.
    ISBN 0-8057-8430-6 — ISBN 0-8057-8439-X (pbk.)
        1. Cuban Americans—History.   I. Olson, Judith E.   II. Title.
    III. Series.
    E184.C97046 1995
    973´.04687291—dc20

                                                                94-34365
                                                                CIP

The paper used in this publication meets the minimum requirements of American National Standard for Information Sciences—Permanence of Paper for Printed Library Materials, ANSI Z39.48-1984. ∞ ™

10 9 8 7 6 5 4 3 2 1 (alk. paper)
10 9 8 7 6 5 4 3 2 1

Printed in the United States of America.

Contents

Ocean, which eventually evolved into colonial establishments in the Caroline Islands, the Marshall Islands, the Mariana Islands, and the Philippines. That same year Hernán Cortés moved into the Valley of Mexico and conquered Montezuma and the Aztec Empire. The Spanish conquest of Central America took place between the 1520s and the 1530s at the hands of people like Pedro de Alvarado, and in the 1530s Francisco Pizarro conquered the Inca empire. From those bases in New Spain, the Caribbean, and Peru, the Spanish empire expanded north into what is today Florida and the American Southwest; south and southeast into Chile, Bolivia, Paraguay, Argentina, and Uruguay; and north into Ecuador, Colombia, and Venezuela.

From its very inception, the Spanish empire was largely a top-heavy political enterprise governed directly, and absolutely, from the mother country. The imperial apparatus was heavy handed, with power resting in the hands of *peninsulares*—political appointees born in Spain who spent several years in the colonies as a means of moving up through the ranks of the civil service, the military, and the church. Spain discouraged the development of indigenous political institutions and a local political consciousness and tried to exercise all power, but nationalistic movements developed in the late eighteenth century in Mexico, Central America, and South America, and late in the nineteenth century in the Caribbean and the Philippines. By that time the Spanish economy had already entered its long period of decline, which eventually left Spain one of the poorest countries in Europe. Spain took thousands of tons of gold and silver out of Mexico and South America, but the riches bought pleasure for the Spanish nobility, the royal family, and the church, not an infrastructure or economic development for the country as a whole. Spanish mercantilist policy, which tried to centrally control every aspect of the colonial economies, eventually resulted in gross economic stagnation and decline. The Spanish population actually declined from eight million to six million people in the late sixteenth and seventeenth centuries. With a declining population and a shrinking economy, Spain could not sustain the empire it had been building since 1492.

During the Napoleonic Wars of the late eighteenth and early nineteenth centuries, Spain was for much of the time cut off from its New World colonies, and in the process the nationalists received a new sense of independence. Between 1810 and 1830 revolutions erupted throughout Latin America, and in the process Spain lost control of its colonies. When the political dust settled, Spain retained only Cuba, Puerto Rico, and its Pacific Ocean and African settlements. With its huge sugar plantations, Cuba became the heart, the "Pearl," of the empire, and Spain was determined to hold on to the island at all costs. But those dreams too were doomed. Cuban nationalists fought sporadically against Spanish rule until the 1890s, when full-scale revolution broke out. A similar revolution was occurring in the Philippines. Those revolutions merged with the Spanish-American War in 1898, at which point the United States arrived on the scene. Spain suffered a humiliating defeat at the hands of the United States, and in the subsequent treaty, the United States assumed a protectorate over Cuba, seized Guam and Puerto Rico, and purchased the Philippines. In 1899 Spain sold the remaining Mariana Islands and the Marshall Islands to Germany.

Spain's once vast, global empire had been reduced to practically nothing. But in human history, the fall of one superpower is usually accompanied by the rise of another. The Spanish empire was no more, but the United States was acquir-

Cuban Americans in Miami use the screening of the 1961 film *Mein Kampf* to protest Cuba's Communist regime, likening Castro to Hitler.

ing one. The acquisition of the Philippines, Guam, and Puerto Rico, along with the establishment of the Platt Amendment over Cuba, was only the beginning. Through sheer economic strength and a variety of noncolonial but nevertheless imperial institutions, the United States managed to establish its influence over much of the earth in the twentieth century. Although the Cuban upper class had long been integrated into the American economy, enjoying the perquisites of money, power, and influence that the United States provided, the lower classes felt exploited and excluded. For them, the Cuban revolution against Spain had been stillborn when the United States intervened; Cuba simply replaced one master with another, and the lower classes still found themselves under the political, economic, and social control of the old-line Cuban elites. Late in the 1950s Fidel Castro took advantage of that resentment and launched the revolution that drove the United States, as well as that Cuban elite, off the island, creating a large, influential Cuban-American community. By that time, of course, the world was engaged in a new struggle for global power, a cold war between the democratic capitalism of the United States and the totalitarian communism of the Soviet Union and the People's Republic of China—and of Fidel Castro's Cuba. Once again, Cuba found itself at the vortex of an international power struggle—this time between the United States and the Soviet Union.

Throughout their history, Cuban Americans have maintained an ongoing, intimate connection with the mother country. They are not, of course, the only

immigrant group to nurture a close relationship with home. Most first-generation immigrants welcomed news from home, read ethnic-language newspapers
describing life in the Old World, and took sides in Old World political disputes. A
deep interest has been particularly acute among such groups as the Arabs, Poles,
Jews, Puerto Ricans, French Canadians, Mexicans, Chinese, and Japanese. But
no group of immigrants has followed so closely the affairs of the mother country
as the Cubans. Part of that relationship was simply a matter of geography.
Havana was just 90 miles from Key West, Florida—a one-day cruise on a
steamship. By the 1920s there were 40 steamers and ferries operating weekly
between New York, Key West, Jacksonville, New Orleans, and Havana. It was
easy and inexpensive to visit relatives and to have relatives come to the United
States for a visit, and that ease made for strong political and cultural connections. But there was also a powerful economic connection between Cuba and
the United States. Throughout the twentieth century, the Cuban economy was
increasingly integrated into the orbit of the U.S. economy, creating a symbiotic
relationship that made Cubans on both sides of the Straits of Florida highly
dependent on one another. Finally, those ties were heavily political. Throughout
the émigré and immigrant communities of the United States, Cuban politicians—from upper-class *criollos* to revolutionaries—organized and lobbied for
political and economic support, hoping to remake Cuba in their own image.

For most immigrants in the United States, the mother country gradually
became more and more remote and less and less relevant, especially to their
children. The Old World for them was simply the recollections and nostalgic
reminiscences of their parents and grandparents. But it was not so for the
Cubans. They could almost see the island from Florida, and it was rarely out of
their minds. All of them had close friends and family members still living in
Cuba, and as the Cuban economy deteriorated in the 1960s, 1970s, and 1980s
and the suffering of Cuban citizens increased, the sympathies and the political
consciousness of Cuban Americans were raised. They also harbored a good deal
of pain and a great deal of resentment for what had happened to them there.
Life in Cuba retained an immediacy for them and served as a passionate force
that continued to shape their cultural and ethnic identity.

one

Ethnogenesis: The Origins of Cuban Culture

Geography and history, not simply coincidence, create destiny, and it was Spain and Portugal that first transcended the insular perspective of medieval Europe and looked across the Atlantic Ocean toward the New World. Their vision would eventually change the world. Bordering the Atlantic and the Mediterranean, Spanish and Portuguese commercial life revolved around the maritime trade with Africa, Northern Europe, England, and the Middle East. From their western outpost on the Iberian Peninsula, the Spanish and Portuguese were the closest to the African coast and to the Canary, Azore, and Cape Verdean islands that became points of departure for the great voyages of exploration and conquest in the fifteenth and early sixteenth centuries. Ever since the early 1400s Spanish and Portuguese vessels had been sailing west and southwest to those islands, conquering the native peoples and transplanting their own social, political, and economic institutions. From there they looked west and south; Spain and Portugal already possessed the naval expertise and the geographic expectations to take advantage of their imagination and passion. The two Iberian powers would take the lead in the imperial enterprise.

But it was that passion and vision, more than maritime skills and geographic experience, that drove the Portuguese south down the coast of Africa and the Spaniards west across the Atlantic. In the eighth century, the Moslem invaders from North Africa began their march across Iberia, and for the next 700 years Spanish Catholics fought a righteous crusade against them. The holy war of the Reconquista gave Spain a reverence for honor, self-respect, courage, integrity, and personal expression. They also had an overpowering conviction that Roman Catholicism was the one true faith and that it was their solemn, moral duty to impose it on the rest of the world. Finally, the Reconquista bequeathed to sixteenth-century Spanish culture a spirit of aggressive adventure and bold opportunism, and it was those feelings that made the conquistadors so successful in the great overseas enterprise.[1]

Finally, in addition to maritime skills, religious conviction, and personal zeal, Spain had the political and financial resources to embark on global conquests. Spain was the first of the European nations to emerge from the decentralized political feudalism of the Middle Ages and to achieve nation-state status. In 1469 Isabella, heir to the throne of Castile, married Ferdinand, King of Aragon.

Her accession to the throne in 1474 united the two kingdoms and provided the impetus for the creation of modern Spain. With her husband, Isabella was responsible for directing the Reconquista. By 1492, with the capture of the Moorish stronghold of Granada, the reconquest was complete, and Isabella became convinced that Spain should expand its trade with Asia. She saw merit in the plan of Christopher Columbus to find a profitable trade route to the Far East by sailing west across the Atlantic.[2]

Columbus reached landfall on 12 October 1492. For nearly two weeks the three ships he commanded plied their way across the Caribbean, and on 28 October they sailed up a large river in Cuba. In his log Columbus wrote that he had "never beheld so fair a thing; trees all along the river, beautiful and green and different from ours, with flowers and fruits each according to their kind, and little birds which sing very sweetly."[3] Cuba was approximately 800 miles long and ranged in width from 160 miles in the east to only 25 miles near Havana. The coastal lowlands were pockmarked with mosquito-infested swamps, peat bogs, and mangrove trees, and heavy jungles covered the Zapata Peninsula. The Sierra Maestra covered southeastern Cuba, and the smaller Sierra Escambray and Sierra de los Organos ranges were farther west. In the central interior there were less fertile savannas covered with wire grass, shrubs, and pockets of palm trees and pines. The rainy season extended from May until October, making Cuba ideal for large-scale agriculture, especially in the western reaches where topsoil was often 20-feet deep.

Here, in what he thought was an Asian paradise, Columbus hoped to make contact with the fabled leaders of "Cipangu" and "Cathay"—Japan and China—and bring home to Spain some of the treasures described two centuries earlier by Marco Polo. Of course, he would also become a rich man himself. Columbus immediately began inquiring about the "Grand Khan," the Asian emperor he wanted to meet. When Indians produced a few bits of gold and told Columbus that they came from "Cubanacán," meaning mid-Cuba, the Admiral mistakenly thought they were saying "El Gran Can."[4] Columbus had no idea, nor would he ever know, that he had discovered a nearly 43,000-square-mile island in the Caribbean—a "New World"—and that the island was destined to become the strategic heart, and last major colonial entity, of the vast Spanish empire.

The people Christopher Columbus encountered were not exactly what he was expecting, although his initial response to the Indians of Cuba was positive and benign.[5] Although scholars disagree about the number of indigenous people living in Cuba in 1492, the consensus today is that they totaled approximately 100,000. At the end of the fifteenth century, Cuba was inhabited by three primary Indian groups: the Guanahatabey, Ciboney, and Taíno. A foraging people, the Guanahatabey lived in the forests of the far western tip of Cuba, migrating constantly in search of fruit, small game, fish, roots, and insects. The Spaniards found them to be hopelessly barbaric, a "savage people," in the words of Diego Velázquez.[6] They nursed no hopes that the Guanahatabey would lead them to wealth.

The other two Indian groups were Arawakan peoples. A peaceful, more technologically advanced group than the Guanahatabeys, the Arawaks had originated in South America and gradually spread throughout the Greater and Lesser Antilles in the thirteenth century. Before the arrival of Christopher Columbus and the Spaniards, the Arawakan Indians found themselves losing a struggle for survival with the more aggressive Karib Indians, who were expanding out of South America into the Lesser Antilles. The Karibs had already conquered the Lesser Antilles and were poised to assault the Arawakan peoples on the Greater Antilles when Columbus appeared on the scene. The arrival of the Spaniards stopped the Karib expansion into Cuba, Hispaniola, and Puerto Rico, even though there was sporadic warfare between Spanish settlers and Karib invaders during the first decades of the sixteenth century.[7] The Arawakan people of Cuba were divided into two primary groups: the Ciboney and the Taíno. The Ciboney maintained a foraging economy and lived in the western half of the island. Far more advanced than the Guanahatabey or the Ciboney were the Taínos, who lived in central and eastern Cuba. Unlike the other Cuban tribes, the Taínos raised manioc, tobacco, cotton, corn, potatoes, and yams. They lived in settled communities with complex social structures and were known for their pottery and textiles. The Taíno were the dominant indigenous group in Cuba and they were the people Columbus first encountered in Cuba.[8]

The Spanish conquest of Cuba, however, was still 20 years in the future. During Columbus's four voyages to the New World, the island of Hispaniola, just to the east of Cuba, became the center of Spanish colonization efforts. The Columbus family eventually established a political dynasty on Hispaniola, and the island became the base of operations for the Spanish conquest of the rest of the Greater Antilles.[9] When the lack of significant amounts of gold on Hispaniola became clear in the early 1500s, and when Indian population decline produced labor shortages, Spain began looking for new conquests. Not surprisingly, they cast their gaze across the Windward Passage to Cuba. Early in the 1500s, Spanish labor contractors and slavers were already raiding Cuba and forcibly seizing Taíno Indians, but in 1507 Spain decided it was time for a more systematic approach to the enterprise. Sebastián de Ocampo received a commission to explore the Cuban coast. During 1508 he became the first Spaniard to circumnavigate Cuba and prove it was an island and not an extension of the mainland.[10]

Diego Velázquez headed the expedition of conquest to Cuba. He landed at Baracoa in 1511 and then headed inland, defeating the Indian tribes and establishing settlements at Baracoa, Bayamo, Havana, Puerto Príncipe, Trinidad, and Santiago de Cuba. By 1514 he had pacified the natives, though he encountered heroic resistance, notably by Chief Hatuey. To consolidate his power, Velázquez used the *encomienda* system, which gave settlers the right to exploit Indian labor as payment for Christianizing and "protecting" them. The most valuable *encomiendas* went to Velázquez's closest associates. He served as governor until 1521, when a political dispute with Hernán Cortés led to his removal. Velázquez was restored to office in 1523 and died in 1524.[11]

Accompanying Velázquez's expedition was an obscure soldier who eventually became one of the Spanish empire's most important moral figures. Bartolomé de las Casas was born on 11 November 1484 in Seville, Spain. He participated in the conquest of Cuba and earned a fortune, but he was horrified by the Spaniards' treatment of the Indians, even though he noted that Velázquez had often tried to be even-handed. Las Casas returned to Spain, gave up his wealth, and at the age of 40 took vows in the Dominican order. In 1522 he wrote the first of his famous treatises in defense of the Indians, "A Very Brief Recital of the Destruction of the Indies." The work graphically and sometimes exaggeratedly detailed the aggressiveness, greed, cruelty, and sadism of the Spanish conquistadors and established Las Casas as Spain's most vocal spokesman for Indian rights.[12]

Although Las Casas's crusade may have benefited some of the indigenous people of the Spanish empire, it was too late for the Indians of Cuba. Unlike much of the rest of Latin America, a large, powerful mestizo culture—represented by people of mixed Spanish and Indian ancestry—did not appear in Cuba, and Indians were not destined to play a significant role in the emergence of Cuban culture. The Guanahatabey, Ciboney, and Taíno Indians were devastated by their contact with Spaniards. A severe population decline—precipitated by epidemics of smallpox, influenza, chicken pox, mumps, and measles—set in long before significant numbers of Spanish colonists arrived to develop the island. Although catastrophic demographic collapses occurred in Mexico and Peru during the sixteenth century, there was still significant intermarriage between Spaniards and Indians and the beginnings of the mestizo class, which would eventually become the majority group in both societies. But in Cuba the Indians were dying out before significant numbers of Spanish settlers arrived. By 1520, less than a decade after the beginning of Velázquez's expedition of conquest, severe shortages of Indian labor were already apparent. The native population dropped from 100,000 in 1492 to 19,000 in 1519 to 7,000 in 1531 and fewer than 3,000 in 1550.[13]

At the same time that Spanish officials in Hispaniola were beginning to look enviously at Cuba as a potential source of wealth, they were also surveying much of the rest of the Caribbean. Francisco Hernández de Córdoba arrived in Cuba in 1511, and the next year Diego Velázquez commissioned him to explore the Caribbean islands and mainland coast of Central America and the Gulf of Mexico, and between 1512 and 1518 Hernández conducted those explorations. He was wounded on the coast of Mexico in 1518 and died of his injuries later that year in Cuba. But before his death he sent back to Hispaniola news of rumored wealthy societies on the mainland, and in 1519 Hernán Cortés began his conquest of the Aztec Empire.[14]

The conquest of Mexico, and later of Peru, transformed the economy of Cuba. Cuba, rather than Hispaniola, became the economic and political base for the lucrative mainland enterprises. As the Taíno, Ciboney, and Guanahatabey Indians died, Spanish settlers took over the farming responsibilities and continued to grow primarily manioc, tobacco, cotton, corn, and potatoes. A small cattle industry developed on the rich grasslands, providing salted meat and hides for other Caribbean settlements, but it was as an "economic service" colony, rather than as a producer, that early Cuban entrepreneurs earned their wealth. Havana, with its fine harbor and strategic location along the Gulf Stream, served as the key port of call for treasure fleets returning to Europe. Havana became Cuba's governmental seat in 1538. The bullion-laden galleons attracted pirates. Pedro Menéndez de Aviles, who governed Cuba in the 1560s, improved the convoy system that guarded Spanish shipping and transformed the capital into a military bastion.[15]

But Cuba also became a backwater of the empire in the sixteenth century. Although Havana enjoyed some prosperity, most Spaniards found the island's climate unhealthy and economic opportunities quite limited. During the 1510s and 1520s, a few Spaniards enjoyed modest success panning for gold, but the huge discoveries of gold and silver in Mexico and Peru dwarfed the Cuban deposits in significance. In 1523 the Casa de la Contratación (House of Trade) in Seville provided financial assistance to a few landowners to transplant the sugar industry from its base in the Canary Islands to Cuba. To replace the dwindling supply of Indian workers, Cubans began importing African slaves in 1523, but even then economic as well as population growth was slow. By 1544 the total population of Cuba was only 6,500 people, consisting of approximately 700 Spaniards, 800 Africans, and 5,000 Indians. By 1600 the population was up to approximately 20,000 people, of whom fewer than 2,000 were Indians and 3,000 were Africans, but the island still paled in economic and political significance when compared with New Spain and Peru.[16] The vast majority of people in Cuba made their living as small farmers. It was on the mainland, not on the isles of the Caribbean, that the heart of the Spanish empire developed.

The island's political system reflected the values of the Spanish crown and the Roman Catholic church. In the political culture of late fifteenth- and early sixteenth-century Spain, sovereignty rested clearly in the monarchy, whose authority to rule was believed to be mandated by God. Nowhere else in Europe was the notion of the "divine right of kings" more thoroughly established. Political power flowed from the top down to the lowliest administrator, and there was no hint of popular sovereignty or democracy. The crown appointed all government and military officials in the colonies. Authoritarianism was celebrated as the only reliable way of governing. The upper classes exercised a political power that they believed came from God and the king—they had a "right to rule." That Spanish legacy of the right to rule was destined to condemn Latin American politics to the curse of dictatorial governments periodically replaced by rebellions and coups d'état, only to evolve once again into totalitarian dictatorships.

Geographic reality reinforced that authoritarianism. The Audiencia of Santo Domingo, the supreme legislative and judicial body for the Caribbean, was established in 1511, and Cuba was included in its jurisdiction. After 1535 the Audiencia of Santo Domingo fell under the jurisdiction of the new Viceroyalty of New Spain, which itself reported directly to the Council of the Indies. Theoretically, the governor of Cuba was subject to the Audiencia, the viceroy, and the council. In reality, however, the governor of Cuba had great discretionary power, even though the Audiencia worked diligently at limiting it. This was especially true after the conquests of New Spain and Peru had relegated the island to second-class status. The tradition of authoritarian rule, bequeathed to Cuba by the Spanish crown, was magnified by limits in the effectiveness of the imperial system of checks and balances.

Finally, there was no separation of church and state on the island. Political and religious authority fused in the *Patronato Real* (Royal Patronage), in which the pope gave the Spanish crown absolute control over the church in the New World. As historian Charles Gibson has written, "*Patronato Real* implied state domination over the church, but it simultaneously allowed for ecclesiastical intrusion into civil and political affairs. In the complexities of law and precedent it was impossible to say where church authority ceased and state authority began."[17] Under the protection of the state, the church acquired enormous power in Cuba. Blessed with the authority to collect the *diezmo*, or tithe, the church steadily acquired more and more property, a phenomenon that was augmented by donations of land to the church in the wills of thousands of deceased

Cubans. The church also rented out its land to peasant farmers, and the income produced by the rent augmented church wealth. As time passed, the Catholic Church in Cuba became a wealthy, conservative institution tied to the interests of the elite that dominated Cuban life.[18] The lower classes, although highly committed to the spirit of Roman Catholicism, were gradually more and more alienated from the institutional church. So both theoretically and practically, the Spanish empire amounted to a theocratic monarchy where political legitimacy revolved around an authoritarian model.

That political authoritarianism in the early colonial period was exaggerated by an ethnic phenomenon in Cuba in particular and throughout the empire in general. The most prominent bureaucratic, military, and clerical appointments in the Spanish colonies went to *peninsulares* (peninsulars)—individuals born in Spain. Most of them were temporary sojourners in the colonies, hoping to use their offices as stepping stones to influential appointments that would take them back to Spain. Those native Spaniards were a minority of the population in the early colonial period, but they wielded great influence. As time passed, however, they became an increasingly smaller minority, and their disproportionate power would eventually fuel the nineteenth-century revolutionary movement in Cuba. Just below the *peninsulares* were the *criollos* (creoles)—people of Spanish descent born in Cuba. Most of them were prosperous farmers or merchants in and around Havana, but they suffered from an increasing resentment of the *peninsulares*, who looked down on the *criollos* as a provincial, uneducated people. Although *criollos* often found positions in the lower bureaucracy, they were usually unable to secure more influential posts in the clergy, military, and colonial bureaucracy.

It was not surprising that native-born Spaniards constituted only a small minority of the Cuban population. Because of the 700-year occupation by the Moors of North Africa, Spanish society had been conditioned to dealing with dark-skinned people. Spanish explorers had also reached the Canary Islands in the early 1400s and conquered the dark-skinned Guanches. When they encountered the Indians in the New World, or when they imported Africans to work their fields, Spaniards found them different and sometimes exotic. There was a powerful color consciousness in Spanish culture, but they did not react as negatively as other Europeans did to the indigenous people of Africa and the Americas. Also, throughout the sixteenth century, there were very few Spanish women living in Cuba. In 1520 there were only a handful of Spanish women in Cuba, and as late as 1600 only 10 percent of the population of Cuba was female. The Spanish men living on the island, as well as the thousands of sailors who went in and out of Havana each year, usually took Indian and African women as wives, lovers, and temporary sexual liaisons. In the early years of the 1500s the mixed population that emerged out of these relationships was of Spanish-Indian descent.[19]

During the seventeenth and early eighteenth centuries, Cuba grew steadily. The population of the island increased from approximately 20,000 people in 1600 to 30,000 in 1660 and then to approximately 50,000 in 1700. The number of African slaves increased from 5,000 in 1660 to approximately 10,000 in 1700. The sugar and cattle industries continued to expand gradually, but tobacco production was the most dynamic sector of the economy during the seventeenth century. By the end of the 1500s, tobacco consumption in Europe began to increase geometrically, as did the number of tobacco farms in Cuba. Small farm-ers—Spaniards, Spaniard-Africans, and Africans—began to move inland from the base at Havana to plant more land in tobacco. As the tobacco farmers moved up the alluvial floodplains, new towns and villages appeared and the Cuban population became more dispersed. Tobacco production in Cuba increased from 2,000 tons annually in the 1730s to 5,500 tons in the late 1750s. Tobacco planters, known as *vegüeros*, became an increasingly powerful interest group in the Cuban economy.[20]

Another influential social group appeared during the seventeenth century. Unlike much of the rest of North and South America, Cuba developed a large class of free blacks. Sugar production was not nearly as intense in Cuba in the 1600s as it was on Hispaniola, Jamaica, and Puerto Rico, so the demand for cheap labor was not nearly as great. African slaves in Cuba enjoyed a legal dis-tinction unknown in most other parts of the empire. Early in the 1500s African slaves received the status of *coartación*—the right to negotiate their freedom. Slaves could save up to purchase their freedom or the freedom of their children, or they could arrange to pay out their owner in installments. The practice of *coartación* was more widely exercised in urban areas, where slaves knew of the law and where their opportunities for extra wage labor were greater, than in iso-lated rural areas where most of them were field hands. Slaves could not exercise the *coartación* until they had already served for seven years, but in most cases the emancipated slaves had been born in Cuba, not in Africa. By 1774 the total Cuban population had increased to 171,620 people. Of that number, more than 75,000 were of African descent and nearly 31,000 of them were free.[21]

Those free blacks came to constitute a large portion of the Cuban working class. Many of them became small-scale ranchers and *vegüeros*, settling in more remote areas of the island in order to raise cattle and tobacco. Other free blacks lived in towns and cities and worked as craftsmen, artisans, teamsters, construc-tion workers, and stevedores. Free black farmers and workers coexisted with working-class whites and mixed-race people, giving Cuban society and culture, at least within the Spanish empire, an unusual sociolegal mixture. To be sure, there was a sense of racial identity in early colonial Cuba, and that sense would become more intense with the large-scale importation of new African slaves in the nineteenth century. Unlike other areas of the Caribbean and North America, however, where the vast majority of black people were slaves functioning under the tight control of a tiny white minority, Cuba enjoyed a large group of free blacks who were politically and economically, if not socially, integrated into the larger society.

By the mid-eighteenth century the Cuban social structure had evolved its own class system. At the top was the *peninsular* elite. Closely related to them was a *criollo* elite who owned sizable estates for raising cattle, tobacco, and sugar, and who owned shipping and mercantile businesses. Their mercantile interests dom-inated commercial life in Havana. There was a middle class of small landowners and urban artisans, tradesmen, construction workers, and clerks, most of whom were Spanish in ancestry but who also included some free blacks and people of mixed ancestry. Beneath them was a lower class of landless peasants, wage laborers, and migratory workers who consisted of poor whites and large num-bers of free blacks. And at the bottom of the social structure were African-Cuban slaves who worked the sugar plantations.

But that mid-century social structure, along with the rest of Cuban life, was destined to change in the last half of the eighteenth century when Spain imposed mercantilist policies on the Cuban economy. In 1717, because of the profits being made off of the tobacco trade, the Spanish crown assumed the exclusive right to purchase all Cuban tobacco. They bought the tobacco at an artificially low price from Cuban planters and sold it in European markets at artificially high prices. The monopoly triggered a storm of protest from outraged planters who wanted to sell their crops at market prices. During the early 1720s a number of *vegüero* rebellions took place in Cuba against Spanish authority, and those rebellions had to be suppressed with military force. For the first time in Cuban history, local groups were protesting imperial policy. In 1740 Spain established the Havana Company, gave it a monopoly on the importation of slaves, and forced Cuban sugar, tobacco, and cattle producers to sell their entire crops to the company at government-mandated, below-market prices. It managed to stifle the Cuban economy and to further alienate the *criollo* elite from imperial policies.

Cuban merchants and landowners did not realize just how oppressive the imperial mercantilist policies were until 1762, when the British navy seized Havana during the Seven Years' War. Although the British controlled Havana for only 10 months, they virtually liberated its economy, abolishing trade duties and declaring the city a free port. Until 1762 an average of 15 vessels entered Havana each year, but during the British occupation that number increased to more than 1,000 vessels. Cuban farmers sold products at market prices, and European and American producers flooded Cuba with consumer goods. The Royal African Company brought 10,000 African slaves into the colony during an eight-month period. The end of the Seven Years' War in 1763 led to the withdrawal of British forces from Havana, but *criollo* merchants, planters, and ranchers would never again tolerate the imperialist policies of the past. Spanish mercantilism stifled the Cuban economy, but it also politicized the *criollo* class.[22]

It was not long after the end of the Seven Years' War that King Charles III of Spain launched a series of reforms that stimulated economic growth in Cuba and further sharpened the *criollo* identity. Charles III assumed the Spanish throne in 1759. Intelligent and deeply concerned about the future status of Spain, he was an enlightened ruler who proved to be the best of Spain's Bourbon kings. At home he tried to stimulate the economy, reduce the stifling power of the craft and merchant guilds, and improve the country's infrastructure through an ambitious program of public works. In 1767, concerned about the growing power and influence of the Jesuit order, Charles III expelled the Jesuits from the New World. He was not the first to take such a step. The Portuguese monarchy banned the Jesuits from Portugal in 1759 and from Brazil in 1760. The absolutist monarchs of Europe had long resented the tendency of Jesuits to interfere in secular political concerns, and in the Spanish and Portuguese colonies, Jesuit priests often aligned themselves with nationalist groups and with indigenous peoples. At the same time, Enlightenment intellectuals condemned Jesuits as too militant in their religious views. In 1773 Pope Clement XIV suppressed the Society of Jesus.[23]

The reign of Charles III had a dramatic impact on economic life in Cuba. In addition to unfettering the economy of Spain, Charles III wanted to modernize Spanish mercantilism. On 16 October 1765 Charles III gave Cuba and the other

Spanish possessions in the Caribbean access to the Spanish ports of Alicante, Barcelona, Cartagena, Gijón, la Coruña, Málaga, Santander, and Sevilla in addition to Cádiz. At the time Cádiz had a legal monopoly over the American trade. The islands were also permitted intercolonial trade in American products and, after 1774, in European goods. Louisiana received legal access to Havana in 1770, and that decision opened up Havana to the huge trade of the American hinterland that came down the Mississippi River to New Orleans. Other Spanish colonies soon gained similar privileges. The mercantilist deregulation reached its culmination in 1778 when Charles III issued the Free Trade Decree, which was designed to eliminate contraband, stimulate the imperial economy, and, through a larger volume of trade, increase tax revenues. For the next two decades the volume of trade and customs receipts increased dramatically. With the outbreak of the American Revolution in 1776, the port of Havana boomed as American products flowed in—lumber, manufactured goods, and foodstuffs—and as the delivery of slaves increased. In return, Cuban planters found new markets for their tobacco, molasses, and sugar. Once Spain formally joined in the war against Great Britain in 1779, the economic links between Cuba and the United States strengthened even more.[24]

The reforms of Charles III had a dramatic impact on Cuban society. Without the old state monopolies and mercantilist regulations, the Cuban economy boomed. Tobacco, cattle, and sugar production skyrocketed, as did the volume of commercial traffic in and out of Havana. *Criollo* political consciousness, fueled by the new prosperity as well as continuing domination of the Cuban military, church, and bureaucracy by *peninsulares*, sharpened even more. Newspapers representing *criollo* interests appeared in Havana: *Gazeta de la Habana* and *El Pensador* in 1764, *Gazeta de la Habana* in 1782, and *Papel Periódico* in 1791. That same year, leading landowners in Cuba established the Sociedad Económica (Economic Society) to disseminate the latest information on ways to improve cattle, sugar, tobacco, and mining production and to advocate increased liberalization of trade. By the 1790s Cuban *criollos* had become a self-conscious group in their own right, and they were more active than ever before in public affairs and more likely to protest Spanish or *peninsular* oppression. The liberalization of the imperial economy had brought in its wake a liberalization of the colonial political culture.

Cuban economic growth and the rising sense of Cuban identity were further stimulated by a population boom in the 1770s, 1780s, and 1790s. Between 1774 and 1791 the total population of Cuba increased from 171,620 people to 272,300 people. Large numbers of families migrated from Spain to Cuba to take advantage of the prosperity, and in the process the white population went from 96,440 to 153,559. Because of the continuing practice of *coartación*, the numbers of free blacks skyrocketed in those 17 years, from 30,847 to 54,151. Finally, free-trade policies made it much easier for planters to import slaves, who simply replaced those emancipated slaves on the plantation. Between 1774 and 1791 the number of Cuban slaves increased from 44,333 to 64,590.[25]

These social, economic, and demographic trends were dramatically accelerated in 1791 when the great slave rebellion erupted in St. Domingue, the large French sugar colony located on the western third of Hispaniola. At the beginning of the decade more than 500,000 African slaves were working the colony's coffee, cotton, and sugar plantations. St. Domingue produced 71,000 tons of sugar in 1791, compared with only 14,000 tons on Cuba. But the slave rebellions precipitated a decade of civil war that devastated agricultural production. A worldwide shortage of sugar developed, and between 1791 and 1795 sugar prices tripled. The coffee industry on Hispaniola was similarly disrupted, and coffee prices doubled. Approximately 30,000 French-speaking refugees fled St. Domingue for Cuba, and many of them brought money, slaves, and expertise in coffee and sugar production with them.[26]

Blessed with unprecedented demand, escalating prices, and worldwide shortages of sugar and coffee, Cuban farmers and planters went on a production binge. For the most part, the French refugees who had been coffee planters on St. Domingue transplanted their industry to eastern Cuba, primarily in the area around Santiago de Cuba and Guantánamo. There were only two coffee plantations in Cuba in 1774, but by 1802 that number had increased to 108 and to 1,315 in 1806. Twenty years later there were more than 2,000 coffee plantations in the region. Coffee production reflected the increased cultivation. In 1792 Cuba exported approximately 178,000 pounds of coffee, but in 1833 that volume had increased to 64,160,000 pounds. The increase in sugar production was equally dramatic. On the eve of the slave rebellions on St. Domingue, Cuba exported 15,423 tons of sugar, but that volume jumped to 28,761 tons in 1800 and 45,396 tons in 1815. Production nearly doubled to 84,187 tons in 1829 and doubled again to 161,248 tons in 1840.[27]

The agricultural revolution led inevitably to ecological and demographic revolutions in Cuba as well. In 1790 there were about 100 sugar plantations on Cuba and more than 10,000 acres in cultivation. By 1830 there were more than 1,000 plantations in Cuba and 500,000 acres under production. Planters laid waste to the Cuban forests in the early decades of the nineteenth century, permanently deforesting whole regions to provide land for sugar cultivation and wood to fuel the sugar processing mills. The number of mills increased from 424 in 1778 to 1,442 in 1846. Sugar production spread throughout the country as planters bought up tobacco land and cattle ranches and converted them to sugar. Although the areas in the west around Pinar del Río and San Cristobal remained in tobacco production, sugar production took over whole sections of western and central Cuba, where the soil was so rich. On a smaller scale it also penetrated eastern Cuba.[28]

The sugar and coffee boom also triggered a demographic revolution. Sugar production was labor intensive, and the demand for African slaves became insatiable. Between 1791 and the early 1860s sugar planters imported more than 832,000 slaves into Cuba, but by 1862 there were only about 350,000 slaves in Cuba. Part of that decline can be explained by the continuing practice of *coartación*, in which slaves earned their freedom. The free black population of Cuba increased from about 114,000 people in 1817 to more than 232,000 in 1861. Much of that, of course, was the result of natural growth, but *coartación* was still in operation. The slave population, on the other hand, was unable to sustain itself. The work was so harsh and debilitating—18-hour days, six-day weeks— that life expectancy was only seven years after arriving in Cuba. It was not at all uncommon for plantations to lose up to 10 percent of their slaves every year, creating a constant, and feverish, demand for replenishment. In 1821 Spain and England had signed an agreement prohibiting the importation of any more African slaves into Cuba, but Spanish authorities and planters regularly ignored the agreement. When Great Britain began to actively suppress the international slave trade, it became increasingly difficult for Cuban planters to acquire new slaves. They worked desperately at smuggling in the slaves they needed, but as the anti–slave trade campaign of the British navy grew stronger in the nineteenth century, the planters began to experience serious labor shortages.[29]

The expanding plantation economy increased the power of *peninsular* merchants, shippers, and traders as well as North American suppliers. Cuba increasingly became dependent on imports of foodstuffs, clothing, and manufactured goods, the bulk of which came from the United States, and Spanish-born mercantile interests controlled the export-import traffic. The long-standing social and political divisions in Cuba between *peninsulares* and *criollos* were aggravated by the division between the mercantile and commercial interests that exercised increasing control over the planter economy.

·The sugar and coffee booms, along with the demographic changes they brought, transformed the Cuban social structure. The arrival of hundreds of thousands of new slaves from Africa gave Cuba a sense of racial identity, and tension, that it had not known before. The social hierarchy in Cuba acquired a strong racial dimension. The most recent arrivals from Africa, who were known as *bozales* or *negros de naciones*, were at the very bottom of the social structure. Most of them labored on the vast sugar plantations of western Cuba. The slaves came from a variety of groups in Africa. Whites used the term "Mandingas" and "Gangás" for slaves whose tribal homelands were among the Malinkes of Sierra Leone. Slaves who were Akans from the Gold Coast were known as "Minas." The so-called Lucumís were actually Yoruban-speaking people from the Bight of Benin. The Ibos and Efiks were known as "Carabalís." The "Congos" were indeed the Congos of Angola, and the "Macúas" were Makwas from Mozambique. Most slaves, however, were Lucumís, and Afro-Cuban culture gradually took on a Yoruban flavor.

Just above the *bozales* in the racially stratified Cuban social structure were Cuban-born slaves. Although many labored on the sugar plantations of western Cuba, significant numbers of them, because of their acculturation and ability to speak Spanish, found positions as artisans, teamsters, dockworkers, liverymen, cooks, washerwomen, wet nurses, gardeners, and urban workers. Because they lived in cities and could communicate with their owners, they were better fed, better dressed, and better treated than the *bozal* field hands, and their opportunities under the *coartación* to earn their freedom were better. Cuban masters found their urban slaves easier to control. The urban slaves, better than any people, knew of the harsh lives of the *bozales*; they also knew that their masters, at any time and for any provocation, could consign them to the sugarcane plantations for an early death.

The mass influx of African slaves into Cuba had a sobering effect on the white population. Large numbers of the slaves came from tribes with strong militaristic traditions. They were culturally conditioned to resistance, not to acquiescence, and the fact that the large majority of them were males did not leave them with families to protect or worry about. Most slaves in Cuba were African-born *bozales* who remembered their freedom and resented their captivity. Escape was one option, and by the early 1800s there were *palenques*—permanent fortresses of runaway Africans—hidden in the mountains of eastern Cuba. Slave rebellions also became increasingly common, culminating in the great uprising in Matanzas in 1844. At the time the English government regularly protested continuation of the slave trade, and abolitionists in Cuba, British as well as Cuban, constantly articulated their opposition to slavery and the rights of black slaves to be free.

Since more than half of the Cuban population was black by the 1840s (436,000 slaves and 153,000 free blacks out of a total population of 1 million in 1841), Spanish authorities and Cuban planters began to fear a slave uprising. To counter the abolitionists, Spain sent Lieutenant General Leopoldo O'Donnell to Cuba in 1843, giving him specific orders to crush any slave insurrection. O'Donnell conducted a "witch hunt." Spanish officials claimed that the rebellion was part of a colonywide conspiracy, and they crushed it with a vengeance, slaughtering as many as 1,000 slaves and free blacks suspected of participating in it. It became known as the "La Escalera" rebellion because so many thousands of Cuban blacks were tied to ladders—*escaleras*—for their floggings and executions. The La Escalera incident created a deep, permanent resentment among Cuban slaves toward the Spanish government.[30]

Free blacks occupied the middle of the Cuba's social hierarchy. Between 1791 and 1841 the number of free blacks increased from approximately 31,000 people to 153,000. Most of them lived in the segregated barrios of Havana, Santiago de Cuba, Puerto Príncipe, Matanzas, and other towns. Since Spanish law excluded them from working in the law, medicine, accounting, pharmacy, universities, and government employment, they were most likely to work in skilled jobs and crafts—butchers, carpenters, cobblers, midwives, undertakers, seamstresses, bloodletters, glaziers, barbers, and hairdressers—or laborers. In more rural areas—especially in eastern Cuba where there were relatively few sugar plantations—there were thousands of free black farmers, drovers, ranch hands, seasonal workers, and peddlers. But even among free blacks the caste of color was important. People of mixed African-Spanish ancestry were known as *pardos*, and they considered themselves, and were so considered by most whites, to be the social superiors of full-blooded African free blacks—the *morenos*.[31]

At the top of the Cuban social hierarchy were whites, but they were also divided into a variety of stratified economic classes. In the early history of Cuba, most colonists descended from people native to southern Spain—especially Andalucía and the city of Seville—and those groups of families came to dominate the planter class as well as the *criollo* mercantile elite. The white families arriving in Cuba in the late eighteenth and early nineteenth centuries were more likely to be Asturians and Catalonians. Canary Islanders—*isleños*—were the largest group of immigrants in the 1820s and 1830s. They constituted more than a third of all foreign-born whites living in Cuba in 1846. At the very bottom were the *monteros*—poor rural whites who labored as herdsmen, teamsters, migrant farmers, slave drivers, slave hunters, sharecroppers, and peasant farmers with only a few acres of land. The *monteros* were so poor that their life-style was not much better economically than that of slaves, but what differentiated them from slaves and free blacks was color, and even the poorest white considered himself superior to any *bozal, pardo,* or *moreno*. Wealthy planters could always rely on the *monteros* for help in crushing slave rebellions.

Just above the *monteros* were urban whites who worked as grocers, tailors, cigarmakers, carpenters, clerks, domestic house servants, physicians, pharmacists, lawyers, accountants, and teachers. Also included in the white middle class were independent sugar, coffee, and tobacco farmers whose landholdings did not give them plantation status. There was also, however, a high level of cultural unemployment among the urban white working and middle classes. Because Spanish culture had traditionally looked down on manual labor as inferior, large numbers of whites would rather do nothing and live as vagrants than find a job to support themselves. Race only reinforced that cultural stigma, since so many free blacks in Cuba worked in the skilled trades. They tended to associate skilled or unskilled labor as something that should be confined to blacks, not to whites.[32]

The white upper class by the early 1840s was the domain of influential *peninsulares* and *criollos*. The *peninsulares* still controlled the governmental bureaucracy, the military, and the church hierarchy, but there were also influential peninsulares who owned import-export and banking businesses in the major cities. The *criollo* elites consisted of the major landowners who controlled the sugar and coffee plantations, as well as businessmen who owned large volumes of urban property in Havana, Matanzas, Santiago de Cuba, and Puerto Príncipe. The traditional division between the *peninsular* and the *criollo* elites still existed—*peninsulares* looked down on *criollos* as unsophisticated provincials, while the *criollos* viewed the *peninsulares* as arrogant snobs whose influence far surpassed their abilities.

Unlike the rest of Latin America, however, where *criollo* resentment of *peninsular* power spawned the revolutionary movements of the early 1800s, Cuba remained a bastion of imperial conservatism. Although the economic boom of the late eighteenth century gave birth to a heightened *criollo* political consciousness, the mass influx of African slaves in the early 1800s subdued it. At the very time when the independence movements erupted throughout Latin America, the sugar boom was enriching Cuban *criollos*. Economic prosperity was not fertile ground for revolution. Beyond that, however, *criollos* feared that the elimination of peninsular authority would inevitably lead to a social revolution that might displace the *criollo* elite as well. There were widespread fears among Cuban whites about the "Africanization" of the island. They needed *peninsular* military authority to keep their slaves under control. A fear of slave rebellions permeated the *criollo* consciousness; the last thing they wanted was the departure of Spanish military support.[33] Upper-class conservatism in Cuba was reinforced by the large-scale influx of royalist refugees from the mainland revolutions. They were a mix of *peninsulares* and *criollos*, but they all came with tales of woe and misery, of social dislocation and revolution. Their stories of what the mainland revolutions had done to the upper classes frightened the Cuban upper class, enhancing their loyalty to the empire. At the same time, large numbers of Spanish troops were shipped to Cuba from the mainland colonies after the independence victories. Cuba became an armed camp. The Spanish empire in Cuba was infinitely more powerful after the Latin American revolutions than it had been before. Cuba had become the premier colony in the shrinking Spanish empire.

Emigrés: The Origins of the Cuban-American Community

If Iberian geography helped create the Spanish imperial destiny, Caribbean geography did the same for Cuban history. With only 90 miles separating the two countries, Cuban fortunes have been inextricably linked to those of the United States. The Caribbean Sea and the Gulf of Mexico have always been vital to American national security, especially after the construction of the Panama Canal, so Cuba has always been an important factor in American strategic debates. And ever since the mid-eighteenth century, Cuba has been intimately connected to and dependent on the larger U.S. economy. And regardless of the direction of Cuban politics, whether oriented to Spain in the eighteenth and nineteenth centuries or to the Soviet Union in the late twentieth century, the economic link to the United States has shaped the island's destiny. America and Cuba have had a love-hate relationship, and neither has been able to ignore the other.

Although Cubans have alternatively sought and loathed the influence of the United States, there has been no escaping, since the nineteenth century at least, the power of the "Colossus of the North." Cubans have tried to use that power when possible to promote their own interests without becoming a political and economic appendage of their gigantic neighbor. In many ways the Cuban national identity in the twentieth century has used the image of the United States as its cutting edge. And because of the proximity of Cuba to the American mainland, Cuban Americans have always been deeply involved in the domestic and international politics of their ancestral homeland. More so than any other group to settle in the United States, the political and cultural links between the immigrants and the mother country have been inextricably entangled.

The first European settlements in North America were in Florida. Ponce de León explored the peninsula in 1513, and, because of the abundant flowers and foliage, he named the land Florida. Most Spanish attempts to explore and colonize there ended in disaster until 1565, when St. Augustine became the first permanent, successful settlement. Spain had high hopes for Florida, but they were never fulfilled, primarily because of territorial conflicts with the British and the French. Florida became British territory after the end of the Seven Years' War in

1763. Several hundred British businessmen and settlers moved to Florida beginning in 1764, and the next 20 years were characterized by peace and economic growth. During the American Revolution, however, Spain fought in the side of the colonists and defeated the English in West Florida in 1779 and in Pensacola in 1781.[1]

The Treaty of Paris of 1783 ended the American Revolutionary War, and as part of its terms Great Britain returned Florida to Spain. Boundary disputes between Spain and the United States erupted within a few years, especially over the border between Florida and Georgia, Alabama, and Mississippi. The matter was not settled until ratification of the Treaty of San Lorenzo in 1785, when both countries agreed to the thirty-first parallel as the northern boundary of Spanish Florida.

Although the Treaty of San Lorenzo settled the legalities of the boundary dispute, it did nothing to stem the tide of American settlers taking up land in Florida. Spain protested the illegal settlement, but there was little either country could do about it. The dynamic of geographic expansion was less a policy of the United States than a vision in the minds of millions of people. In 1803 the United States completed the Louisiana Purchase with France, bringing New Orleans under American sovereignty, and between 1810 and 1813 the United States annexed West Florida. East Florida remained under Spanish control. During the War of 1812, General Andrew Jackson invaded Florida. He seized Pensacola in November 1814 but then quickly withdrew to defend New Orleans. During the First Seminole War in 1818, Jackson invaded Florida to attack the Seminoles and to punish the Spanish for assisting them. When Secretary of State John Quincy Adams and Jackson demanded that Spain either control the territory or surrender it, Spain agreed to negotiate. The Adams-Oñis Treaty was signed in Washington, D.C., on 22 February 1819. Under its terms, the United States received sovereignty over East Florida, and Spain recognized the earlier United States seizure of West Florida. The treaty defined the western boundary of the Louisiana territory.[2]

Spanish citizens in Florida became part of the United States. Scholars estimate that there were approximately 5,000 people of European and African descent, in addition to the Seminole Indians, living in Florida in 1819. Most of them were in northern Florida and in the panhandle—white southerners from Georgia carrying the U.S. flag and looking for new land. They were accompanied by their slaves. Deeper in the interior were bands of runaway slaves from Georgia whose owners had not been able to find them. There were British merchants in Pensacola and St. Augustine and Hispanic settlers in the mission settlements of the east coast. A few hundred people lived in South Florida. Some of the Hispanic settlers had formerly been in Cuba. So at the time of the American acquisition of Florida in 1819, there were probably a handful of Cubans scattered throughout the colony.[3]

By the early 1800s a new political restlessness was spreading throughout Cuba. Joaquín Infante led a rebellion against Spain in 1809, and in the early 1820s José Francisco Lemus, with assistance from Simón Bolívar, the great leader of the South American independence movements, tried to proclaim the Republic of Cubanacán and establish a formal political alliance with Colombia. The Aguila Negra Conspiracy occurred in Cuba early in the 1820s. Inspired by Mexico's successful revolution, several Cuban exiles in Mexico City, led by

Simón de Chávez, established a Junta Patriótica and tried to secure support from such prominent Mexicans as Guadalupe Victoria and Antonio López de Santa Anna. The conspirators linked up with José Julian Solís and Manuel Rojo in Cuba, and their calls for independence began to attract a following. Simón de Chávez, a former Roman Catholic priest, was known as Aguila Negra, or Black Eagle. Spanish authorities arrested and imprisoned the Cuban leaders in 1825, and the movement was aborted. Another rebel was Joaquín Agüero. Born in Camagüey Province in 1816, Agüero was raised and educated in Havana, and as a student he became an outspoken advocate of independence for the slaves. Spanish authorities identified him as a dangerous radical, a posture he only magnified when he began to call for Cuban independence as well. In the late 1840s Agüero became president of the Sociedad de la Liberación (Liberation Society) in Camagüey, and he also constructed secret printing presses to reproduce revolutionary literature coming from New York. Joaquín Agüero was arrested for treason in 1851, tried, and executed.[4]

Throughout most of the nineteenth century, all of the early insurrectionist movements aborted. Felix Varela y Morales advocated a variety of church reforms as well as abolition of slavery and Cuban independence in the early 1820s. To avoid arrest Varela fled in 1823 to New York City, where he formed the nucleus of what became a vocal Cuban émigré community. Varela lived out his life in New York City, serving as vicar-general of Roman Catholics there and publishing a Cuban newspaper, *El Habanero*. He became Cuba's first revolutionary hero. Varela saw to it that the newspaper was smuggled into Cuba, where it garnered a significant following. Spanish authorities were angry enough with the newspaper to send assassins to New York City in an unsuccessful attempt to kill him. José Antonio Saco, a professor of philosophy at the San Carlos Seminary, emigrated to New York in the 1850s, where he published *El Mensajero Semanal* and eventually called for Cuban independence.[5]

In the beginning the *criollo* liberals had only the vaguest notions of just how to reshape the island's political relationship with Spain. There were the philosophical extremes. Some of them were classical liberals who continued to advocate further relaxation of trade restrictions, reduced taxes, fewer bureaucratic restrictions, and less centralization of authority. For them the true liberation of Cuba had to begin with economics. The radicals like Varela and Saco wanted complete independence from Spain. Others called for "autonomy"—some system in which Cuba would govern itself internally with fewer external trade regulations, but in which Spain provided for military defense and the general direction of foreign policy.

For a time in the 1850s, some Cuban liberals flirted with the notion of annexation by the United States. During the early 1800s the social and economic relationship between Cuba and the United States had grown stronger. By the 1840s Cuba's foreign trade with the United States exceeded its trade with Spain, and increasing numbers of Cubans were traveling to the United States on business and vacations. Many Cubans had also been inspired by the Texas rebellion against Mexico in 1836. After a 10-year period of independence, Texas was annexed by the United States in 1845. Cuban *criollos* hoped for the same. They still feared that independence from Spain would deprive them of the military means to defend themselves against a slave uprising. They were also concerned that the increasingly powerful antislavery movement in Great Britain might eventually force Spain to abolish slavery in Cuba. Annexation by the United States, where slavery was firmly entrenched, would solve both problems: they would be rid of Spain, but they would still have a powerful military force capable of maintaining the existing social order. The annexationists established the Club de la Habana (Havana Club) to promote their agenda, and for a time, with financial backers in the United States, they tried unsuccessfully to sponsor anti-Spanish uprisings in Cuba.

Cuban annexationists were also encouraged by expansionst sentiments in the United States. During the late 1840s the spirit of Manifest Destiny spread throughout the United States as Americans expressed a collective desire to see the country reach from the Atlantic Ocean to the Pacific Ocean. The Oregon Treaty of 1846 and the Treaty of Guadalupe Hidalgo ending the Mexican War fulfilled that dream. In 1854 President Franklin Pierce offered Spain $130 million for Cuba, but Spain refused. Later that year the U.S. ministers to Spain, Great Britain, and France met in Ostend, Belgium, and called on the State Department to renew the offer, but the so-called Ostend Manifesto was refused again.

By the 1850s there were perhaps 1,000 Cubans living in the United States, and many of them promoted annexation. Cristobal Madán, a prominent Cuban sugar planter, founded the Consejo de Gobierno Cubano in New York. Madán's wife was the sister of John O'Sullivan, the New York journalist who coined the phrase "Manifest Destiny" in the 1840s and who advocated American expansionism. The Consejo published *La Verdad* and lobbied throughout the United States for annexation. Madán and his associates also distributed copies of *La Verdad* throughout Cuba, although the Spanish government prohibited it. The advocates of territorial expansion and Cuban annexation had joined hands. Some of the more vociferous advocates of annexation added a violent dimension to their campaign. In the late 1840s and early 1850s Narciso López launched a series of filibustering, or small-scale military, expeditions against Cuba. He enjoyed the support of the Consejo in New York and the Club de la Habana in Cuba, and with money from both groups he tried to invade Cuba and inspire insurrection in 1848, 1849, and 1851. The expeditions all failed to inspire the desired uprising, and at Bahía Honda in 1851 López was captured and executed.[6]

But the annexationist alternative ran head on into the political debate over slavery in the United States and could not sustain its momentum. The Ostend Manifesto in particular, and the entire debate over the expansion of slavery in general, raised a storm of protest in the North. Concern about the expansion of slavery into the territories had been mounting ever since the 1820s. Congress had already debated the Missouri Compromise, Texas annexation, the Wilmot Proviso during the Mexican War, the proposals of the Liberty party and the Free-Soil party, and the Compromise of 1850, all of which had revolved around the question of the expansion of slavery to U.S. territories and newly annexed states. Some northerners opposed the expansion of slavery because they hated slavery, while others opposed it because they hated blacks. Most northerners worried that the entrance of new slave states into the union would give control of Congress to southerners. When the Kansas-Nebraska Act was passed in 1854, raising the possibility that slavery would be permitted in Kansas, the resulting controversy led to the creation of the new Republican party. It was based exclusively in the North and was dead set against the expansion of slavery. At the time there were more than 225,000 free blacks in Cuba and perhaps 350,000 African slaves. After Kansas-Nebraska, there was simply no way northerners would tolerate the purchase of Cuba, with its slave-ridden sugar plantations.[7] The Civil War in the United States dealt the final blow to the ideas of annexation. The Emancipation Proclamation in 1863 and the Thirteenth Amendment to the Constitution in 1865 ended slavery in the United States. Cuban slaveowners would find no protection there.

After the American Civil War, Spain appeared to be in a more conciliatory mood. Santo Domingo, or the Dominican Republic, had finally completed its break with Spain in 1865, shrinking the once great Spanish empire even more, and the prospects of losing Cuba, the "Pearl of the Empire" as the Spanish often called it, were unthinkable. The revenues from its sugar plantations were the last real source of wealth in the empire. To appease *criollos*, Spain established a Junta de Información that met in Madrid in 1866 and 1867 to discuss the possibilities of political reform. The Junta, which was composed primarily of Cuban *criollos*, recommended Cuban representation in the Cortés (the Spanish legislature), basic civil liberties, gradual emancipation of the slaves, and enactment of civil and criminal codes in Cuba, which were the same, procedurally and substantively, as those in Spain. There was a brief period of euphoria among the Cuban representatives, but their hopes were soon dashed. The Spanish government repudiated its recommendations, increased taxes, and prohibited reformist public meetings and publications.

The growing presence of North Americans in Cuba also raised *criollo* economic expectations. During the 1840s and 1850s American economic penetration of Cuba became more and more significant in the local economy, especially in terms of the industrial and transportation infrastructure. American architects, engineers, machinists, merchants, bankers, and shippers came to Cuba to live, and they built highways, railroads, port facilities, water and sewage systems, and bridges. The Cuban economy became more and more dependent on their technical services. There were 1,256 Americans living in Cuba in 1846, and that number jumped to 2,500 in 1862. After the Civil War several thousand southerners relocated to Cuba, many of them bringing their slaves with them. By 1868 the number of North Americans living in Cuba had increased to as many as 5,000. Very few of them shared any elements of a Hispanic political culture, with its centralized, nondemocratic view of sovereignty and power. They lived along the northern coast of Cuba, especially around Havana. Suspicious of big government and committed to free enterprise, they helped imbue Cuban *criollos* with a more well-developed resentment of Spanish heavy-handedness. They brought to Cuba the same political philosophy—states' rights and anticentralism—that southerners had brought to Texas in the 1820s and 1830s.

To more and more *criollos*, the need for reform gave way to the need for revolution. It had become increasingly clear to most of them that Spain was willing to risk losing the "Pearl" completely rather than make any reasonable concessions. But whites still faced the old dilemma—how to make the break with Spain without destabilizing the social structure. Spain was still under considerable pressure from the British to abolish slavery in Cuba. In the words of historian Louis A. Pérez, Jr., "Creole elites could not plot to end Spanish sovereignty as a way of defending slavery without provoking Spain into ending slavery as a way to defend sovereignty."[8] Technology soon provided a way out of that historical trap. During the 1850s and 1860s it became more and more clear that the invention of labor-saving devices had the potential of limiting the need for slave labor. Such mechanization would require a major capital investment—something that would be easier for large plantation owners to afford than small landowners. At the same time, Cuban planters in general realized that they could import contract labor from China and from other parts of the Caribbean and Latin America to work the sugar plantations, thus eliminating the need for slaves.[9]

Developments in agricultural technology and immigration made it possible for the planting elite to accept the idea of abolition. Once they could even ponder such a possibility, they were able to escape the slavery-sovereignty dilemma that had trapped them ever since the beginning of the sugar boom. They also enjoyed new possibilities for political alliances with free blacks and slaves. Ever since the brutal repressions of the La Escalera Conspiracy in 1844, black resentment against Spain had run very deep. *Criollo* liberals had been unable to exploit that resentment, however, because of their own fears of abolition. With those fears lessening, they could call for revolution and abolition, and in doing so they, along with Cuban black people, became the dominant political majority. Cuba was ripe for revolution.

The revolution began in 1868. Its leading figure, Carlos Manuel de Céspedes, was born near Havana in 1819. As a young man he traveled widely throughout Europe and the United States and acquired a powerful sense of Cuban nationalism. During the 1840s and 1850s Céspedes became a successful sugar planter, but he continued his agitation for Cuban independence from Spain. He was a leader of local *criollo* nationalists, especially those active in the Masonic movement. Carlos Céspedes became famous throughout Cuba on 10 October 1868, when he proclaimed independence and the establishment of the Republic of Cuba in the town of Yara in Oriente Province. The proclamation launched Cuba on the Ten Years' War. By the end of October, Céspedes had nearly 15,000 followers, and by the end of the year he was in virtual control of Oriente Province. In 1869 he assembled a convention that drafted a constitution declaring Cuban independence, abolishing slavery, and annexing the country to the United States. The delegates to the convention also elected Céspedes as the first president of Cuba.[10]

The rebellion soon drew a number of individuals who emerged as revolutionary leaders. One of them was Máximo Gómez, a native of Santo Domingo. Gómez spent his early years fighting against Spanish authority, but in the civil war that devastated Santo Domingo in the 1860s, he lost all of his possessions and fled to Cuba. When the Ten Years' War began in 1868, Gómez joined up with Céspedes and quickly rose through the army ranks because of his leadership skills and unmatched zeal for independence. Eventually he became secretary of war under Céspedes. Another prominent leader was Antonio Maceo y Grajales. Maceo was born in Santiago de Cuba in 1848 to a mulatto family, all of whom, after the La Escalera witch hunts, were absolutely committed to Cuban independence. Eventually his father, 10 brothers, and Maceo himself died in the war against Spain. He became a major general in the revolutionary army and a folk hero among the Cuban black population.[11]

Another prominent revolutionary leader to emerge during the Ten Years' War was was José Martí. Born in Havana in 1853 to a military family, Martí as a student came under the influence of Rafael María de Mendive, an anti-Spanish Cuban nationalist. When Céspedes launched the Ten Years' War in 1868, Martí became an enthusiastic exponent of Cuban independence. In 1869, along with his close friend Fermín Valdés Domínguez, Martí wrote *El diablo cojuelo*, a satirical political document on freedom of speech and of the press. Martí's first dramatic play, *Abdala*, was a plea for Cuban independence published in 1869. That same year he was arrested for sedition and sentenced to six years in prison. He worked at hard labor in prison until early 1871, when he was deported to Spain and released. He received a law degree at the University of Zaragoza in 1874 but continued his campaign for Cuban independence.[12]

By that time, however, Spain had gained the upper hand in the rebellion. Céspedes had been unable to keep control of the movement. His decision to abolish slavery alienated many conservatives, as had his October 1869 decision to go along with the plan of Máximo Gómez to destroy many sugar plantations to rob the Spaniards of their economic base in Cuba. Many conservatives were also disturbed by power of Antonio Maceo. They worried that his popularity among Cuban blacks would lead to a racial rebellion and a real socioeconomic revolution in Cuba. But when Céspedes grew jealous of the popularity of Máximo Gómez and removed him from military command, he lost much support among radicals. In 1873 other revolutionary leaders removed him from the presidency. Carlos Manuel de Céspedes was ambushed and killed by Spanish soldiers in 1874. That army then proceeded to crush the rebellion, and in February 1878 the rebels agreed to an armistice in what became known as the Pact of Zanjón.[13]

The turmoil that had beset Cuba politically since the 1850s and socially and economically in the late 1860s increased the number of Cubans settling in the United States. The U.S. Census of 1870 listed approximately 5,300 people of Cuban descent living in the United States. Because of the economic disruptions brought on by the Ten Years' War, some Cuban cigar manufacturing concerns relocated their factories to the United States, drawing Cuban workers there, and political refugees also relocated to continue their campaigns for Cuban independence. Also, the rise of sugar beet production in Utah and Idaho provided new competition for Cuban sugar, undermining prices and bringing a depression to the island. By 1880 there were nearly 7,000 Cubans living in the United States. Most of them were in the Gulf Coast and Atlantic coast cities—New Orleans, Mobile, Pensacola, Tampa, Key West, Miami, Baltimore, Philadelphia, New York, and Boston. Key West, with more than 2,000 settlers, had the largest concentration. Just five years later there were more than 5,000 Cubans in Key West alone, and there were 91 cigar factories on that island. The growth continued during the early 1890s, and along with the settlers came businesses—barbershops, cafés, restaurants, grocery stores, and so forth. By 1900 the population of Key West exceeded 18,000 and Tampa more than 23,000.[14] Both cities were known as "Little Havana." From those places the immigrants continued to campaign and plan for Cuban independence. There were also the political refugees still functioning in New York City, Philadelphia, and Boston.

Typical of the political refugees was Calixto García Iñiguez. García became committed to Cuban independence as a young student, and during the Ten Years' War he joined revolutionary forces fighting the Spanish army. By 1872 he was second in command to General Máximo Gómez. Spanish forces captured

Cuban-American cigar workers in Tampa, Florida, in the 1930s. *Courtesy Florida State News Bureau*

García in 1874, and he spent the rest of the war in prison. After his release in 1878, however, he relocated to New York City, where he organized the Cuban Revolutionary Committee to raise money and promote the independence movement. In August 1879, just a year after the end of the Ten Years' War, García met with Antonio Maceo in Jamaica and planned an insurrection. They issued the Kingston Proclamation calling for insurrection and then went back to Cuba. Convinced that Maceo's African ancestry would be a political liability, García removed him from military command and personally led an invasion of Cuba in May 1880. It failed miserably, and García was captured in August 1880. After spending several years in prison in Spain, García returned to Cuba in 1895 and once again rose to become second-in-command to Máximo Gómez.[15]

Other Cuban revolutionary leaders had similar experiences. In 1875 José Martí went to work as a journalist in Mexico City for *La Revista Universal*. When the Pact of Zanjón ended the Ten Years' War in 1878 and declared a general amnesty for all revolutionaries, Martí returned to Havana. He immediately resumed his political activities, and late in 1878 Spanish authorities exiled him once again. Spain was still unwilling to countenance any political opposition. Martí moved to New York City, where he spent the next 15 years raising money and promoting the cause of Cuban independence. Martí left New York in the spring of 1895 and joined up with the revolutionary forces in Cuba. Antonio Maceo, fully aware of Spain's historical intransigence about colonial independence, refused to accept the Pact of Zanjón ending the Ten Years' War, and Spanish authorities exiled him from Cuba. He fled to Mexico in 1880 and then spent time in Haiti, Honduras, Mexico, New York, and Panama, agitating for Cuban independence. Like José Martí, Máximo Gómez also refused to accept the Pact of Zanjón. Gómez moved to Honduras. He went to the United States in 1885 and became part of José Martí's effort to organize a new war for independence in Cuba.

In many ways the social and political attitudes of the Cuban émigré community in the United States reflected the opinions of their counterparts on the island. Because of the severe economic problems in Cuba during the 1880s and early 1890s, large numbers of people emigrated from the island. Thousands of them settled in the United States. Between the 1840s and the 1890s separatist thought among Cuban Americans evolved from an economic liberalism envisioning annexation to the United States to absolute Cuban independence, complete with vast social and economic change. The evolution of Cuban-American political attitudes passed through three general stages. During the 1840s and 1850s most of the Cuban émigrés living in the United States were upper-class *criollos* with powerful economic interests to defend. Even though few in number, they were well-organized politically and very vocal, especially in New York, Philadelphia, and New Orleans. Those Cuban émigrés living in New York City had the greatest influence in the early years. Most of them—including people like Cristóbal Madan, José Luis Alfonso, Gaspar Betancourt Cisneros, Porfirio Valiente, José Sánchez Iznaga, and Juan C. Zenea—possessed an upper-class, liberal point of view. For them, Cuba's future, as well as their own, would best be fulfilled by free trade, representative government, and the gradual elimination of slavery with fair, market-value indemnification to slaveowners. They were also convinced that only through political annexation to the United States could those values, along with separation from Spain and preservation of the existing social order, be realized. They also believed that the transition from Spanish to U.S. sovereignty should be completed peacefully and diplomatically.

But in the 1850s, when the possibilities of annexation became more and more remote, political leadership of the Cuban-American émigré community shifted from New York City to New Orleans, where a more radical group lived. Instead of the cautious, diplomatic approach of the New York junta, they wanted to use armed force against Spanish power in Cuba. People like Cirilo Villaverde, Juan Manuel Macías, and Plutarco González formed the Sociedad Republicana and published a newspaper—*La Voz de América*—to promote their views. They pursued a violent, insurrectionary strategy rather than diplomacy, and they emphasized Cuban self-determination rather than simple annexation. They did not want to exchange one master for another. In doing so, the New Orleans radicals appealed to Cuban nationalists who did not want to become part of the United States as well as to the older annexationists, providing a way for the two factions to unite, temporarily at least. Their main point was that once Cuba was free of Spain, it could decide whether to become independent or part of the United States. The key, however, was to first cast off Spanish imperialism.

The Sociedad Republicana then took the bold step in 1866 of advocating immediate abolition of slavery. The death of slavery in the United States had all but doomed slavery in Cuba, and mechanization and contract immigrant labor could probably fill labor demands anyway. By advocating immediate abolition, they hoped to gather support for the independence movement from free blacks and slaves in Cuba and from mulatto Cubans in the émigré communities. That would broaden their base of support. The Sociedad also called for the abandonment of the notion that the exiles would have to bring about the insurrection through an external invasion. The filibustering expeditions of people like Narciso López had not triggered any spontaneous uprising, and what was needed was a broad-based political movement inside Cuba to bring about the uprising.

When the Ten Years' War erupted in 1868 there was a brief resurgence of annexationist sentiment, primarily because of the arrival in New York and New Orleans of people like José Morales Lemus, José Antonio Echeverría, and Manuel M. Mestre, all of whom were well-to-do *criollo* liberals. But their influence was short-lived because of the intense, separatist nationalism of the Sociedad Republicana, which argued that annexation was actually anti-Cuban and not to be tolerated. To counteract the new annexationism in New York, separatist nationalists like Carlos and José Gabriel del Castillo, Miguel Bravo y Sentéis, José J. Govantes, and José de Armas y Céspedes established the Sociedad de Artesanos Cubanos de New York in 1870. They called for armed insurrection against Spain and an immediate abolition of slavery, and they rejected any postrebellion political arrangement that left Cuba under any form of U.S. control. The separatist point of view prevailed. By the end of the Ten Years' War the annexationists had been thoroughly discredited in the émigré communities, and the *independentistas* triumphed. The political culture of the émigré communities in the early 1880s was intensely nationalistic, abolitionist, and committed to insurrection and independence.

The Pact of Zanjón ending the Ten Years' War, however, led to another, though brief, change in direction of the political thought in the émigré communities. The hope of the Sociedad de Artesanos Cubanos that the insurrection against Spain could be internally driven lost some credibility when the Ten Years' War ended, and once again many people in the émigré communities came to view themselves as central to the revolutionary debate. For them, the liberation of Cuba could only come if the émigré communities provided financial support and triggered the initial stage of the insurrection through an invasion. The geographic center of Cuban-American political activity shifted from New York and New Orleans to Florida, and the movement assumed a military dimension it had never had before. The leadership of the movement changed to military figures like Calixto García, Ramón Bonachea, Máximo Gómez, and Antonio Maceo, all of whom began organizing filibustering raids against Cuba. Most of them had refused to accept the Pact of Zanjón and had participated in the abortive Guerra Chiquita in 1879–80, a short-lived attempt to revive the Ten Years' War.[16]

But the filibustering activities soon raised doubts among such émigré intellectuals as José Martí and Enrique Trujillo. Martí was convinced that any successful insurrection in Cuba would have to be democratically inspired and internally driven, and he felt the filibusters would achieve neither. The military leadership of the filibusterers was politically inept and not inclined to democratic rhetoric, and they were all based in Florida. Without intimate connections between the filibusterers and the masses in Cuba, along with careful planning, there would be no spontaneous uprising on the island. Martí wanted to move away from the notion that the émigré communities were to be the prime force in the insurrection. Although the émigré communities were politically divided over the issue in the 1880s, Martí's faction eventually emerged triumphant. All of the filibustering expeditions failed, and in 1886 Gómez and Maceo admitted as much. Cuban leaders in Key West then abandoned the filibustering ideal in 1889 and organized La Convención Cubana (Cuban Convention), a group dedicated to the establishment of revolutionary cells throughout Cuba.

By that time, however, the separatist debate in the émigré communities had shifted again. From the 1830s to the late 1870s, the Cuban-American émigré communities had been primarily white and middle to upper class in composition. But in the 1870s, when the cigar industry developed in Key West, and in the 1880s, when another cigar industry emerged in Jacksonville and Tampa, Florida, the composition of the Cuban-American community began to change. Large numbers of the immigrants were working-class and multiracial in background. By the mid-1880s more than 80 percent of Cuban émigré were blue-collar workers, and more than 20 percent were black and mulatto. Conditions in the cigar factories were abysmal, and while the poor workers suffered, the white Cuban entrepreneurs prospered. Labor leaders began to emerge in the Cuban-American communities—people like Ramón Rivero, Enrique Messonier, Enrique Creci, Carlos Baliño, Guillermo Sorondo, and Francisco Segura. Those Cuban workers, especially the Afro-Cuban workers, were almost as resentful of the white Cuban upper class as they were of Spain. Their migration to Florida added a class dimension to the Cuban-American community that had not existed in earlier years.

The vanguard of Cuban workers heading to Ybor City near present-day Tampa, Florida, began in 1886. By 1890 there were 1,313 Cubans living there, and those numbers jumped to 3,533 by 1900. Because of the proximity of the island, the interchangeability of work skills in the cigar industry, and the ease of travel, these workers returned frequently to Cuba during holidays and slack work periods. During the 1890s between 50,000 and 100,000 people passed annually between the United States and Cuba. The immigrants came primarily from Havana and the small towns outside the capital, especially Bejucal, San Antonio de los Baños, Santiago de las Vegas, and Cardenas. Approximately 13 percent of the Cuban population in Ybor City consisted of Afro-Cubans.[17]

For the most part, labor organizers from the Cigar Makers International Union and Knights of Labor found it difficult to recruit Cuban workers. Cuban labor organizers had already formed their own immigrant unions in the émigré communities, and those unions were noted for their political activism. Part of that political activism stemmed from a deep sense of ethnic solidarity. By the early 1890s there were as many as 20,000 Cuban and Spanish workers in Florida, and more than half of them were Cubans. Highly resentful of *peninsular* power in Cuba, they took it out on the poor Spanish cigar workers, refusing them membership in the immigrant unions. Although American labor organizers tried to impress on the Cuban workers a sense of class solidarity, it was of little use. The Cubans wanted nothing to do with the Spaniards.

But beyond that heightened sense of ethnic identity, the working-class leaders felt it was hypocrisy to discuss the political liberation of Cuba from Spanish oppression unless there were also plans for genuine social change. It was a common practice in the cigar factories to have the *lectura* going on in which workers would read out loud to one another while they worked. Their topics of discussion were often political, and although the Cubans felt a sense of patriotic duty to liberate the island, they were also intent on real social and economic reform. Freedom from Spain for the Cuban lower class would mean little to them if they remained economically exploited. Their sense of political activism was sharpened even more by the tactics of some of the cigar manufacturers. Vicente Martínez Ybor, a prominent cigar manufacturer in Key West and Tampa, attempted to crush the activism by building company towns and trying to run them according to the "patrón-peon" models so common in Latin America. The workers would have nothing to do with them. He also used strike-breaking activities that would have made the most reactionary American manufacturer proud. Middle- and upper-class Cuban Americans who refused to acknowledge the political activism and the social and economic agenda of Cuban-American workers were destined to fail.[18]

Racial issues also began to divide the Cuban-American community, as they always had divided social life in Cuba. For years the issue had been abolition, but by the late 1870s the question of slavery in Cuba was rapidly reaching a point of resolution. On 5 November 1879 Spain provided for the gradual abolition of slavery in Cuba. The new law established an eight-year transition period in which the slaves had to continue to work for their former owners, but the plantation owners, for their part, had to provide adequate food and clothing and a monthly wage. The planters soon realized, however, that mechanization and the availability of poor whites and Asian contract laborers made the new system even more expensive than slavery. During the old days they had to provide slaves with food and clothing, but not with a monthly wage. And under complete freedom they could hire the former slaves only during peak seasons, not having to pay them the wage throughout the year. Many planters became abolitionists because of economic self-interest, and on 7 October 1886 Spain abolished slavery outright.

Spain did not realize, of course, that the very process of emancipation and the transition from slave to wage labor would increase the politicization of the lower classes and stimulate the independence movement. Cuban blacks had long deeply resented Spanish authority, particularly because of the brutality with which government officials had suppressed slave rebelliousness. But the condition of slavery did not allow for legitimate political or social protest. Outspoken slaves encountered not only the opposition of the state but the ire of their owners. Once emancipation had occurred, working class individuals had more freedom to express their points of view, particularly after labor organizers began to work among them. They became very blunt advocates of political independence, even though Spanish authorities often punished them for it.[19]

What Cuban blacks and mulattos, as well as their counterparts in the United States, soon realized, however, was that the abolition of slavery did not mean the abolition of racism and exploitation. Blacks were encountering discrimination in the sugar fields of Cuba as well as the cigar factories of Florida, and they especially resented the prejudice they experienced at the hands of Cuban whites. Black protest leaders began to emerge in the émigré communities—Carlos Borrego, Guillermo Sorondo, Joaquín Granado, Cornelio Brito, and Francisco Segura in Florida and Martín Morúa Delgado and Rafael Serra in New York. They rejected outright the old economic liberalism—free trade and laissez-faire policies—of traditionalists in the émigré communities and instead proposed changes ranging from political and economic reform to revolution. By the end of the 1880s the Cuban-American émigré communities were badly divided between conservative separatist leaders and revolutionaries.[20]

At that point José Martí emerged as a coalition builder among Cuban Americans. He knew that if a successful revolution was ever going to develop in Cuba, the traditional factionalism of Cuban politics would have to be transcended and a unified revolutionary party had to be forged—one capable of attracting the loyalties of traditional separatists as well as the larger group of socially alienated poor Cuban workers and Cuban blacks. Toward that end, Martí established the Partido Revolucionario Cubano (Cuban Revolutionary party), or PRC, in 1892. The PRC took a determined stand against the filibustering philosophy by calling for a broad-based, internally inspired uprising in Cuba, but because the PRC was centrally organized and authoritarian at the top, it attracted the support of old-line separatists and military filibusters who understood that only political unity, not endless factionalism, was going to bring about independence.

Martí also realized, however, that the PRC would eventually have to attract support among working-class and black and mulatto émigrés. In his speeches and articles, Martí began calling for a revolution that benefited all Cubans, not just the white elite. He regularly condemned racism and discrimination, demanded that cigar factory employers treat their workers fairly, and urged those workers to oganize themselves into effective labor unions. At the same time, Martí condemned anarchism and any notions of the inevitability of class struggle.

Martí possessed an elaborate, complex political philosophy. He passionately believed that Spanish colonialism had to be destroyed and replaced with an independent, republican Cuban government. Martí further believed that the legacy of colonialism would also have to be obliterated, that the Spanish system of government—with sovereignty resting in upper-class elites and power flowing down from them to other social groups—was antidemocratic and conducive to dictatorship. The role of government, therefore, was to achieve social justice so that a cooperative spirit, rather than a competitive one, would prevail between the various social and economic groups.[21]

Central to that sense of liberty and cooperation was property. The poor people of Cuba—blacks, whites, and mulattos—needed a stake in the society, and the best stake they could ever have was land. Martí did not propose taking from the rich and giving to the poor; such a proposal was guaranteed to alienate powerful *criollo* interests from the movement. Instead, he advocated redistribution of some government and church property to the poor. Martí was an admirer of what capitalism had accomplished in the United States, although he was concerned about its excesses. He believed firmly in the values of individual initiative, competition, and private property, and so naturally he was an opponent of monopolies and tariff protecitonism, both of which stifled competition and concentrated economic power in the hands of the few. The role of government should be to protect all citizens against exploitation by a tiny corporate elite, and the best way of achieving that objective was through vigorous antitrust activity and free-trade policies. By emphasizing worker participation in the PRC, social justice, and racial equality, Martí was able to gain the support among the lower classes he knew the rebellion so desperately needed. Antonio Maceo and Máximo Gómez joined forces with Martí's PRC. So while the PRC was busy flooding the Cuban-American émigré communities as well as Cuba itself with Martí's increasingly popular political philosophy, La Convención Cubana continued to organize revolutionary cells all over the island.

But José Martí was also a realist about the long-term relationship between Cuba and the United States. In terms of population size, economic power, and military might, the United States would always be in a position to threaten Cuba, and because of the self-righteous arrogance of Anglo-American culture, Cubans would always have to be on guard, watching out for those powerful North American interests eager to exploit the island's people and resources. Martí also knew the danger of eliminating Spain as a Caribbean power; although it was necessary for Cuban liberation, it would leave a geopolitical vacuum that the United States would quickly fill. Cubans would have to be shrewd about winning and keeping their independence—otherwise it could be won and then lost again in an instant.[22]

Economic and political events on the island were playing right into Martí's hands. Large numbers of *criollos* had suffered during the Ten Years' War. The fighting destroyed many plantations outright, and the depression in the sugar industry that followed in the 1880s forced many *criollos* to sell their land or declare bankruptcy. In either case, significant amounts of land were transferred in the 1880s from *criollo* to *peninsular* interests—an event that only sharpened *criollo* resentments. At the same time, Spain showed no inclination toward reform or autonomy. Once again the Spanish capacity to risk everything rather than compromise on anything was abundantly clear. Finally, the Ten Years' War gave Cubans a sense of nationhood they had not possessed before. Fighting during the war had ranged widely throughout the island, overcoming some of the regionalism that had always dominated ethnic identities. The war also produced heroes and symbols that had not existed before. A Cuban patriotism had emerged in the 1880s and 1890s that fueled the trend toward revolution. When José Martí, Máximo Gómez, and Antonio Maceo issued the call for an uprising on 24 February 1895, Cuba was ripe for insurrection. The "Pearl of the Spanish Empire"—the "Ever Faithful Island"—was about to become independent.

three

Revolution and Reaction, 1895–1955

With the call to arms of 24 February 1895, thousands of people in the émigré communities of the United States headed back to Cuba, including José Martí, Máximo Gómez, Antonio Maceo, and Calixto García. The dream of a revolution launched by external manipulation but joined immediately by a broadly based, spontaneous internal uprising was about to become reality. The Cuban population in the United States quickly dropped to only 11,000 people. The émigrés had gone home to win the freedom of the fatherland. At first Spanish officials reacted predictably, expecting the rebels to self-destruct in an orgy of ideological disagreement and political betrayal. But this rebellion was destined to be different from its predecessors. Under the command of Máximo Gómez and Antonio Maceo, the insurgent armies broke out of their bases of support in the eastern mountains and invaded deep into the planter heartland of western Cuba—regions where even the Ten Years' War had not penetrated. Never before had the planter elite seen real war and personally experienced the devastation of armed rebellion. Recruitment of new guerrilla troops became easier and easier, and by 1896 there were insurgent armies fighting in every province of Cuba.[1]

The rebels also decided on a change in tactics, implementing a scorched-earth policy and destroying the plantations of those wealthy *criollos* whom they felt were making the Spanish cause easier. In earlier years, Cuban rebels had targeted *peninsular* officials as their real enemies, and the essence of rebel thought had simply been separatism—throwing off the Spanish yoke. After the Ten Years' War, however, separatist thought developed a social and economic agenda, calling for elimination of Spanish imperial exploitation as well as the social and economic oppression of the *criollo* elite. It was the broadening of the revolutionary agenda that made the rebellion of 1895 different and that gave the rebels so much success in recruiting supporters from the lower classes. Rebel leaders called for an end to all sugar production, destruction of the planter aristocracy, and widespread redistribution of property. General Máximo Gómez best characterized the rebel policy: "It is necessary to burn the hive to disperse the swarm." That military policy was a direct political corollary of José Martí's call for massive social change in addition to independence.[2]

To deal with the rebellion, Spain turned to Arsenio Martínez Campos. Born in Spain in 1831, Martínez Campos had spent his career as an officer in the Spanish army. As a young general in 1874, Martínez was given command of

Spanish troops trying to subdue rebel forces in the Ten Years' War in Cuba. He succeeded in crushing the rebellion through brilliant military maneuvers and astute political conciliation, in which he offered amnesty and financial rewards to Cubans agreeing to a peaceful settlement. When the war was over he was appointed captain-general of Cuba. Martínez tried to be an enlightened leader, campaigning for a wide range of civil liberties, tax reductions, and free trade, but he encountered much resistance from Madrid.[3] He spent the late 1880s and early 1890s back in Spain, but when the Cuban rebellion began in 1895 was returned to command of Spanish forces in Cuba. Martínez tried once again to use the tactic of political conciliation and compromise, but this time the rebel leaders were just as recalcitrant as Spain had always been. There would be no compromise.[4]

With the rebellion rapidly getting out of hand, and with Martínez Campos's conciliation policies collapsing, Spain decided to pursue a policy of violent repression, and it turned to Valeriano Weyler to do the job. The days of Spanish vacillation were over. Weyler was the Spanish military attaché to the United States during the Civil War. He went to Cuba and served as an officer for the Spanish army during the Ten Years' War, and in 1896 he was appointed governor of Cuba and told to crush the rebellion—a task he undertook with enthusiasm and an iron hand. One of the most frustrating problems Spanish military officials were facing was the guerrilla nature of the war. The insurgent armies were living off the land, requiring a tenth of the logistical support Spanish troops needed, and Spanish troops were unable to distinguish the rebel soldiers from the civilian population. The guerrillas used unconventional hit-and-run tactics against Spanish troops and then melted into the civilian villages and towns. Weyler instituted a policy of herding the rural population into garrisoned towns, where they could be controlled and where the Cuban guerrillas could not recruit or use them for support. In 1896 and 1897 Weyler relocated more than 300,000 people into camps where hunger, disease, and starvation were the rule. Innocent people died by the tens of thousands in Weyler's "reconcentration camps."

Weyler's policies made life more difficult for the insurgents in the short term, but they were political disasters in the long term. In Madrid, Spanish liberals described Weyler's policies as brutal and inhumane. In the United States the émigré newspapers made the most of Weyler's program, advertising the mass suffering in the relocation camps and supplying a steady stream of similar stories to the large metropolitan dailies in Boston, Philadelphia, New York, and Chicago. Millions of American readers began to sympathize with the rebels in ways that would have been impossible a few years before, and those sympathies found political expression in the attitudes of a number of prominent congressmen. Whatever tactical advantage Weyler enjoyed because of the concentration camps was squandered in the overwhelming political opposition it generated in Cuba, Spain, and the United States.

The rebellion transcended the charismatic personalities of its major leaders. José Martí died in battle 1895, but the rebellion survived the news of his death. On 7 December 1897 Spanish troops ambushed General Antonio Maceo in San Pedro, just outside Havana. Maceo was killed in the skirmish. Maceo was already a warrior-hero to the Cuban masses, and Spaniards could not imagine their continuing the fight with Maceo gone. Three days later, when Valeriano Weyler learned of Maceo's death, he was so convinced of ultimate victory that he convened a group of his officers and celebrated it. Calixto García died a little while later.[5] Despite of the deaths of its leaders, however, the insurrection continued to gather momentum. Martínez Campos was unable to dislodge the rebels in the east, and Weyler was similarly unsuccessful in the west. By early 1898 it was clear on both sides of the Atlantic that Spanish rule was doomed.

That realization created a sense of panic among the Cuban *criollo* elite. Ever since the large increase in the numbers of slaves arriving in Cuba in the early 1800s, they had viewed Spanish rule as the only way of preserving the social order—making sure that the black and mulatto population did not rise up, overthrow white rule, and redistribute property and power. When the revolution assumed its radical dimension, complete with the rhetoric of true revolution and destruction of planter property, the conservatives became even more convinced of the need for Spanish protection. But by 1897 and early 1898, when it became increasingly clear that Spain would be unable to provide any protection, and that violent class warfare was a real possibility, the Cuban elite began to look for another protector. The only place they could expect any help was up north—in the United States. Once again the annexationist theme assumed a prominent place in Cuban political debate.

By that time the United States had become deeply interested in the revolution. During the 1880s and early 1890s American investment in Cuba had grown dramatically. As sugar production became more highly mechanized, many Cuban planters were desperate for capital to make the conversion. Much of that capital came from U.S. firms. At the same time, large numbers of Cuban planters had been ruined by the Ten Years' War, and during the 1880s American investors bought up land from the bankrupt owners. Many plantation owners who retained their land did so only by incorporating and selling stock to American investors. By the mid-1890s American investment in Cuban land exceeded $50 million, and American imports of Cuban sugar and tobacco totaled $76 million annually. The markets for Cuban sugar were also changing dramatically. The European sugar beet industry developed dramatically in the 1880s, eliminating that market for Cuban sugar. By the early 1890s more than 94 percent of the Cuban sugar product was marketed in the United States.

Traditionally, the interests of the United States and the *criollo* upper class had been one and the same. With equal fervor both groups feared and opposed social unrest, racial equality, and political instability, all of which might emerge from an independent Cuba. Although annexation to the United States had often been the most popular idea, the preservation of Spanish sovereignty in Cuba was preferable to rule by a rabble of lower-class, Afro-Cuban workers. The continuation of Spanish rule was good for one reason: it meant the protection of private property, economic privilege, and social order. For those American corporate interests heavily invested in the Cuban sugar industry, the prospects of a rebel victory were frightening. When Cuban planters began appealing to President William McKinley for U.S. intervention, they found a ready ally in the business community. The war was devastating the Cuban economy. In 1894 Cuban planters harvested more than 1 million tons of sugar, but that dropped to 225,000 tons in 1896 and 212,000 tons in 1897. American imports from Cuba dropped from $76 million in 1894 to less than $15 million in 1898. In 1895 there had been more than 3 million head of cattle grazing on the island, but by 1898 that number had dropped to only 200,000. Nor could Cubans purchase

American goods in significant volumes. U.S. exports to Cuba dropped by more than half during the same four-year period.[6]

While American corporate interests were becoming increasingly concerned about the direction of events in Cuba, the public was being whipped into a frenzy of anti-Spanish sentiment by the "yellow journalism" of people like Joseph Pulitzer and William Randolph Hearst. Pulitzer published the *New York World*, while Hearst's paper was the *New York Journal*. In their competition for readers, they sensationalized events in Cuba, making Spain appear as the embodiment of evil and the Cuban rebels as symbols of virtue and freedom. American public opinion became decidedly anti-Spanish in 1896 and 1897, providing political support for the interventionist demands of the Cuban *criollos* and American investors. By early 1898 public pressure on President William McKinley to do something to help end the bloodshed led to American efforts to get the Spanish government to agree to a cease-fire and to grant internal self-government to the Cubans. This American interference was widely resented both in Spain and by pro-Spanish people in Cuba.[7]

When the U.S.S. *Maine* exploded in Havana harbor in February 1898, American interference became an American war. President McKinley sent the battleship to Havana as a show of force after riots erupted in Havana against Spain's reform policies. The ship arrived in Havana on 25 January. For reasons that remain mysterious, the ship exploded and sank on 15 February, killing 252 sailors. Another eight died of their injuries. Most Americans blamed Spain, and the demand for war escalated. The United States held Spain responsible, although the cause of the explosion has never been firmly established. The cry "Remember the *Maine*" made it impossible to resist the clamor for war to free the Cubans; Congress declared war on 25 April 1898.[8]

Although the American mobilization effort was haphazard at best, the war was over in a matter of months. On 1 May, Commodore George Dewey destroyed the Spanish fleet at Manila Bay in the Philippines. U.S. naval vessels blockaded Cuban ports. Early in July the Spanish fleet made a desperate but ultimately unsuccessful attempt to break through the blockade. When the smoke of battle cleared, four Spanish cruisers and two torpedo boats were destroyed. The U.S. Navy emerged from the battle virtually unscathed. American troops invaded Cuba on 22 June 1898, and a month later a Spanish contingent of 17,000 soldiers in Santiago surrendered. On 12 August 1898 Spain agreed to a cease-fire. The next day Manila fell, and Spanish forces in the Philippines surrendered.

At the Paris peace conference Spain agreed to harsh terms, at least for the future of its empire. Cuba was awarded its independence, and the United States annexed Guam and Puerto Rico. The United States also paid Spain $20 million and assumed sovereignty over the Philippines. Diplomats signed the treaty on 10 December 1898, and on 6 February 1899, after an intense debate on the merits of an overseas empire, the U.S. Senate ratified the treaty. Because of the war, the United States gained a foothold in the western Pacific, and the Caribbean had become an American lake.[9]

The American intervention into the war changed its complexion altogether, transforming it from a Cuban-Spanish conflict into the "Spanish-American War." In his war message to Congress, President Mckinley said nothing about Cuban independence, only about the need to end the war and restore order.

Indeed, American corporate interests did not want independence, at least not the revolutionary independence being articulated by people like Máximo Gómez. Historian Louis A. Pérez wrote,

> North Americans early detected in the shattered ranks of the creole property owners natural allies in its pursuit of control over Cuba. Both opposed Cuban independence. Both opposed Cuban government. Policymakers needed supporters, property owners needed security. The United States searched for a substitute for independence; *peninsular* and creole elites sought a substitute for colonialism. The logic of collaboration was compelling. There was an inexorable choicelessness about this collaboration. . . . The old colonial elites in need of protection and the new colonial rulers in need of allies arrived at an understanding.[10]

The budding arrangement was not without its opponents, in Cuba as well as the United States. Anti-imperialists in Congress were suspicious of the motives of the McKinley administration; they realized that American intervention was not simply an expression of altruistic concern for the suffering of the oppressed Cuban masses. They worried that the declaration was simply a cover for corporate adventurers interested in using the U.S. government to promote their economic interests abroad. To secure congressional support for the war message, McKinley had to agree to the Teller Amendment, in which the United States "hereby disclaims any disposition of intention to exercise sovereignty, jurisdiction, or control over said island except for pacification thereof, and asserts its determination, when it is accomplished, to leave the government and control of the island to its people."

But the Teller Amendment was hardly worth the paper it was written on. The United States established a military government over Cuba in 1899 under the command of General John Brooke (January–December 1899) and General Leonard Wood (December 1899–May 1902). Both men were convinced that Cuba was not ready for independence, and they urged President McKinley to oppose the idea. The president concurred and told Congress that the United States should not cut its ties to the island. Those words were music to the ears of corporate interests in the United States as well as to the *criollo* elite in Cuba.

Back in the early 1890s José Martí had expressed his fears about the United States. Although he admired the country's political democracy and the sheer strength of its economy, he had an intense dislike for American materialism and the hedonistic nature of American culture. He also feared the United States. The fact that Cuba had fallen into American economic orbit was especially worrisome to Martí, since he was convinced that economic union automatically led to political union. He believed that America would not want a truly independent Cuba in the Caribbean,[11] and he was right. When the period of the military occupation came to an end in 1902 and U.S. troops prepared to withdraw, Congress granted Cuba a nominal independence, but only under the terms of an amendment proposed by Senator Orville H. Platt. In addition to limiting the ability of the new Cuban government to contract a public debt and guaranteeing the right of the United States to maintain military bases on Cuba, the Platt Amendment prohibited Cuba from entering into any treaties with foreign governments without the express permission of the United States, which also had the "right to intervene for the preservation of Cuban independence, the maintenance of a government adequate for the protection of life, property, and individual liberty, and for discharging the obligations with respect to Cuba imposed by the Treaty of Paris on the United States, now to be assumed and undertaken by the government of Cuba."[12] General William R. Shafter was more blunt: "As I view it, we have taken Spain's war upon ourselves."[13]

The American military occupation between 1898 and 1902 had a dramatic impact on Cuba. First of all, there was considerable resentment among all but the most conservative of the *criollo* elite about the nature of the American involvement and the significance of the Platt Amendment. American military commanders had virtually taken over the war, and American diplomats had negotiated the final settlement with Spain. Cuban military figures and revolutionary political leaders were excluded from meaningful participation. Many Cubans worried that they had traded one colonialism for another, and that Cuban sovereignty had been put on the back burner. Juan Gualberto Gómez, the prominent black Cuban general, remarked despondently that the "Platt Amendment has reduced the independence and sovereignty of the Cuban republic to a myth."[14]

Many Cuban veterans resented the outcome of the war. They also faced a Cuban economy that lay in ruin. Tens of thousands of plantations, ranches, and farms had been destroyed, and many of the poor soldiers and their families squatted on land they did not own. The American military government found itself with a major pacification problem—restoring peace to the island while doing the bidding of the *criollo* elite and pushing the squatters off the land. The United States organized native militia units to carry out the pacification, and when it proved impossible to secure convictions for looting, squatting, or banditry, the militia received authorization to perform summary executions of the accused. Anti-American hostility increased throughout the rural countryside.[15]

The years of war and occupation brought dramatic changes in land tenure. During the early 1890s Cuban planters and farmers had gone deeply into debt, mortgaging their land in order to boost production, but the war devastated the economy. More than 70 percent of the total value of all urban and rural land in Cuba was mortgaged. In 1900 there were only 207 sugar mills, out of 1,100 in 1894, still operating. Cuban property owners emerged from the war with neither the capital to rebuild nor the credit to pay the mortgages. The U.S. government declared a moratorium for two years on debt payments, bringing some temporary relief to land and mill owners, but when the moratorium expired, bankruptcies skyrocketed. When the United States authorized the reconstruction and expansion of the railroad system, the right of way laws also led to large land transfers. Such corporate entities as the Cuban Railway and the Cuban Central Railway bought up large tracts of land for depots, towns, and right of way. Finally, the United States insisted on the rationalization of land titles in Cuba. Historically, those titles were notoriously vague, and much land was owned in common by large numbers of small farmers. But when the phalanx of lawyers and surveyors was done with it, many farmers had lost their land.[16]

The land transfers reinforced the prerevolutionary social structure. Large *criollo* planters often retained or even expanded their holdings. During the war, by making hefty contributions to the rebel cause or hiring their own private armies, they had saved their land from devastation. Only they could afford the lawyers and surveyors to secure titles to their land. Wealthy U.S. syndicates and land corporations moved in, buying up bankrupt property, paying back taxes, commissioning land surveys, and acquiring new titles. American companies like the Cuban American Sugar Company, the United Fruit Company, and the Cuban Land Company acquired enormous tracts. By 1906 U.S. investors owned about 20 percent of the island's land and had taken over more than 75 percent of the cattle ranches. Also during the first 10 years after the war, more than 300,000 Spaniards emigrated to Cuba. Since the U.S. government guaranteed property rights, Spanish merchants—*peninsulares*—retained much of their influence.[17]

The American occupation had a dramatic impact on the Cuban economy— exactly what corporate investors and *criollo* planters and merchants had expected. Cuba was quickly integrated into the North American economy. In addition to large purchases of land, American companies made deep inroads into banking, public utilities, transportation, and lead, manganese, copper, and iron ore mining. They controlled the railroad, telephone, electricity, urban transit, and banking industries, while American-owned construction firms built most of the bridges, roads, and public buildings in Cuba in the early 1900s. The Cuban economy was also completely dependent on the American machine tool industry for its progress in industrialization. By 1911 American investment in Cuba exceeded $200 million, and it went over $1 billion by the early 1920s. Thousands of U.S. citizens also moved to Cuba, hoping to do there what earlier generations of settlers had done in Oregon, California, Texas, and Florida. Most of them bought up small to medium-sized farms. By 1910 more than 60 percent of all rural land in Cuba was controlled—either owned or leased—by foreign companies or foreign-born settlers, while another 15 percent was in the hands of resident Spaniards. When Congress passed the Reciprocity Treaty of 1903 reducing tariffs of Cuban products, the integration of the Cuban and American economies only accelerated.[18]

In addition to economic domination, the popular culture of the Cuban elites took on a decidedly North American flavor. The occupation government insisted that English be taught in all public schools, and it was clear to all middle- and upper-class Cubans that fluency in English would be a prerequisite to economic success. The Cuban elites became bilingual. The United States also sponsored teacher education programs so that Cuban teachers could travel and study in the United States, and by the 1920s more than 90 percent of all public school teachers in Cuba had participated in the program. Protestant churches in the United States launched aggressive proselytizing missions in Cuba, and they established well-heeled private schools where the Cuban elite sent their children. These schools were confined to white Cubans. Usually, the Protestant schools received financial support from the large American corporations doing business in Cuba. American magazines, movies, newspapers, and books flooded the island, as did American-produced consumer goods and sports, especially baseball. The Americans also formed their ubiquitous civic and social associations such as the Chamber of Commerce, YMCA, Rotary Club, and Lions' Club, and they invited the Cuban elite to join. American tourists created a huge industry in Cuba, increasing from 35,000 visitors a year in 1914 to 100,000 a year in 1930. The Havana economy became especially dependent on the tourist industry, and English-speaking skills became necessary for even working-class groups like waitresses, taxi drivers, tour guides, bus drivers, and telephone and telegraph operators. What had happened in Cuba as a result of the revolution was more land concentration, more foreign economic domination, and more power in the hands of the white upper class.[19]

The situation for Afro-Cubans was particularly dismal. The rhetoric of equality and social reform expressed by people like José Martí had inspired broad support for the revolution among black people. About half of the enlisted troops and perhaps 40 percent of the officers in the rebel army were Afro-Cubans, but when the war ended they were mustered out into a ruined economy. Many of them lost their land to foreign investors, railroads, or *criollo* entrepreneurs. As the sugar plantations expanded in size, the amount of land available for subsistence agriculture decreased. At the same time, large numbers of poorer immigrants and contract laborers from Haiti and Jamaica increased unemployment and reduced wages for poor Afro-Cubans. Unemployment among Afro-Cubans by 1907 exceeded 30 percent. Although blacks totaled 610,000 out of a Cuban population of about two million, they were woefully underrepresented in the professions, the civil service, and the postwar military. Plagued by a sense of profound betrayal, Afro-Cubans founded the political party Agrupación Independiente de Color to promote their needs, but in 1910 the government outlawed the organization. In 1912, primarily in Oriente Province, a political uprising against the government had overwhelmingly racial overtones. The rebels attacked sugar property, especially that owned by foreigners. They also attacked railroads and Spanish-owned bodegas and cantinas. To suppress the rebellion, the government suspended civil rights and reopened the concentration camps to separate the rural population from the rebels. The United States landed troops. It proved to be a ruthless pacification campaign in which 6,000 Cuban blacks were slaughtered.[20]

With the Cuban elites and middle classes thoroughly integrated into the North American economic and social network, the Cuban working classes— black as well as white—began to develop a dual enemy that revolved around the upper class as well as the United States. Class conflict in Cuba acquired a decidedly nationalistic tone. For poor Cubans, things had not changed that much. They had traded Spanish and *criollo* masters for American and *criollo* masters and were probably worse off because the size and power of the United States made real change even more unlikely. The domination of Cuba by U.S. capital and upper-class *criollos* set in motion a powerful revolutionary movement.

Moderate nationalists focused their resentments on the presidential administration of Gerardo Machado. He came to power in 1924 with a reformist reputation—a man able to balance off the demands of U.S. interests on the island with the rhetoric of Cuban sovereignty. But Machado lost most of his support when sugar prices collapsed in 1925 and later when the Great Depression descended on Cuba in 1929. The depression devastated poor workers, students, and the middle class, and they adopted the weapon of Cuba nationalism to criticize the economic system causing so much suffering. Even upper-class interests turned on Machado because they feared that a continuation of the status quo would only lead to a real socioeconomic revolution that could destroy them. There was no way Machado could survive, especially once the United States recognized his vulnerability. A revolution dislodged him in 1933.

The new Cuban leader was Carlos Manuel de Céspedes, but he stayed in power only three weeks. With strong ties to the United States, he could not inspire any support among large numbers of Cubans. He was replaced by Ramón Grau San Martín, who immediately tried to forge a new political coalition. The government abrogated the Platt Amendment, reduced utility rates by 40 percent, lowered interest rates, enfranchised women, and passed a series of social legislation that included a minimum wage, eight-hour day, workers' compensation, and a requirement that at least half of all workers in commerce, manufacturing, and agriculture had to be Cuban natives. It was a middle-of-the road, reformist political agenda, but it doomed the Grau government. U.S. economic interests hated the labor legislation because it would cut profit margins, but Cuban radicals felt the government had not gone far enough in promoting revolutionary change. At the very minimum they wanted the breakup of the large sugar estates, nationalization of native and foreign-owned public services, and a highly progressive taxation system. They were not going to get those demands from Grau. Without real political support on the left or the right, the Grau government dissolved. By 1934 new power had appeared on the Cuban political stage—Fulgencio Batista.[21]

Fulgencio Batista was born in Banes, Cuba, in 1901, and spent his early career in the army, rising to the rank of sergeant by 1928. He, too, was a member of the large group of disaffected soldiers and civil servants who joined together to overthrow Machado and his successor, Carlos Manuel de Céspedes, in 1934. He later turned on Grau and became the dominant political force in Cuba. Batista became chief of staff of the army in 1934 and for the next seven years controlled the Cuban government from that position. Although he established more than 1,000 new schools and improved social services, his government was an absolute dictatorship. Batista became president of Cuba in 1940 and then a member of the Senate in 1948, and in 1952 he carried out a coup d'état, proclaimed himself chief-of-state, and suspended the constitution.[22] Batista, however, was no different from earlier generations of Cuban rulers. The country remained dominated internally by rich and well-to-do white *criollos* and externally by U.S. economic institutions.

In fact, the trends of earlier years—more North American economic and cultural penetration as well as increases in the gap between the rich and the poor in Cuba—only intensified during Batista's reign. U.S. concerns like International Telephone and Telegraph, American and Foreign Power Company, Western Railroads of Cuba, and Consolidated Railroads of Cuba controlled more than 80 percent of the railroad industry and 90 percent of public utilities. American land corporations controlled more than 40 percent of sugar production, and American banks held more than 40 percent of Cuban deposits. The petroleum and mining sectors of the economy were also American dominated. American-owned companies produced the bulk of the cement, glass, fertilizers, paper, textiles, soft drinks, publishing, and chemicals. There were nearly 7,000 North Americans living in Cuba and running those concerns, and more than 300,000 tourists from the United States were visiting Cuba annually. Large gambling, drug, prostitution, and pornography industries materialized to serve the tourists. Huge hotels and casinos, complete with the latest American entertainers, popped up in Havana and Santiago. Tens of thousands of American sailors on Caribbean duty took their liberties in those two cities. Along with the booming vice industries came tens of millions of dollars of mob money from organized crime in the United States. Prominent American mobsters like Meyer Lanksy,

Lucky Luciano, Joe Bonano, and Frank Costello worked closely with the Batista government to secure lucrative gambling concessions, and in return government officials received millions in bribes and payoffs.[23]

The domination of the Cuban economy and society by U.S. capital and upper-class *criollos* eventually set in motion a powerful revolutionary movement. In the beginning of the twentieth century, Cuban nationalism was primarily modest and accommodationist in tone, with its adherents—middle-class professionals, civil servants, military officers, smaller planters, and small businessmen—hoping to bring about less control by the United States without altering the traditional social order. U.S. military intervention occurred between 1906 and 1909 and again in 1912, and at various times during the 1920s and 1930s the threat of military intervention was raised. Not surprisingly, the Platt Amendment became a point of increasing resentment among many Cubans. Ironically, however, American economic power in Cuba blunted the force of conservative nationalism. Cuban planters, bankers, manufacturers, and merchants were increasingly dependent on the United States, even though many of them wanted more political control. The old fear of well-to-do Cubans—that removal of Spanish or American political power would lead to social upheaval—still exerted enormous influence on the island, and in the long run it eviscerated the impact of conservative nationalism.

Instead, Cuban nationalism assumed a revolutionary flavor. Conservative nationalism did little to address the needs of other constituencies in Cuba, especially the large lower class. Whether the administrations of Tomás Estrada Palma, Gerardo Machado, Fulgencio Batista, or any other Cuban presidents, the basic Cuban social structure did not change. The poor were still poor, very poor, and increasingly irritated with the status quo. Out of their plight emerged a powerful revolutionary nationalism that had strong allies among students and intellectuals. In the late nineteenth century, because of economic depression and oppressive Spanish attitudes about labor unions, the Cuban labor movement took on a decidedly radical tone. Anarcho-syndicalism became the dominant theme of labor values in the early 1900s. During the 1920s the Cuban government launched an attack of political terrorism on the radical unions, crushing strikes and deporting, imprisoning, and even killing prominent radical leaders. By the end of the 1920s the left wing of the labor movement had been all but destroyed. A political vacuum appeared on the Cuban left, and when the Great Depression developed in the 1930s the Cuban Communist party had considerable success organizing sugar mill and cane field workers. The Cuban Communist party filled the void created by the government's destruction of the labor unions.[24]

Other radical, anti-Batista groups emerged during the 1950s, but Fidel Castro's 26th of July Movement became the dominant left-wing political force on the island.[25] He was born in Mayarí, Cuba, in 1927 and received a law degree from the University of Havana in 1950. On 26 July 1953 Castro led a daring attack on the Cuban army barracks at Moncada in Santiago de Cuba, and although the attack failed and he was arrested, its boldness thrust Castro into the anti-Batista limelight. He spent several years in prison, and on his release in 1955 he immediately began plotting against the government, emphasizing armed struggle and social justice. Operating out of the Sierra Maestra region of Oriente Province in eastern Cuba, Castro steadily gained strength. Like previous

Cuban insurrectionists, he looked for support and money in the émigré communities of the United States, and he found a considerable amount of it among the Cuban cigar workers of South Florida.[26] Once again the Cuban-American connection was playing a critically important role in Cuban political life.

On the Eve of the Great Migration:
Cuban America in the 1950s

During the first half of the twentieth century the Cuban-American community grew only incrementally. At the turn of the century, there were approximately 11,000 people of Cuban ancestry living in the United States. Most of them lived in South Florida, especially in Key West and Ybor City, but there were smaller communities in New Orleans and New York City. Almost all of the Cuban Americans functioned within the economic context of the cigar industry. There was a fairly steady flow of immigrants from Cuba between 1900 and 1950. Between 1901 and 1910 a total of 40,159 Cubans entered the United States. More than 8.5 million other immigrants settled in the United States during that decade. Between 1910 and 1920, largely because of World War I, the number of Cuban immigrants dropped to 27,837, and general immigration to the United States totaled only 5.5 million. Cuban immigration fell during the 1920s to 15,608, primarily because of anti-immigrant and anti-Cuban vigilante activities by the Ku Klux Klan in South Florida, severe labor unrest in the cigar industry, and the collapse of the Florida real estate economy, all of which constituted serious social and economic disincentives for prospective immigrants. Total immigration to the United States fell to 3.9 million during the 1920s. The Great Depression of the 1930s all but eliminated immigration to the United States. Only 471,000 people immigrated during the decade, and only 4,122 of them were Cubans. Between 1941 and 1950 a total of 15,451 people arrived in the United States.[1]

But although more than 100,000 Cubans immigrated to the United States between 1900 and 1950, the Cuban-American community did not really grow substantially during those years. The immigration figures are deceptive. Because of the proximity of Cuba to Florida and the regular steamship routes, travel between the two countries was cheap and efficient. Cubans frequently came to the United States for short periods, returning to Cuba after a few months or a few years only to return again when they needed work or wanted to visit friends and relatives. Since the National Origins Act of 1924 specifically exempted Western Hemisphere immigrants from the quota restrictions, there were relatively few obstacles to the Cuban immigrants. In 1959, on the eve of the great migration from Cuba to the United States, there were only 30,000 Cubans living in the United States.

The key political issue in the Cuban-American émigré communities before 1898 was the status of Cuba itself. In Key West the Instituto San Carlos functioned as an emigrant aid society as well as a center for Cuban nationalism. In New York such groups as El Ateneo Democrático, La Sociedad Republicana de Cuba y Puerto Rico, Liga Patriótico, Artesanso de Cuba, La Auxiliadora de Cuba, and La Sociedad de Independencia performed similar functions. Such Cuban-American newspapers as *El Eco de Cuba, El Filibústero, El Separatista, La República,* and *Patría* played central roles in disseminating nationalist ideas.[2]

After independence, however, subtle changes came to the Cuban-American community. Most of those people who considered themselves to be political émigrés returned to Cuba, but economic opportunities there were limited. Many Cuban Americans employed in the cigar industry made the decision to stay in the United States, and in the process they began to make the transition from émigrés to immigrants. The separatist press and the independence clubs disappeared quickly in Key West and Tampa. There was no point anymore to promoting independence: independence had been achieved. With the exodus of patriot leaders back to Cuba, radical activists from the Cuban-American working classes began to shape the political culture in Tampa and Key West. That radical culture survived in the Cuban-American community until the Great Depression in the 1930s, when mechanization, changing tastes, and economic decline all but destroyed the hand-rolled cigar industry in South Florida.

Other changes came to the Cuban-American community as well. Before the Revolution, Cuban-American leaders worked hard at creating multiracial sensitivities in order to enjoy political solidarity. The idea of *Cubanidad* (being Cuban), they emphasized, transcended racial divisions. But after Cuba achieved independence, those old racial divisions reasserted themselves in the Cuban-American community. They came just when the Jim Crow system was descending on the American South. New organizations appeared to replace the older patriot organizations, and membership was based on race. In Key West the new Sociedad Cuba admitted only whites, as did the Círculo Cubano in Tampa. Afro-Cubans in Tampa formed the Unión Martí-Maceo, which was only for blacks.[3] Racial divisions would plague Cuban Americans for the rest of the century.

Throughout the late nineteenth and twentieth centuries, the size of the Cuban-American community had fluctuated according to the political winds. During periods of economic dislocation or political instability—such as the Ten Years' War (1868–78), the depression of the 1880s and early 1890s, the uprising of 1912, or the political turmoil of the early 1920s and the early 1930s—the Cuban émigré and immigrant community increased in size and visibility, only to shrink back when good times returned to the island. During the years of the Batista dictatorship between 1952 and 1959, the Cuban population of Miami increased from 20,000 to 50,000 people.[4] Despite that ebb and flow, however, the size of the Cuban-American community gradually increased over time. In 1960 the Bureau of the Census reported that there were 124,416 people of Cuban descent living in the United States. Of that group, 79,150 were Cuban-born and 45,266 were born in the United States to Cuban parents. Distinct Cuban-American communities existed in New York City, across the Hudson River in New Jersey, Philadelphia, Chicago, Boston, Mobile, Los Angeles, and New Orleans, but the bulk of Cuban Americans lived in Florida—Miami, Jacksonville, Tampa, Key West, and Pensacola.[5]

Some Americans had long been aware of the small Cuban presence in the United States, but it was not until the 1950s that a handful of Cuban Americans found themselves in the limelight. Not surprisingly, entertainment and sports were the vehicles for their prominence. Traditionally in American history, sport and entertainment were the first avenues for success among immigrant groups. It was as if racism and ethnocentrism could be set aside if an individual exhibited talent in one of those areas. As long as racism and prejudice closed off other opportunities for immigrants, sports and entertainment were industries where immigrants could achieve success.[6]

Although large numbers of Cuban Americans came from economically prosperous families who were closely connected to major North American corporations or estates in Cuba, the sports and entertainment connection nevertheless functioned for some Cuban Americans. The stereotypical Cuban American of the 1950s was Desi Arnaz, Jr. Arnaz was born as Desiderio Alberto Arnaz y de Archa III in Santiago de Cuba in 1917 to a wealthy landed family. With the Batista revolution of 1933–34, the family estates were confiscated by the government and Arnaz's father was imprisoned. Desi and his mother fled penniless to Miami. He went to work with Xavier Cugat's band in 1937 and formed his own band in 1938. It was the age of the big band in American entertainment, and Arnaz earned a following. In 1940 Arnaz went to Hollywood with a part in the film *Too Many Girls*. Lucille Ball also had a part in the film, and they fell in love and were married later in the year. During the 1940s she continued to make movies, and he toured the country with his band. They both became celebrities in the 1950s when they produced and starred in the television comedy "I Love Lucy." Arnaz played the role of Ricky Ricardo, a Cuban-born bandleader at the Tropicana nightclub in New York City. Actually, Arnaz was straightman for the zany antics of his wife, Lucy, whose obsession with show business provided a story line for dozens of episodes. "I Love Lucy" was the most popular television show in American during the 1950s, and although Arnaz was not the major character, Americans fell in love with his fractured English, gentle humor, "Ba-ba-loo" lyrics, and conga drum rhythms. They also formed Desilu, Inc., a production company that made both of them multimillionaires by producing other situation comedies in the 1950s and 1960s.[7]

Other Cuban-American entertainers and sports figures also made a mark on the American popular culture consciousness. During the 1920s Cuban dances began to take the country by storm, changing the musical repetoires of bands and orchestras, dance clubs, radio shows, and nightclubs throughout the country. The rumba was the most popular during the 1920s and 1930s, and in the 1930s and 1940s Desi Arnaz, Jr., popularized the conga. Other Cuban dances also became cult fads—the danzón, son, bolero, mambo, pachanga, and the cha-cha-cha. In New Orleans, Miami, and New York City and then throughout the country, Afro-Cuban music mixed with jazz and became part of the larger musical culture. Prominent band leaders like Dizzy Gillespie, Nat King Cole, Duke Ellington, Cab Calloway, Stan Kenton, and Louis Armstrong hired Cuban musicians for their shows. Mario Bauza, Armando Peraza, Carlos Valdéz, Ernesto Lecuona, José Curbelo, Cándido Camero, Xavier Cugat, Miguelito Valdés, and Arsenio Rodríguez all earned national reputations that transcended the Cuban-American commmunity.[8]

Nor was there any shortage of Cuban sports stars in the American limelight. Kid Chocolate and Kid Gavilán became popular boxers and regular fighters on

Gillette's "Friday Night Fight" television series in the 1950s, but it was in base-ball that Cuban athletes really made their mark. Early in the 1870s baseball gained popularity in Cuba. Visiting American merchant sailors played the game and began to organize Cuban teams for opponents. From there the game spread across the island. Baseball also became very popular in the émigré communities of Tampa and Key West. The *criollo* elite in Cuba, enamored of everything North American, brought the game from the United States, and by following it while abandoning the Spanish bullfights they used sports for political expression. Upper-class Cubans increasingly eschewed Sunday afternoon bullfights in favor of baseball games. The Cuban League of Professional Baseball was established in 1878, and baseball was on the track to becoming the Cuban national pastime. When radio began broadcasting games in the 1920s and 1930s, the names of American players became household words to generations of Cuban children.[9]

Although major league scouts were aware of the depth of baseball talent in Cuba, they were unable to do much about it because of the color line in the sport. Major league baseball in the United States was a white man's game, and people of Latin and African heritage were confined to playing in the Negro Leagues of the United States or the professional leagues of Mexico, the Dominican Republic, Puerto Rico, and Cuba. They could only dream of playing in the big leagues. But in 1946 Branch Rickey, general manager and owner of the Brooklyn Dodgers, decided to break the color barrier in major league baseball by signing Jackie Robinson to a contract. Over the next decade every team in the National League and the American League integrated their lineups.[10] Baseball scouts began scour-ing the United States and the Caribbean for new talent. Cuba proved to be a gold mine. From those scouting trips and contract signings came such Cuban stars as Bert Campaneris, Mike González, Tony Oliva, Cookie Rojas, Sandy Amorós, Mike Cuéllar, Orlando Peña, Pedro Ramos, Camilo Pascual, and a host of others.[11]

But there was another, larger reality to Cuban-America beyond the baseball diamond, the dance clubs, and great bands, and the "I Love Lucy" show. Cuban America was hardly a monolithic community. In fact, like every other ethnic community in the United States, Cuban America was divided by a series of pro-found racial, economic, religious, and political differences. Political and social life in the Cuban-American community revolved around a kaleidoscope of rich and poor, black and white, Catholic and Protestant, and liberal, conservative, and radical perspectives. The Cuban working classes in the United States were struggling for economic survival. Cigar manufacturers had first moved to the United States in the 1870s to avoid political and social instability on the island and secure a good supply of cheap labor. Depending on where the political atmosphere was most propitious for low wages and labor exploitation, cigar manufacturers would shift economic assets and investment capital back and forth. It was clear to them as well as to the workers that Key West, Tampa, and Havana were all within a single economic orbit. Workers sympathized with one another's problems and supported one another's strikes. Unless they could estab-lish a united front, they stood no chance of improving their economic circum-stances. Cuban workers in Florida and Cuba believed in labor organization, labor legislation, and a liberal social and economic agenda. They were highly politicized and acutely aware of their own economic predicament. Their managerial and corporate counterparts in Cuba and the United States, not surprisingly, were conservative and anti-union.

The Cuban workers in the United States found themselves in difficult political and social circumstances, primarily because Florida was part of the deep South. Southern tobacco, cotton, and sugar planters had always been notoriously anti-union; the last thing they wanted was the large-scale organization of poor blacks and whites in the fields and mills. In fact, many Florida whites were especially anti-Cuban because of the popularity radical political theories had traditionally had among Cuban-American workers. Although there were profound differences in philosophy between Karl Marx and José Martí, southerners were not aware of them. Most southerners viewed the Cuban workers as a kind of radical vanguard, and by the 1950s, during the Red Scare, more than a few southern politicians voiced concern about the possibility of Communist cells in South Florida.[12]

Many Cuban-American workers also faced the dilemma of being black in the American South. Most of the workers were Afro-Cubans, and most white southerners had no love lost for black people, whether they spoke Spanish or English. The fact that the Afro-Cubans were also highly politicized only made them appear more threatening. During the labor strikes of the 1930s and 1950s, especially when integration fears were blossoming after the Supreme Court's *Brown v. Board of Education of Topeka, Kansas,* decision in 1954, the Ku Klux Klan targeted what it called the "Cuban niggers" for a reign of terror. With the tacit and sometimes enthusiastic support of local law-enforcement agencies, the Klan joined forces with manufacturers to crush strikes, intimidate workers, and beat up and kill union organizers. The Klan's ubiquitous burning crosses often lit up the night in the Afro-Cuban neighborhoods. At the same time, the FBI and the CIA launched clandestine investigations of those communities, hoping to turn up secret Communist groups planning anti-American activities.[13]

South Florida was not much more hospitable for poor Cuban whites. During the nineteenth and early twentieth centuries, immigrants to the United States did not normally settle in the South. Its reputation for racism and ethnocentrism kept many immigrants away, as did its retarded economy and system of labor exploitation. The vast majority of southern whites in the 1950s were descendents of those English and Scots-Irish immigrants who had arrived in the United States during the eighteenth and nineteenth century. Not surprisingly, southern whites were not very accustomed to immigrants or ethnic diversity. Also, because of the outcome of the Civil War, they often had an extremely negative, hostile attitude about racial and ethnic differences. For them, moral virtue in any decent society was concentrated in the white community. Far more so than in the great immigrant cities of the Northeast, native southern whites had no sense of cultural pluralism. And the only real enduring diversity in southern ethnic life—the division between whites and blacks—had been a source of strain and violence, not strength. Afro-Cubans were forced to live in separate neighborhoods, and Afro-Cuban children were segregated into separate schools with southern black children. The children of Cuban whites were forbidden to speak Spanish in the public schools, even during lunch and recess. Drop-out rates were very high, and the resulting poverty severe. Job discrimination and such phrases as "Cubans need not apply" became all too common.

Religion was also a distinguishing feature of the Cuban working class in Florida. Southern white culture was dominated by Protestantism—a fundamental Protestantism that was imbued with unusual passion and that played a central role in the cultural identity of the region. During the nineteenth century the major Protestant denominations of the South—Baptists, Presbyterians, Methodists, and Episcopalians—had split with their northern brethren over the slavery issue. The notion of being a white Baptist or a white Presbyterian or a Pentecostal acquired a great deal of power. During the twentieth century, as biblical criticism and modern scholarship progressed in northern universities, southerners became more and more committed to a strict interpretation of their "old time religion." They interpreted the Bible literally, rejected outright any belief in evolution, and maintained a powerful evangelical point of view.

They were also intensely anti-Catholic. To southern Protestants, Roman Catholicism represented an alien religion inherently different from the spirit of American institutions. For Catholics, spiritual sovereignty was contained in the priesthood authority that emanated from the pope in Rome to bishops and then to parish priests and finally to individual worshipers. That seemed antidemocratic to most white southerners, who believed in congregational autonomy and in the idea that no living human being controlled the gates of heaven. From the 1920s into the 1950s southern Protestants felt they detected all kinds of Roman Catholic plots and conspiracies to take over America; they were especially concerned about the large-scale Roman Catholic immigration to the United States from Ireland, eastern and southern Europe, and Latin America. During the twentieth century, the Ku Klux Klan added Catholics and Jews to its list of enemies of the United States. The Klan also spread out of the South into the urban centers of the North where resentment about immigration was increasing.

So in addition to being African and Hispanic in background as well as highly politicized in their backgrounds, the working-class Cubans in Florida were also heavily Roman Catholic, which made them even more suspect as far as southern Protestants were concerned. The irony, of course, was that Cubans were the least religious, at least in terms of formal Catholicism, of any Roman Catholic group in the United States. In the Spanish colonial empire, the church was responsible for the moral and spiritual guidance of the people, but the Catholic clergy was under imperial control. Because of the Patronato Real, church and state in Cuba did not really separate in Cuba until after 1898, when the independence movement triumphed during the Spanish-American War. Spain had enjoyed a papal grant of power allowing the king to appoint, assign, and dismiss priests and collect tithes. Highly dependent on the governing classes, the church became a conservative social and political force identified closely with the interests of the elite. During the Ten Years' War and the independence struggle, the Catholic church sided with the empire and called on Cubans to accept Spanish authority. The fact that the church owned large amounts of property, which it often rented out to peasants or sharecroppers, also gave it a landlord profile that was increasingly resented by poor people. Throughout the seventeenth and eighteenth centuries, because Cuba was considered an economic and political backwater of the Spanish empire, it did not attract good-quality priests. More than a few scoundrels were assigned to Cuban parishes, especially the rural parishes, where peasants came to suspect and disrespect them.[14]

Because of its upper-class bias, links to the conservative forces of the Spanish crown, intense opposition to the independence movement, and ownership of enormous tracts of land, the church alienated large numbers of Cubans, who equated it with economic corruption, political conservatism, and authoritarian control. By the late 1950s there were only 200 parishes serving the 6 million people on the island, and there were only 700 priests working in those parishes. While Ireland had one parish for every 3,000 people and one priest for every 450 people, Cuba had one parish for every 30,000 people and one priest for every 8,500 people. Even Mexico, with all of its anticlerical history, had one parish for every 14,500 people and one priest for every 3,700 people. Although the vast majority of Cubans were Roman Catholic in terms of their personal religious identity, they were not nearly as loyal to the institutional church as many other ethnic Catholics.[15]

The Cuban church for the most part served the needs of the urban middle and upper classes during the colonial period. Cuban priests almost always came from the upper classes, and even as late as the 1950s approximately 80 percent of all Roman Catholic priests working in Cuba were Spanish-born *peninsulares*. At a time in the 1950s when more than 90 percent of Latin Americans identified themselves as Catholics, only 72 percent of Cubans did. Because rural parishes usually had no resident priest, the population rarely attended church services. Even urban areas were underserved, since most priests in Cuba were teachers in private schools and universities rather than pastoral ministers. The reputations of those priests, for intellectual ability as well as moral honor, was less than exemplary.[16] Although most Cuban-American Catholics reflected the religious characeristics of the mother country, southern white Protestants were nevertheless highly critical of their Catholicism.

Even those Cubans living in the United States were held in more than a little contempt by the Roman Catholic nuns and priests trying to serve them. Very few of the Cubans living in Florida in the 1880s and 1890s were actively practicing their faith by attending Mass and receiving the sacraments regularly. American Catholics were determined to rekindle the Cuban faith. The Redemptorists established missions among the Cubans of South Florida in 1869, 1870, and 1876. The Sisters of the Holy Names opened a parochial school for Cuban girls in 1873, but the school—Our Lady of Mercy School—attracted few Cuban-American girls and had to close five years later. Because the Cubans would not attend church, the priests succeeded in building a separate chapel for Cubans in 1879—Our Lady of Charity del Cobre. Still, most of the church's attempts to strengthen the faith of the Cuban Americans in South Florida failed. The Cubans simply did not trust the institutional church or its priests. A frustrated Jesuit priest working in the area in 1904 said that

> I never once asked them for money, on the contrary I always explicitly said to them that I would baptize, marry, and bury them *gratis*. . . . We cannot visit them socially; if we try, as I have tried it hundreds of times, we are misjudged, sinister intentions are attributed to us. We should not dare go when the husbands are not at home and when these are home, the women are relegated to the back rooms of the house. It is a God-forsaken race, at least those we have in Key West. Nothing but a miracle of grace will save them.[17]

This is not to say, of course, that the Cubans were not a religious people. Despite their lack of passion for formal Roman Catholicism, many of the Cuban immigrants to the United States, especially those of Afro-Cuban descent, were faithful to one of the syncretic religions that had fused traditional Catholic beliefs and rituals with African folk beliefs. Among large numbers of Cuban and Cuban-American blacks as well as lower-class Cuban whites and those of mixed ancestry, religious belief revolved around syncretic Afro-Catholic rituals. Although most upper-class *criollo* whites believed that the cults were based on barbaric superstitions, as did the Roman Catholic church hierarchy, the lower classes, especially the Africans, were drawn to them. It was often difficult to distinguish Roman Catholicism from such religious traditions as Santería, Abakua, Mayombería, Regla de Palo, and Regla Conga.[18]

Of course, the presence of these religions among the Afro-Cubans in Florida did little to endear them to the southern white majority or to the minority of American Catholics for that matter. If anything was worse than Catholicism, in their point of view, it was Catholicism that had been combined with African tribal practices. The feelings, however, were mutual. Ironically, the fears of radicalism became self-fulfilling prophecies. Afro-Cubans resented the racism of the South, while poor white Cuban workers hated the ethnocentrism. Both groups despised the self-serving conservatism of the planter and manufacturing elite, whether Cuban or American. They felt like second- and third-class citizens and became highly resentful of American culture. Many of them returned in disgust to Cuba. Those who stayed behind did indeed become a radical political constituency. PCC (Cuban Communist party) groups were organized in the working-class neighborhoods, and a variety of other socialist and anarchist groups tried to build a political base there.[19]

Among the most successful was Fidel Castro and the 26th of July Movement. There were large numbers of *fidelistas* in the working-class neighborhoods of South Florida—especially Key West and Ybor City—in the 1950s. Castro preached the same message as José Martí had preached in the early 1890s, except this time the regime to be toppled was that of Fulgencio Batista, not the Spanish empire. The workers organized 26th of July clubs and raised money to purchase arms and supplies for Castro's guerrilla army. As that band grew into an army, the Florida workers celebrated Castro's successes and openly called for the abdication of the corrupt Batista regime. Late in November 1955, Castro came to South Florida to raise more money, and perhaps even to recruit some more fighters, and he told a working-class audience in Tampa that the "Republic of Cuba is the daughter of the cigarmakers of Tampa."[20]

There were, of course, plenty of other Cuban Americans who wanted nothing to do with Fidel Castro or with revolution. A substantial number of middle-class Cubans and their descendents had moved to the United States during the twentieth century purely for economic reasons and found prosperity. Because the economy of Cuba was so heavily vested in large-scale commercial agriculture—coffee, sugar, and tobacco—there was little room for a middle class. Cuban society was divided by a huge lower class, a tiny upper class, and a middle class that was not much larger. There were not enough rich people to consume the services of large numbers of middle-class professionals, nor were there enough poor people who could afford them. Consequently, the United States became the beneficiary during the twentieth century of a steady flow of highly educated teachers, lawyers, accountants, physicians, dentists, engineers, librarians, professors, pharmacists, journalists, nurses, technologists, architects, and scientists. They simply could not make a living in Cuba. There was also a small group of wealthy Cuban-American families involved in the cigar-manufacturing business. The Vicente Martínez Ybor family, for example, had relocated their cigar factories to Florida in the late nineteenth century and there acted like "Robber Barons," with attitudes not unlike those of Andrew Carnegie or George Pullman. In fact, they had also moved their operations from Key West to what became known as Ybor City outside of Tampa to escape organized labor. Ybor City was originally a company town where the lives of workers were completely controlled by management. Other prominent cigar-manufacturing families, such as the Gatos and the Piños, created similar barrios where organized labor was not permitted. Although that company-town mentality had disappeared by the 1950s, there were nevertheless several thousand Cuban Americans whose wealth had come from the cigar sweatshops of the late nineteenth and early twentieth centuries.[21]

Finally, on both sides of the Straits of Florida, there were tens of thousands of Cubans whose economic livelihood depended on the continuation of the status quo. Unlike the Cuban-American working classes, who were often radical in their politics, mixed in their racial background, and Catholic-Santería in their religion, the more well-to-do Cuban Americans were politically conservative, white, and often Protestant. A great economic, social, and political chasm divided the two groups, and it was not unlike some of the class divisions on the island that would soon bring about another revolution.

It was not surprising, given the close economic ties between the Cuban elite and the United States, that they were almost as much American as they were Cuban, sharing a great deal with upper-class Cuban Americans. The devastation of the Ten Years' War convinced thousands of well-to-do Cubans that their investment capital was safer in American banks than in Cuba. Large numbers of Cubans increased their dollar investments as a way of protecting themselves economically against political instability in Cuba. Each time Cuban politics erupted in civil war or revolution, the flow of capital to the United States increased and the linkages between upper-class groups in Cuba and the United States grew stronger.

The Cuban elite developed an even more unique strategy for protecting themselves against instability on the island. Beginning late in the nineteenth century, increasing numbers of well-to-do Cubans sought and achieved U.S. citizenship. Thousands of rich Cubans became naturalized American citizens, which then allowed them to appeal for U.S. protection of their property. When local disputes caused property damage, these "Cuban Americans" could demand reparations and expect U.S. support for their demands. And because there were so many well-to-do Americans living in Cuba and managing corporate assets there, a good deal of intermarriage occurred between the children of the two elites over the years. Since the child of a U.S. citizen was automatically an American citizen or was eligible to apply for it, there were thousands of "Cuban Americans" on the island who had never really lived in the United States for any extended period. Like their counterparts in the United States, they had only the most conservative expectations of a Cuban government.

But money was not the only thing upper-class *criollos* were sending to the United States. Because school facilities were so lacking on the island, the Cuban elite usually sent their children to the United States for an education. An American education was also an entré for economic success on the island. Many well-to-do Cuban children attended private primary schools, secondary schools, and colleges in the United States, spending their entire childhood and adolescence away from home, becoming more American in outlook than Cuban. Many of them married school sweethearts and took out American citizenship. They even adopted English as their primary language, using Spanish only when they returned home to Cuba for visits.[22]

With their money and their children often living in the United States, they found themselves frequent travelers in America. By the 1940s and early 1950s the regular steamship and ferry traffic between several American ports and Havana was augmented by regular air service between Havana and New York City, Chicago, Philadelphia, Baltimore, New Orleans, and Miami. Wealthy Cubans traveled to the United States to visit their children, relatives, and corporate clients, as well as to hit the most popular vacation spots. They came to the United States to secure sophisticated medical treatment. Finally, and most often, they came to America to shop. That process too had a tremendous effect on Cuban society because the Cuban elite began to use an American frame of reference in judging economic success. That they were well off compared to Latin American standards was no longer enough; they also wanted to be well off by North American standards.

In addition to adopting American consumer culture, many Cubans converted to Protestantism. After the Spanish-American War a variety of Protestant denominations began evangelizing crusades in Cuba, dividing up the island into spheres of influence. Baptist, Methodist, Congregationalist, Lutheran, Presbyterian, and Quaker ministers and missionaries fanned out across the island trying to win converts. They encountered a great deal of success, some because there were religiously devout people looking for an alternative to Catholicism, and others simply because conversion to Protestantism seemed to be socially and economically prudent given the American domination of the island. By the 1950s there were more than 400,000 Protestants in Cuba, and the number of Protestant ministers and chapels outnumbered the number of Catholic priests and churches. Although Catholics still far outnumbered Protestants on the island, Protestants probably outnumbered Catholics on Sunday morning in terms of church attendance throughout the island.[23]

What evolved over the course of the twentieth century was the creation of an upper class in Cuba that had been educated in American schools and was often bilingual in English and Spanish, Protestant or nominal Roman Catholic in religion, conservative in political and economic orientation, intimately linked with the American corporate world by investment or employment, and familiar with or faithful to the products of the American consumer culture and the icons of American popular culture. There are literally thousands of examples of this profile in the Cuban upper class. Tomás Estrada Palma, the man the United States designated as the first president of an independent Cuba in 1902, was a naturalized U.S. citizen, a Quaker, and a fluent speaker of English. Mario Menocal, who served as president of Cuba from 1912 to 1920, had a degree from Cornell University and had been a longtime employee of the Cuban-American Sugar Company. Demetrio Castillo Duany, who became governor of Oriente Province, was a naturalized American citizen who had lived in New York City and studied at the New York School of Commerce. Perfecto Lacosta, longtime mayor of Havana, had a degree from the University of Pennsylvania. With their North

American friends, they had joined the yacht, jockey, Rotary, Lions, Kiwanis, and Optimists clubs; they joined the chambers of commerce, Masonic Lodges, country clubs, American Legion, Daughters of the American Revolution, women's clubs, tennis clubs, athletic clubs, Little League, United Spanish War Veterans, YMCA, YWCA, Women's Christian Temperance Union, and a host of other recreational and civic organizations. If "Little Havanas" existed in some of the cities of South Florida, there were "Little Americas" in several cities of the north coast of Cuba, and in most cases certain Cubans were invited to join.

Unlike any other group of ethnic Americans in the 1950s, or throughout U.S. history for that matter, the Cuban-American community existed in the new country as well as in the old. There were nearly 125,000 people of Cuban descent living in the United States, but there were thousands more in Cuba whose cultural, economic, and political ties to America were extremely tight. There were nearly 6 million people living in Cuba in the mid-1950s. In addition to the 10,000 or 15,000 people who were truly upper class, there were another 600,000 Cubans who worked as middle-class professionals, corporate managers, office workers, and marketing personnel, and most of them directly depended on the links between the Cuban and North American economies. When Fidel Castro marched triumphantly into Havana in 1959, there was a strong anti-American, class dimension to the revolution. The lives of those hundreds of thousands of white, English-speaking, Protestant, well-to-do, conservative Cubans were vulnerable to dramatic change. They would become the "Golden Exiles" to the United States.

The "Golden Exiles":
Cuban Immigration, 1959–1970

Although Fulgencio Batista managed to overthrow the government of Carlos Prío Socarrás in 1952, the dictatorship he established did nothing to address the serious economic and social problems facing Cuba. In fact, in no time at all the political crisis grew more severe, as did the island's economic troubles. The resentment among peasants, particularly Afro-Cubans, over their economic and social situation, remained unabated, and it was among those groups that Fidel Castro found the support that broadened the movement from its student and intellectual base. Less than 8 percent of the Cuban population owned up to 70 percent of the land, and peasants had long hoped for a redistribution of property. Although Afro-Cubans constituted just over one-fourth of Cuba's population in the mid-1950s, they were grossly underrepresented in positions of political power and economic significance. Centuries of antiblack racism among the Cuban upper classes had exacted a terrible toll on the Afro-Cuban community. The guerrillas Fidel Castro assembled in the Sierra Maestra of Oriente Province all nurtured an intense hatred for the racism, wealth, and power of the Cuban upper classes. Most of the peasants there lived in a state of desperate poverty, and in Fidel Castro they felt they saw an answer to their plight.[1]

For the Cuban lower classes, Fidel Castro became the symbol of freedom and liberation; for the Cuban elite, and subsequently for the Cuban-American community, he was the embodiment of oppression, the man who had robbed them of their birthright and their country. In the early 1940s Castro was a student at Belén High School, a Jesuit school in Havana, and there he came under the influence of the *hispanidad* philosophy, an intellectual movement claiming that lack of social reform and the displacement of Spanish culture by alien, Anglo-Saxon values had doomed Latin America to a position of dependency in the world. Neither Marxism-Leninism nor Anglo-Saxonism was the answer for Latin America. Castro began to call for social reforms. In the early 1940s Fidel Castro was hardly a revolutionary, but he was already committed to totalitarian models of political organization, and that commitment would shape the character of the revolutionary movement.[2]

During the late 1940s Castro studied law at the University of Havana and became very active in student politics. Fidel Castro's political vision was a curious mixture of philosophical commitment and personal ambition. During those early years, he was hardly an ideologue; he seemed interested in any rebellion that might also serve to elevate his own political career. If he had any real commitment to Marxism-Leninism or even socialism in late 1940s and early 1950s, it was not at all evident. He seemed more interested in denouncing the existing status quo, whatever it happened to be, and in denouncing the political and economic influence the United States continued to exert in Cuban affairs.

In 1947 Fidel Castro trained in eastern Cuba and joined an abortive effort to overthrow Rafael Leónidas Trujillo, the dictatorial head of the Dominican Republic. A year later, Castro participated in the "Bogotazo" riots in Bogotá, Colombia, after the assassination of Jorge Eliecer Gaitán, leader of the Liberal party. Castro was in Bogotá for meetings of the Latin American Union of Students, and on the day Gaitán was assassinated he took to the streets and participated in anti-United States rioting and demonstrations against the conservative Colombian government. After the coup d'état that brought Fulgencio Batista to power, Castro began working against the new government. He led an abortive attack on the Moncada army barracks in 1953, hoping to inspire a general rebellion, but it only resulted in his own arrest and imprisonment. The arrest proved to be a godsend to Castro's career. During his incarceration, he earned a national reputation in Cuba. When he was released from prison in 1956, he launched the guerrilla crusade that eventually toppled the Batista regime.

But the early 1950s was not the first time that the Cuban lower classes had expressed hatred for the people who ruled them. Again and again during the previous century and a half they had risen up against Spaniards, Cuban elites, and the United States, but their frustrations had never found an effective political expression. The rebellions were always crushed and the rebels killed, imprisoned, or dispersed. Under Fulgencio Batista, however, the malaise in Cuba spread to most other groups as well. Among the urban working classes during the 1950s, unemployment increased from less than 10 percent to nearly 20 percent, even while wages were falling by 20 percent. Price increases on foodstuffs, so important to the budgets of poor people, reached hyperinflation levels. The Cuban middle class, which had at first welcomed the Batista coup d'état, soon became disgruntled. The cost of living in Havana was one of the highest in the world, while city services and social services were wretched, at least compared with those in the United States. Although the Batista regime claimed that the Cuban living standard was the best in Latin America, the Cuban middle and upper classes did not have a Latin American frame of reference, at least in terms of economic prosperity and the consumer culture. Their model was the United States, and by that standard, Cuba was woefully lacking. They, too, became disenchanted with the Batista regime, especially when news began to leak out about the huge, multimillion-dollar accounts regime leaders had accumulated in Swiss banks.[3]

The social deterioration became more and more visible. The numbers of homeless people, beggars, peddlers, panhandlers, petty thieves, prostitutes, pickpockets, pornographers, and gangs increased dramatically, to the point that the middle and upper classes felt unsafe almost anywhere in the cities and major towns. Crime, juvenile delinquency, and suicide shot up alarmingly. Castro's guerrilla army in eastern Cuba expanded and succeeded in completely disrupting the economy. Sugar production declined, the infrastructure broke down, and shortages of oil and gasoline brought the transportaton system to a standstill. Urban terrorism and rural warfare—complete with assassinations, bombings, arson, and sabotage—terrified American tourists and sent the industry into a depression. In February 1958 Fidel Castro did what Máximo Gómez had done 60 years before—announced a war against the sugar mills, oil refineries, factories, highways, railroads, bridges, public utilities, and corporate property of Cuba—a war against the economy. And just like the *criollo* elite of 1898, the Cuban upper class in 1958 was terrified of the social and economic possibilities should Castro succeed.

During the nearly 400 years of Spanish rule, the Cuban upper class had relied on the empire to enforce order and maintain the social structure. During the 1890s, when Spain proved unable to maintain that order, the *criollo* upper class had turned on the empire and looked to the United States for the imposition of a new regime capable of upholding the social and economic status quo. The Cuban upper class felt the same way by the late 1950s. It was not that they disagreed with Batista's politics; they simply realized that the government no longer had the power to protect their property and way of life. The United States came to the same conclusion. As distasteful as most Americans found Fulgencio Batista's dictatorship to be, he had protected American assets on the island.[4] Preservation of corporate assets, known to an earlier generation as "dollar diplomacy," remained the primary focus of U.S. foreign policy in the Western Hemisphere. Now all that seemed to be failing, and American policymakers decided it was time for Batista to go. On 14 March 1958 President Dwight D. Eisenhower imposed an arms embargo on Cuba. Eisenhower also prohibited Batista from using military units that had been trained and equipped by the United States against rebel forces. United States officials were not supporters of Fidel Castro; they just knew that Batista had to go. The dictator was doomed. On 1 January 1959 Castro called for a revolutionary general strike that sent Fulgencio Batista into exile.[5]

The success of the Castro rebellion was unprecedented. Not only had the rebels succeeded in inflicting military defeat on a superior army and driving a corrupt government into exile, they had done it with no help from the United States. There were no debts to pay this time, no hidden agendas, and the Cuban elites—the military, higher civil service, and economic upper class— were thoroughly discredited. All of them were seen as either *batistianos* or *yanquís,* and they were immediately banished from power. Many of them were also brought to trial for crimes against the fatherland. Unlike any time since 1898, the United States had no internal base in Cuban politics, no powerful allies who would make sure that political rebellion did not turn into social and economic revolution.

During the 1950s Castro had raised the expectations of his followers, and early in 1959 he immediately set out to fulfill them. In the process, of course, he also fulfilled the worst fears of the *criollo* elite and American investors in Cuba about the future. Within a matter of a few months, the new government passed a series of Urban Reform Laws and Agrarian Reform Laws. The Urban Reform Laws reduced all rent payments under $100 a month by 50 percent, $100 to $200 a month rents by 40 percent, and rents over $200 a month by 30 percent. In an attack on the American-owned public utilities, Fidel Castro drastically slashed telephone and electricity rates. Minimum wages were raised substantially and a series of social and labor legislation was passed. The Agrarian Reform Laws limited the size of land holdings to 1,000 acres, except for sugar, rice, and livestock production, in which case the limit was 3,333 acres. Castro then nationalized all land in excess of those limits—a decision that took 2.5 million acres from the *criollo* elite and American corporations. In no time at all he had exhilarated the Cuban lower classes who had for so long felt oppressed by Spanish, American, and Cuban elites.[6]

A sense of despair and outrage permeated the *criollo* elite and American interests in Cuba, and they vigorously protested Castro's policies. Although Fidel Castro was not a Communist himself in 1959, at least in any formal intellectual or organizational sense, he did see to it that Cuban Communists got their fair share of government jobs in the armed forces, mid-level civil administration, and in provincial and municipal offices. The more the United States protested, the worse it got, at least for the Cuban elite and corporate properties. The combination of domestic political forces demanding radical social change and the bitter protests of U.S. interests, as well as subtle threats that the United States would not tolerate the actions of the Castro government, only inspired more radicalization of the revolution. Cuban officials became only more convinced that U.S. influence in Cuba had to be completely eliminated.[7]

The reaction of the Catholic Church, in both Cuba and the United States, to the Castro revolution only provided more ammunition to the radicals. Traditionally, the church had been closely allied with the *peninsular* and later the *criollo* elites in Cuban history. Within weeks of Batista's fall, Richard Cardinal Cushing of Boston publicly warned Castro against seizing any church property and upheld the sanctity of private property as church doctrine. As soon as Castro began confiscating private property in the spring of 1959, priests throughout Cuba condemned the action. Manual Artimé of Agrupación Católica similarly condemned seizures of private property and organized a counterrevolutionary group known as the Movimiento de Rescate Revolucionario (MRR). The CIA was funding the movement and planning to destabilize the regime. Artimé soon went into exile and emerged as a militant, anti-Castro leader in Florida with close ties to the CIA. In May 1960 Archbishop Enrique Pérez Serantes of Havana said, "We cannot say that communism is at our doors, for in reality it is within our walls, speaking out as if it were at home." The Castro regime and his supporters were hardly surprised at the conservative position adopted by the church.[8]

The decisions of the Castro government during its first six months in power set in motion emigration of what became known as the "Golden Exiles" from Cuba. Between 1 January and 30 June 1959, a total of 26,527 Cubans immigrated to the United States, the vast majority of them settling in Miami. Almost all of them were members of the Cuban elite who had been closely associated with the Batista government or with American-owned businesses on the island. They left the island when they lost all of their property, or because they feared being arrested for supporting Fulgencio Batista, or because they were certain that the revolution would develop its own excesses, label them as counter-revolutionaries and enemies of the state, and punish them and their families. They came to the United States full of bitterness about what they had lost in Cuba, and full of commitment about overthrowing the Castro regime and regaining their assets.

Relying on their sense of history, they thought the rebel government would be short-lived, that the United States would manage, as it had so often done in the past, to restore the upper class to power and protect its own investments on the island. Some of them even began to revive the old filibustering activities of the nineteenth century, in which American-based Cuban exiles planned the overthrow of the Cuban government.[9]

The exodus of thousands of upper-class Cubans, the threats of the United States, and the strident counter-revolutionary rhetoric of the Cuban elite had a domino effect on the course of the revolution, inspiring more radicalization, more anti-Americanism, and more pro-Soviet policies on the part of the Castro regime. As the exodus from Cuba took place, the opposition forces inside Cuba became weaker and weaker. In the last six months of 1959 another 30,000 people left for the United States, and their exodus constituted the exporting of whatever hopes there were for counter-revolution. As the anti-Castro forces relocated to the United States, and as the United States continued to condemn the revolution, the ideology of revolution and nationalism became even more closely entwined. As historian Louis H. Pérez, Jr., has written, "The defense of the revolution became synonymous with the defense of national sovereignty."[10] Castro condemned the Catholic Church as a foreign, American-dominated body, just as he condemned the large corporations and landowners in Cuba. He also charged that the United States had supported the efforts of organized crime to penetrate Cuba and bring with it the evils of gambling, prostitution, pornography, and drugs. As the legitimate opposition dwindled in size, the revolution became more revolutionary, and with the threat of economic, political, and military action from the United States, Castro turned more and more to the Soviet Union for support.

The Soviet Union saw a great opportunity to penetrate the Western Hemisphere. Not only was Cuba engaged in a genuine revolution, but the Communist party was playing a role in it. At the same time, the United States was threatening the Castro government with destruction. In the spring of 1960 the Soviets resumed diplomatic relations with Cuba, which they had suspended in 1952 when Batista came into power; promised to purchase 425,000 tons of sugar now and 1 million tons annually thereafter; extended $100 million in economic assistance to Cuba; and agreed to sell petroleum to Cuba at below market prices. The United States' reaction was swift in coming. The Eisenhower administration prohibited Texaco, Shell, and Standard Oil from refining the Soviet oil. At the end of June, Castro nationalized all foreign refineries. Early in July, Eisenhower announced that the United States would no longer purchase Cuban sugar. One month later, Castro nationalized all American-owned public utilities, sugar mills, and petroleum facilities. He followed that up with the takeover of all North American–owned banks in Cuba. In October the United States imposed a complete economic embargo on Cuba, and Castro then nationalized all American-owned publishing facilities, insurance companies, import-export businesses, port facilities, hotels, casinos, textile firms, chemical companies, mines, railroad and bus facilities, food-processing plants, and pharmaceutical concerns. Early in January 1961 the United States severed diplomatic relations with Cuba. By that time Cuba had already become part of the Soviet bloc.[11]

The complete elimination of American business in Cuba proved to be a disaster for the Cuban middle class. More than 150,000 Cubans had been employed by American corporations in Cuba, and their wages had been substantially higher than those enjoyed by workers in other sectors of the economy. During the last six months of 1960, more than 30,000 Cubans left Cuba for the United States, bringing the total number of immigrants in 1959 and 1960 to more than 110,000 people. Almost all of them were upper- and middle-class Cubans whose livelihoods had been destroyed, or at least severely compromised, by the revolution. History seemed about to repeat itself. As in the past, the Cuban elites turned to the United States to restore the status quo and protect their economic positions, and once again the United States seemed ready to oblige. By the end of the year the United States decided to overthrow the Castro regime, and in the exile community of South Florida, the Eisenhower regime started to sow the seeds of counter-revolution, beginning its search for the recruits who would go home at the CIA's bidding and overthrow the Castro regime.

Late in November 1959 the Eisenhower administration made a decision to work to oppose the Castro regime, although at the time the methods to be used were primarily economic coercion and propaganda campaigns. Within the CIA, however, there was a strong movement to take positive steps to destabilize the Castro regime. Fidel Castro represented a Communist beachhead in the Western Hemisphere, and his presence there was intolerable to many Americans. CIA head Allen Dulles was convinced that in the long run the United States could not tolerate the Castro regime in Cuba. Dulles organized within the CIA a special Cuban task force, which recruited 30 Cuban exiles to return to Cuba as local guerrilla leaders. They also formulated plans to commit acts of sabotage against Cuban military and economic installations. Early in 1960 Eisenhower approved Dulles's proposal to overthrow Castro through covert action. CIA radio stations began broadcasting anti-Castro messages over Cuban airwaves.

In August 1960 the Eisenhower administration formally funded what the CIA was calling Operaton Pluto and authorized the Department of Defense to assist the CIA in building a paramilitary force composed of Cuban exiles living in South Florida. The CIA was confident, based on extensive interviews of the Cuban exiles, that the Castro regime was politically marginal and that it would not be too difficult to inspire a mass uprising against him. The fact that they were gathering their intelligence from upper- and middle-class exiles, and that a natural anti-Castro bias was built into their opinions, did not affect CIA planning. They had already concluded that Fidel Castro's regime in Cuba was illegitimate and unpopular with the masses. The radio broadcasts were to prepare the Cuban population for an uprising, and an invasion of the island by the paramilitary expeditionary force would bring it about spontaneously.

The challenge the administration faced in putting together an exile political organization and paramilitary unit was its composition—no simple task given the philosophical differences in the Cuban-American community. There were large numbers of *fidelistas* in the working-class Cuban communities of South Florida who were extremely fond of Castro, and even in the exile community there were a good number of former members of the 26th of July Movement, known as M-26ers, who had split with Castro when the radicalization process began but who still had at least nostalgic feelings about him and more than a little respect for his success. At the same time many *batistianos* had followed Fulgencio Batista to Miami. The administration did not want to use former members of the Batista regime in the counter-revolutionary movement, but they also worried about being infiltrated by M-26ers still loyal to Castro or even closet *fidelistas*.

After carefully surveying the political landscape, the CIA established the Cuban Democratic Revolutionary Front in May 1960 and headquartered them in Miami. Howard Hunt, who would later mastermind the 1972 break-in at the Democratic party headquarters in the Watergate Hotel, was placed in charge of planning for the operation. The CIA also began training guerrilla radio operators near Fort Myers, Florida, and recruited exiles to begin guerrilla military training at Fort Gulick in the Panama Canal Zone. Included in these first training groups were José Pérez San Román, Manuel Artimé, and José Blanco, each of whom would become a leading figure in the exile community. Just in case the CIA would need to train a larger army, the agency established a training facility, named Camp Trax, in Guatemala. The first exile recruits arrived at the end of August 1960. The CIA also purchased Southern Air Transport Company to transfer men, weapons, and supplies to Camp Trax. To provide combat air support, the CIA assembled a contingent of B-26 bombers and C-46 transports and recruited American pilots from the Alabama Air National Guard. Finally, for naval transport and support the CIA purchased ships from a bankrupt company known as Mineral Carriers in Key West. In November the CIA increased the size of the paramilitary unit to battalion level, but news of the training group also began to leak out to the press. Operation Pluto would not be a secret. Its scale was way too large for a covert action. By that time the CIA had also decided to change the nature of Operation Pluto from guerrilla infiltration in favor of a conventional amphibious landing. The timing for the invasion was set for March 1961.[12]

By early February 1961 there were about 1,400 exiles in training in Guatemala under the command of José Pérez San Román. They called themselves Brigade 2506. The name came from the recruit number of Carlos Rodríguez Santana, who had died in a mountain fall during training. Brigade 2506 was divided into six small "battalions" and a heavy weapons group. There was also a commando group of 168 troops scheduled to make a diversionary attack on the island. The CIA had also arranged for another 500 troops to be staged in the Miami area and prepared to back up the main units if reinforcement proved necessary. The exile air force of 30 aircraft was commanded by Manuel Villafaña and stationed in Guatemala. By early February, as the training reached completion, the numbers of stories in American and Havana newspapers about the groups had completely blown whatever covert intentions the CIA had. Although the new president, John F. Kennedy, would not permit any overt U.S. naval or air support for the planned invasion, he enthusiastically approved it.

The invasion, which took place in mid-April at the Bay of Pigs, was an unmitigated disaster. The diversionary invasion failed to take place because of heavy seas, and the CIA's promise that Castro's air forces would not be able to respond to the invasion for at least two days was woefully wrong. Because of all the publicity about the training of the exile army, Castro had placed his own armed forces in a state of readiness. Within hours the Cuban Air Force had sunk two supply ships. Also, the CIA promise that more than 5,000 anti-Castro Cuban guerrillas would join Brigade 2506 went unfulfilled. Only 50 Cubans joined the brigade once it had hit the beaches. The CIA had also scattered the 1,400 troops along more than 36 miles of beach. Three days into the operation, Brigade 2506 had used up all of its ammunition. Brigade 2506 broke up and dispersed into the swamps, and Castro's troops then arrested them one by one. Eventually, the Cuban government captured 1,214 members of the brigade.[13]

The Bay of Pigs invasion was an unbelievable propaganda coup for Fidel Castro, who could not have been more pleased at the CIA folly in planning the invasion and its bungling of the entire affair. He now had proof for all the world to see that the United States was a counter-revolutionary entity bent on his destruction. Although the CIA expected the Cuban people to rise up en masse against the Castro regime once the exile brigade had landed, exactly the opposite took place. Castro enjoyed widespread support among the Cuban lower classes. Once it was clear that the invasion was American-backed, Brigade 2506 was doomed to failure. In that sense the Bay of Pigs helped even more to legitimize the revolution throughout Cuba. When it became clear that Manuel Artimé and a number of Agrupación Católica members had actually assisted the invasion, Fidel Castro retaliated against the Catholic Church in Cuba, closing down Agrupación and nationalizing all parochial schools. That decision prompted the exit of thousands of school administrators, teachers, priests, and nuns.[14]

Although the botched invasion was a political disaster for the new president, he took full responsibility for it in a national television address. And although Kennedy was increasingly suspicious of the CIA's ability to carry out covert operations, American policy toward the Castro government had still not changed, and the administration approved Operation Mongoose to replace Operation Pluto. The CIA set up Zenith Technical Enterprises, placed it on the campus of the University of Miami, and gave it an annual budget of $50 million. Its mission was to overthrow the Castro government. The company purchased hundreds of motor boats, hired hundreds of Cuban exiles, and began conducting paramilitary assaults on Cuba from the Florida Keys. At the same time, there was an increase in the filibustering and paramilitary campaigns of independent exile groups, such as the Second Naval Guerrilla group and Alpha 66. The CIA tried to assassinate Fidel Castro using its own agents, and even hired Mafia contract killers to do the job. Organized crime had been as upset about the Castro revolution as the American corporations and upper-class Cubans had been. Once in power, Castro shut down the gambling casinos, eliminated much of the drug trafficking, and outlawed prostitution, all of which had been extremely lucrative to mob interests in the United States. At the same time, Operation Mongoose involved commando raids to sabotage Cuban railroads and public utility plants. By the early 1960s an astonishing 12,000 Cuban émigrés were on the CIA payroll.

While Operation Mongoose was under way, the Kennedy administration was also negotiating for the return of the Brigade 2506 prisoners of war. Because the U.S. embargo of Cuba had hurt the Cuban economy, Castro demanded $53 million in heavy equipment, medical equipment, drugs, and baby food from Kennedy in exchange for the troops. He also hoped to humiliate the United States on the world stage, gaining even more from the propaganda bonanza the Bay of Pigs fiasco had provided. The president placed his brother, Attorney General Robert F. Kennedy, in charge of a private fund-raising campaign to get the money, and on 22 December 1962 the final agreements for the return of Brigade 2506 were signed in Washington, D.C., and Havana. Of the 1,214 brigade members who had been captured, Castro returned 1,179 of them, as well as 20 CIA agents who had also been captured.[15] President Kennedy met with the members of Brigade 2506 at a special ceremony in the Orange Bowl in Miami on 29 December 1962 and told them,

Your small brigade is a tangible reaffirmation that the human desire for freedom and independence is essentially unconquerable. Your conduct and valor are proof that, although Castro and his fellow dictators may rule natons, they do not rule people; that they may imprison bodies, but they do not imprison spirits; that they may destroy the exercise of liberty, but they cannot eliminate the determination to be free.[16]

The speech was delivered with all the style and charisma John F. Kennedy could muster, and it became a virtual call to arms to the émigré community to continue its crusade against Fidel Castro. Cuba was still a major stage in the cold war, and Kennedy was determined to play a starring role in its outcome. Long impressed by the fact that presidents who display weakness never earn the laurels of history, Kennedy knew that he had to do something to erase the Bay of Pigs from his reputation.

The Cuban missile crisis of October 1962 became the event he wanted to use to change the international political landscape. The combination of the economic embargo of Cuba and the CIA's campaign against Fidel Castro had only served to drive the Cubans more deeply into the Soviet camp. Soviet premier Nikita Khrushchev wanted to cement that relationship, and the Bay of Pigs had inspired him. Raised in the world of realpolitik, Khrushchev had been confused by the temerity of Kennedy's effort to overthrow Castro. Why had not the Americans simply invaded Cuba outright using regular military forces, just as the Soviets had done in Hungary in 1956? Khrushchev concluded that Kennedy was a weak leader who would back down when bluffed. But at the very moment Khrushchev was reaching that conclusion, Kennedy had decided that his political future depended on demonstrating toughness and strength. He would never back down again. The stage was set for the missile crisis.

Early in October American U-2 reconnaissance flights over Cuba revealed the presence of inter-regional ballistic missile silos, indicating that the Soviet Union intended to bring Cuba under its nuclear umbrella. The missiles could deliver warheads up to a distance of 1,500 miles, bringing most major American cities within Soviet range. President Kennedy weighed his options and decided on a forthright military policy. He informed Khrushchev that Soviet nuclear missiles in Cuba were unacceptable, imposed a naval blockade of Cuba with the intention of searching Soviet vessels for missile and warhead components and destroying those implements, and expressed his willingness to go to war—even nuclear war—over the issue. Fidel Castro pleaded with Nikita Khrushchev to launch a nuclear first strike against the United States, a request that the Soviet leader rejected as insane. In the end, Khrushchev was not willing to go to war over Cuba. It was too peripheral to Soviet national security. Khrushchev agreed to remove its missiles from Cuba. In return, as a face-saving gesture to Khrushchev, Kennedy promised that the United States would never again invade Cuba. The Cuban missile crisis was over.[17]

Although the administration had promised not to invade Cuba again, Operation Mongoose continued. Since July 1961 the CIA had trained 2,659 exiles to form a new invasion brigade, but the missile crisis agreement guaranteed that they would not be used in that capacity. Operation Mongoose was scaled down to a series of harassment raids on Cuba, with no real hope that they would destabilize the Castro regime. The administration was also increasingly concerned about the raids on Cuba by independent exile groups. Between 1962 and 1964, several thousand of them were carried out, and one of them in March 1963 actually damaged several Soviet merchant ships off Oriente Province. Secretary of State Dean Rusk worried that the "hit and run raids by Cuban exiles may create incidents which work to the disadvantage of our national interest. Increased frequency of these forays could raise a host of problems over which we would not have control."[18] In 1964 and 1965 the CIA began to discourage the raids and closed down its bases in Miami and the Florida Keys.

The Cuban missile crisis introduced a new level of tensions in Cuban-American relations, and in October 1962 Fidel Castro stopped granting exit visas. During those first four years of the Castro regime, the government had debated the issue of emigration, vacillating between two points of view. On the one hand, the government felt that the emigration of discontented groups constituted a "purification" process for the revolution, making it less and less likely that any opposition group would enjoy enough support to pose a threat to the government. On the other hand, however, it was clear to even the most ideological officials in the government that the exodus constituted a "brain drain" for Cuba. When the revolutionary government began expropriating American-owned property in 1959, the more than 6,500 North Americans living in Cuba left, and their departure posed an economic crisis of its own, since they took with them a great deal of technical expertise needed to keep an industrial economy operating. The loss of tens of thousands of Cubans with similar skills was a real economic crisis. Nevertheless, the advocates of "purification" held sway between 1959 and the end of 1962, and during that time more than 250,000 Cubans left on Pan American flights from Havana to Miami. But all that ended in October 1962. Those flights were suspended during the missile crisis. Cuba was sealed.

Until the severance of diplomatic relations between the United States and Cuba on 3 January 1961, it was relatively easy for prospective emigrants to make the journey across the Straits of Florida. They would simply go to the U.S. embassy in Havana or the U.S. consulate in Santiago de Cuba and fill out the necessary paperwork, purchase the airfare, and fly into Miami. Castro was happy to see them go as part of his purification process, and the United States was happy to see them arrive as proof that Cuban communism was a failure. The exodus would also drain Cuba of its technologically gifted middle class and provide a large pool for recruits to be used in anti-Castro programs. After 3 January 1961 the process became more difficult, since Cuban exiles had to leave Cuba and head for Spain or Mexico before turning around and coming to the United States, but they were still able to get the exit visas and make the journey. It was just more complicated, time-consuming, and expensive.

After the Cuban missile crisis the migration was much more difficult. Without diplomatic relations between the United States and Cuba, the acquisition of the proper documentation was extremely difficult, and regular flights from Havana to the United States had been suspended. Emigrants had to secure exit visas from a reluctant Cuban government, and even that was risky because they had exposed themselves as counter-revolutionaries. They then had to make their way to a third-party government, where they had to make politial and economic arrangements to get to the United States. If that convoluted process was too expensive and too difficult, many refugees tried to get across the Straits of

Visa-seeking Cubans wait in line outside the U.S. embassy in Havana in the early 1960s. *Courtesy U.S. Information Agency*

Florida to the Florida Keys in small boats or even inner tubes lashed together—a dangerous journey that often cost people their lives. From the end of 1962 to late in 1965, approximately 35,000 Cubans made their way to the United States, a number substantially smaller than that of 1959–62.[19]

In September 1965 Castro announced a change in emigration policy. As the tension from the Cuban missile crisis eased during 1963, and as Soviet-American relations improved with the beginning of détente, the political atmosphere for prospective Cuban emigrants changed. The presence of so many Cubans in the United States raised expectations among their relatives back on the island, and Fidel Castro decided to allow another emigration wave. Cubans with relatives in the United States could begin emigrating in October, with the departures taking place by boat from the small port city of Camarioca in Matanzas Province. Almost immediately a flotilla of small boats began crossing the Straits of Florida to pick up their relatives and return them to the United States. In the process a number of boats sank and many people died. During those two months 4,993 people came by boat from Cuba. Both the United States and Cuba wanted to avoid any more such tragedies, so they signed a "Memorandum of Understanding" which authorized "Freedom Flights." Arranged by the Swiss embassy in Havana, they were also known as the "Aerial Bridge" or "Family Reunification Flights."

An extraordinary level of cooperation between the United States and Cuban governments occurred with the Freedom Flights. The joint agreement provided that relatives of exiles already in the United States had priority in emigrating. First in line were husbands, and wives, then parents, and then siblings. Both governments put together lists of those who claimed relatives in the United States and who claimed relatives in Cuba, and then both governments jointly decided who would emigrate. Prospective emigrants with critical job skills had to wait in Cuba until replacements could be located and trained. The expected influx of so many new immigrants from Cuba required the INS to make preparations for them. Congress passed the Cuban Adjustment Act of 1966 to provide for the processing of the immigrants. The legislation stated that any native or citizen of Cuba who was officially processed by the Immigration and Naturalization Service only had to maintain residency in the United States for one year to establish his or her right to remain in the United States indefinitely.

The INS established the Krome Service Processing Center in southwest Dade County, Florida, to handle the influx. For legal immigrants arriving with appropriate visa documents, the processing was immediate. For illegal Cuban immigrants, however, it was somewhat more complicated. They were transported to the Krome Service Processing Center for evaluation. Those without visas were declared "excludable" and the INS began deportation proceedings. If that "excludable" Cuban immigrant had family in the United States or someone willing to sponsor him by assuming financial responsibility, the INS would allow him to leave the processing center. But because there were so many Cuban immigrants arriving in the United States on the Freedom Flights, the INS processing dockets were long and time-consuming. The Cuban Adjustment Act of 1966 only required Cuban immigrants to live in the United States for one year before establishing permanent residency. It took the INS longer than one year to deport them, which meant that virtually any Cuban arriving in the United States, legally or illegally, was allowed to stay.

The Freedom Flights took place between Varadero airport east of Havana and Miami. Two flights a day left Cuba. It was common for people to be fired from their jobs once they applied for an exit visa; they often then spent months and even years working in the fields until they were cleared for departure. During the next seven years those flights carried between 3,000 and 4,000 people out of Cuba every month. By late 1969, another 230,000 Cuban immigrants had arrived in the United States.[20]

The first wave of Cuban immigrants were a unique group, different from most other immigrants. Historically, the vast majority of immigrants to the United States were working-class people, not the upper classes. But the Golden Exiles were different. In terms of their occupational background, more than 68 percent of the 1959–65 Cuban immigrants were white-collar workers, although only 23 percent of the Cuban work force enjoyed that status. Although only 4 percent of Cuban society consisted of high school graduates in 1959, 36 percent of the immigrants had reached at least that educational level. Although only 31 percent of Cuban society in 1959 lived in a large city, more than 83 percent of the immigrants came from major metropolitan areas. Also, more than 82 percent of the Cuban immigrants in the 1960s were whites, while only 2 percent were Afro-Cuban. Approximately 15 percent were of mixed racial background.[21]

In terms of their political attitudes, the Golden Exiles were intensely anti-Castro and convinced that the revolution had benefitted only the Communists, criminals, and the Soviet Union. There was, of course, a great range in political opinion. Some of the exiles were *batistianos* who wanted to overthrow Castro and restore the status quo, but most of the emigrants were somewhat more progressive. Until the Bay of Pigs disaster, the Cuban Revolutionary Council was an umbrella organization for all the exile groups, and its most influential member was the People's Revolutionary Movement (PRM). The PRM advanced the "betrayal of the revolution" concept—that Cuba needed substantial social change but that Castro had gone way too far. What cemented the exile groups together, however, was a powerful anti-Castro, anti-Communist ideology. They also believed that the vast majority of Cubans who remained behind in Cuba shared that point of view but just had not taken the opportunity, or did not enjoy the means, to register their resentment by emigrating. About 40 percent of the immigrants had actively worked against the Batista regime and initially felt positively disposed toward the Castro rebellion, at least until it took its radical turn. Their reasons for leaving were many, but most of them departed because they feared the impact the regime would have on their lives; had lost property, employment, or income from the Castro takeover; had been imprisoned or feared that imprisonment and political persecution were imminent; or simply hated the extent to which the revolution had disrupted the Cuban economy and Cuban social life.

By the mid- to late 1960s, there was a modest but nevertheless clear change in the backgrounds of the immigrants. The Castro regime had set its expropriation and nationalization sites first on large landowners and major corporate entities in Cuba, but as time passed the middle-class, small-business sector of the economy became a victim of the revolution. Beginning in 1964 more and more skilled and semiskilled workers, small businessmen, and small farmers constituted the core of the immigrants, although they still represented a higher socioeconomic group than the average Cuban worker. In fact, they constituted a continuation of the drain out of Cuba of people with technical and administrative skills. Like their somewhat more prosperous predecessors in the Golden Migration, however, they harbored considerable hostility for Fidel Castro and the revolution.[22]

In the beginning, most of them, as well as most Americans in and outside of Washington, D.C., believed that their sojourn in the United States would be temporary, that the Cuban government would quickly give way to internal rebellion or external conquest. The belief that they would probably not be permanent residents helped the settlement process, but so did the long history of political, social, cultural, and economic connections between the United States and the Cuban upper and middle classes. Unlike many immigrants who experienced overwhelming culture shock on arrival in the United States, the Cuban immigrants were quite familiar with American popular culture and with American economic rhythms. They were also familiar with urban life and did not experience all of the problems rural peasants had when moving into a large city. Although life in Miami was a challenging experience for them at first, it was not as difficult as it might have been if the immigrants had come from rural areas and were completely unfamiliar with American popular culture.[23]

Historians have long understood that immigrants traditionally come to America in "chain migrations," following the routes and settling in places where friends and relatives from the Old World had already visited or in which they had lived. The pattern of chain migrations was especially true for the Cuban immigrants. Most of them also had close friends and relatives already living in the United States. In the early years of the migration, more than 70 percent of the immigrants to Miami already had close relatives living in South Florida. The percentage was somewhat less for Cubans settling in New Jersey's Union City–West New York area, and slightly more for those moving to San Juan,

Cuban Americans at Miami International Airport greet relatives arriving from Havana in May 1961.
Courtesy UPI/Bettmann Newsphotos

Puerto Rico. By 1968, however, more than 93 percent of the Cubans living in Union City–West New York had relatives in the United States, and the numbers for San Juan and Miami were more than 99 percent. Also, the Cubans living in San Juan and Miami tended to live in overwhelmingly Cuban-American communities. The presence of so many relatives gave the Cuban community a unique resource base for survival and then for success in the United States.[24]

Most Americans had mixed feelings about the arrival of so many Cuban immigrants during the 1960s. The fact that they were a freedom-loving people fleeing a Communist dictatorship guaranteed a certain level of political sympathy in the United States. And their middle-class and upper-class status reassured many Americans that the Cuban immigrants were hardworking and would not become a burden on public services and social resources. On the other hand, however, there were so many Cubans arriving in so short a time. Demographers have known for a long time that the speed and density of a migration can be alarming to the society receiving new immigrants. The United States has certainly been no exception to that general rule. Between 1959 and 1969 more than 400,000 Cubans settled in the United States, and most of them decided to stay in South Florida. Even though they tended to be a highly educated, ambitious group, their arrival nevertheless increased the competition for jobs and housing in Dade County and placed expensive pressures on the public school system. Not only did the Cuban immigrants have some adjusting to do to American society, native-born Americans had to adjust to them as well.

Social historians trying to explain the continuing migration to the United States from around the world have used the "push-pull" phenomenon as a model. At any given time there are political, economic, and social forces in the Old World driving, or "pushing," people out, while there are also a series of circumstances in the United States that are "pulling" them in. For Cuban immigrants, the push factors were obvious; the revolution had deprived them of so much and threatened to deprive them of even more. In the United States they saw a place where political freedom, private property, and social opportunity were valued, so they settled here.

The U.S. government also made it easier for them. The INS established the Cuban Refugee Emergency Center in December 1960 to assist and process the refugees, and it later was institutionalized as the Cuban Refugee Program (CRP) to assist the newcomers. Because the Miami economy was initially unable to absorb so many refugees, the CRP tried to resettle them in various *colonias* around the country. Although there were small Cuban communities in such major cities as Denver, Minneapolis, Houston, and St. Louis, more than 87 percent of Cuban Americans, according to the 1970 U.S. census, lived in Florida (45.5 percent), New York (16.4 percent), New Jersey (12.7 percent), California (9.1 percent), and Illinois (3.6 percent). The largest concentrations of Cuban-Americans were in Miami and South Florida and in New Jersey's Union City–West New York corridor.[25]

The U.S. government was intensely interested in encouraging the emigration, not only to maximize the propaganda benefits of the flight from Cuba but also to exacerbate the island's economic problems. Visa restrictions were eased in 1960 and then abolished altogether in 1961. Future immigration from Cuba was to be unlimited. The government passed legislation making it easier for Cubans to become U.S. citizens by reducing the residency requirement and the difficulty of the application process. In doing so, the immigrants acquired at least some degree of political clout in an unusually short period of time. The government also provided them with a wide range of entitlement programs. It was quite clear from the very beginning of the mass exodus from Cuba that the economy of Miami not would be able to absorb all of them. One objective of the Cuban Refugee Program (CRP) was to resettle as many of the immigrants as possible all over the country. The CRP worked closely with four private agencies: the National Catholic Welfare Conference, the Church World Service, the United Hebrew Immigrant Aid Service, and the International Rescue Committee. Eventually, between 1963 and 1972, 296,806 of the Cuban immigrants were resettled in 2,400 communities in all 50 states.

Between 1961 and 1971 the federal government spent more than $730 million on the Cuban immigrant aid programs—job-training programs; English-language acquisition programs; low-cost loans for college tuition; free certification programs for Cuban optometrists, college professors, teachers, lawyers, physicians, pharmacists, and nurses; medical care, housing subsidies, food stamps, surplus food distribution, cash allotments, and citizenship exemptions for specified jobs. Between 1962 and 1976 the CRP provided more than $34 million to 16,100 Cuban-American college students. It also spent $130 million in Dade County public schools on bilingual education and multicultural awareness programs. Immigrant Cuban businessmen were declared eligible for loans from the Small Business Administration, and the Department of Health, Education, and Welfare provided extra federal funds to public schools with high concentrations of Cuban-American children. Never before in U.S. history had a refugee group been so well taken care on its arrival in the country.[26]

Despite all the factors in their favor—high educational levels, family support, familiarity with the host society, and substantial government benefits—the Cuban immigrants nevertheless had a difficult time adjusting economically. Part of the problem was that so many of them had previously enjoyed upper- and middle-class income levels and expectations, and once in the United States their lack of resources or problems with the English language confined them to lower echelon positions in the construction or service sector. Still, their confinement to those economic levels proved to be temporary, and the reason they became known as the "Golden Exiles" was the rapidity with which they improved their economic circumstances. By the late 1960s and 1970s the popular press in the United States was infatuated with stories of the "Cuban success story." In October 1966 *Fortune* magazine ran the article "Those Amazing Cubans." *Business Week* claimed in 1966 that "Cuba's New Refugees Get Jobs Fast." A 1967 article in *U.S. News and World Report* was entitled "Cuban Success Story in the United States."[27]

There were a number of reasons for the success, even though most Americans tended to misinterpret the nature of that success. The vast majority of the Golden Exiles were well-educated and highly literate in Spanish. Although most of them had difficulties speaking English in the beginning, they were far better equipped than illiterate immigrants to learn to read and write English. Many of the early immigrants were quite familiar with U.S. managerial and administrative procedures and philosophies, and more than a few of them already had important business and professional contacts here. Also, because so many of them lived in Cuban enclaves, they were able to use Spanish in most of their social and economic relationships. The fact that they lived in Cuban enclaves served the immigrants in another important way. The Cuban ethnic enclaves, especially in Miami, had a vibrant entrepreneurial spirit. By the late 1960s nearly 10 percent of the businesses in Miami were Cuban-owned, and new immigrants were able to find jobs there. With economic units linked by ethnic affinity, the immigrants' chances for economic survival, and success, were vastly improved. The ethnic enclave was not, of course, an unmixed blessing for the new immigrants. There was a good deal of paternalism operating there, and immigrants arriving in the enclave after 1966 were less likely than those living outside the enclave to establish their own businesses. For the most part, however, the presence of the enclave provided the Cubans with unique economic opportunities. Most immigrants to the United States had to enter an open labor market, usually in peripheral sectors of the economy. But large numbers of Cuban immigrants found jobs within the enclave economy. Although their wages were not much higher than those of other immigrant groups at the same time in the 1960s, the ethnic affinities in the enclave provided the Cuban immigrants with an informal but powerful network system.

It should also be understood, however, that the initial economic success of the Cuban immigrants was not an individual phenomenon, as so many Americans assumed. Cuban economic success in the United States was a family phenomenon unique among many immigrant groups. First, Cuban-American women were more likely to have jobs outside the home than other Hispanic women in the United States or women in general. Because of that, by the early 1970s, Cuban-American family income was higher than the national average. Second, the fertility rate of Cuban-American women is among the lowest in the United States. Historians and economists generally understand that fertility rates drop as income and educational levels increase, and because so many of the early Cuban immigrants were middle and upper class, they tended to have smaller families. Cuban-American fertility rates were far lower than those for African Americans and other Hispanics, and even lower than the average for other white Americans. Economic historians also understand that children, who may be an economic asset in an agricultural society, are an economic liability in an urban, industrial setting. With fewer children to support, Cuban Americans enjoyed surplus resources to put into other education and business endeavors. Third, the Cuban immigrants had an unusually large elderly population. The elderly were more likely to be discontented from the results of the revolution, and Fidel Castro was more willing to let them emigrate, as opposed, for example, to young men of military age. While the average age of Mexican Americans in the mid-1970s was only 23, the average age of the Cuban Americans was 37. Most of the elderly Cubans lived with their children and grandchildren. Because of that, they were able to contribute to family income in two important ways: by taking care of grandchildren during the day, they permitted both parents to work outside the home; and most of the elderly received Social Security or public assistance checks. Finally, Cuban Americans were traditionally more likely than most other immigrant groups to enroll in public education, from preschool programs to postsecondary learning. As a result of all of these factors, the Golden Exiles enjoyed a social mobility unknown in other immigrant quarters.[28]

six

Change and Assimilation, 1970–1980

During the early 1960s, the arrival of the Cuban immigrants in the United States constituted a major issue for American immigration and foreign policy. Fidel Castro brought communism to the Western Hemisphere, embarrassing the Eisenhower administration and constituting a thorn in the side of the Kennedy administration. In 1962, during the Cuban missile crisis, the problems surrounding Cuba brought the world to the brink of nuclear holocaust. Cuban immigration, Cuban-American politics, and the cold war were inextricably linked for American and Soviet policymakers, as well as for the American public. In fact, no other immigrant group in American history has had its own internal politics as well as its external image shaped so consistently by foreign-policy issues. Political life in Cuba continued to be by far the most important issue in Cuban-American identity.

In the late 1960s, however, Cuba as an issue in American politics declined in significance and was replaced by the growing public controversy over the war in Vietnam. At first the two conflicts seemed similar. The Kennedy and then the Johnson administrations both discussed Vietnam as a simple case of Communist aggression, not unlike Fidel Castro's illegal takeover of the Cuban government. As the Vietnam War became more and more controversial, however, public perceptions of communism and American foreign policy began to change. The conflict in Vietnam exposed American vulnerabilities, politically and militarily. As the Vietnamese Communists seemed more and more successful in resisting the American military adventure there, Fidel Castro became more and more confident and more and more influential in hemispheric affairs. The United States no longer appeared to be an invulnerable superpower, and Castro's predictions of socialist success and capitalistic failure seemed somewhat more credible, at least to some of his own people. That confidence and influence, however, would be short-lived.

The flow of emigrants from Cuba to the United States in the 1970s was continually influenced, as it had always been throughout the twentieth century, by the changing political and economic relationship between the two countries. During much of the 1960s the United States was bent on the destruction of the Castro regime, although that commitment waned somewhat during the Vietnam debacle. Central to U.S. Caribbean policy was the disruption of the Cuban economy—by isolating Cuba from the world economic markets; encouraging the emigration of its "best and brightest" businessmen, professionals, and technicians; fomenting domestic unrest in a futile attempt to destabilize the Castro regime; and limiting its access to world capital markets. By insisting that pro-American nations around the world stop their purchases of Cuban sugar, the United States was able to reduce Cuban international trade by more than 80 percent between 1962 and 1963. The only international airlines flying into Cuba were Cubana Airlines out of Mexico City and Iberia Airlines from Madrid, Spain. Cuba was almost completely cut off from the world's financial and consumer markets. Although the single-mindedness of American foreign policy raised more than a little criticism around the world and in Latin America, Presidents John Kennedy, Lyndon Johnson, and Richard Nixon stayed the course.

The impact of American foreign policy on the Cuban economy was cata-strophic. No less catastrophic for Cuban economic growth was Fidel Castro's ide-ological evolution toward Marxism-Leninism. Whether the U.S. policy drove him in that direction out of necessity, whether it was internally motivated, or whether it was a combination of the two is still a controversial question, but regardless of its origins, Fidel Castro became more and more committed to the idea that indi-vidual pecuniary interests must be subordinated to the needs of the society as a whole. Individual self-interest would have to be sacrificed to equality—not equal-ity of opportunity but to equality of condition. Under Castro's direction the Cuban economy was about to be force-fit into an ideological mold. By the 1990s that vision would reduce Cuban economic life to nearly premodern standards.

U.S. policy and the revolutionary drift of Castro's economic thought rein-forced each other perfectly. When the United States insisted that Cuban policies respect private property, Castro only became more militantly socialist, and the more socialist he became, the more committed was the United States to his destruction. When the United States severed all economic relations with Cuba, the island's economy went into a tailspin. All of the machinery, equipment, and supplies used in Cuban industry and agricultural processing, along with spare parts, had come from the United States, and because of the ease of shipment, telephone orders were the rule, eliminating the need for stockpiling spare parts and replacements. Within a year of the revolution, severe shortages of machine goods had developed, slowing down the economy. Much of Cuban industry depended on the importation of American chemicals, which suddenly became unavailable. Buses, automobiles, railroad cars, and aircraft could not be repaired. To keep machinery running, parts had to be scavenged from other equipment, further reducing available inventories. The flight of the 6,500 North Americans from Cuba, as well as substantial portions of the Cuban upper and middle class-es, and its technicians, during the 1960s only aggravated the island's economic problems, just as the United States had intended. It also became impossible to bring in American technicians as contract workers. Fidel Castro had to turn to the Soviet Union as a market for his boycotted sugar and as a source of machine tools, technicians, investment capital, and petroleum products.[1]

The loss of so many talented Cubans had to be stopped. In May 1969, how-ever, the Cuban government refused to accept new applications for exit visas, and by August 1971 Fidel Castro began to sporadically interrupt the Freedom Flights.[2] The pool of people who had applied for visas before May 1969 was shrinking, and Castro argued that the original purpose of the Freedom Flights—to reunite families—had for the most part been achieved. Economic problems were at the forefront of his thinking. In the more than a decade since the beginning of the revolution, he had made no progress in moving the economy past sugar monoculture to more diversification. The U.S. embargo explained a good deal of Cuba's economic problems, but so did the large exodus of talented people from Cuba during the 1960s. No less important was the fact that in an aggressively socialist, totalitarian state, individual incentive, the grease of all economic life, had been effectively eliminated. Castro was determined to keep the "best and the brightest" at home, even if he had to do so forcibly. By 1972 the number of people leaving had dropped considerably from earlier levels, and on 6 April 1973 Fidel Castro terminated the Freedom Flights.[3]

Although Cuban Americans protested the decision, primarily because there were still 94,000 people eligible to emigrate under the stated rules of the program, the U.S. government did not offer any vigorous condemnation of Castro's decision. Controversy surrounding the Vietnam War preoccupied American policymakers, and the Cuban immigration question was simply not a priority issue. For several years criticisms of the Cuban migration had begun to mount, and the State Department found itself having to defend the program. Deputy Assistant Secretary of State Robert Hurwitch said of the airlift that "experience has indicated that as long as hope for escape to freedom exists, people living under oppression resist committing themselves to the regime's goals. . . . The refugee airlift, a route to freedom, forestalls the certainty of accommodation to communism of the Cuban people."[4]

But the support was increasingly fainthearted. With the accession of Richard Nixon to the White House, a subtle reevaluation of American policy toward Cuba occurred, and the administration modified the expressed opinion of the previous 10 years that the Castro regime was only temporary. It was becoming increasingly obvious that Fidel Castro was well entrenched and that the emigration policy of the United States had actually made his political position on the island more secure. The more hostile the United States behaved toward Fidel Castro, the easier it was for the dictator to fulminate about Yankee imperialism and maintain his political control. Even though the Cuban economy was declining, Castro could easily blame the United States for Cuban suffering, and he still maintained the personal charisma that so mesmerized the Cuban masses.[5]

Future emigration was not likely to weaken him in any tangible way. At the same time, there was growing domestic criticism of the Cuban immigration program. The Immigration and Naturalization Act of 1965 had imposed an annual quota of 120,000 immigrants from the Western Hemisphere, and when that number went into effect in 1968, many people assumed that the Cuban immigrants consumed more than their share of the total. Between 1968 and 1973, when the quota allowed for a total of 600,000 Western Hemisphere immigrants into the United States, the unlimited Cuban migration took up 40 percent of the total. Mexican-American activist groups began to complain about the discriminatory nature of the program. Actually, the Cuban Adjustment Act of 1966 provided that the vast majority of Cuban refugees were "paroled" into the United States by virtue of executive action and did not count as part of the 120,000 quota from the Western Hemisphere. Even then the federal government tried to count Cuban refugees granted permanent residence against the general quota for the Western Hemisphere.

Those Cubans enjoying "parole" status then faced the challenge of securing permanent resident status. Those who could afford it usually traveled abroad, acquired resident visa applications there, and then returned to the United States on those visas. By the end of 1966, however, only 70,000 of the 300,000 Cuban "parolees" had been able to pay for such a journey. Political protests from South Florida prompted Congress to address the problem, and in November 1966 President Lyndon Johnson signed legislation exempting Cuban immigrants from the visa requirement. The new law allowed them to acquire resident visas without leaving the United States.

In 1972, with the presidential election looming on the horizon and Republicans hoping to win Florida for President Richard M. Nixon, Cuban Americans in Miami began lobbying on behalf of approximately 30,000 Cuban refugees living in Spain. They were unable to enter the United States because of the red tap surrounding the Immigration and Naturalization Act of 1965. President Nixon expressed sympathy for their plight and set in motion a series of executive decisions allowing them to enter the United States as refugees from the Eastern Hemisphere. In 1974 the Nixon administration launched the "Expanded Parole" program, which exempted Cuban refugees from the 120,000 Western Hemisphere quota and, in doing so, satisfied Mexican-American critics who did not want Cuban refugees counted against the quota.

There were other critics of Cuban immigration. Some African-American groups in South Florida complained that Cubans were taking jobs away from native workers and depressing general wage levels, and that government assistance programs made it difficult for small businessmen without such assistance to be competitive. Others complained about the expense of the program—the $727 million spent on the 1961–71 entitlement programs as well as the $50 million in airline tickets paid by the State Department. Some people wondered why those programs should continue when all the news shows were talking about how successful the Cuban immigrants were. For all of these reasons, American policymakers were secretly relieved to see the Freedom Flights come to an end.[6]

By that time the Cuban-American community was in a state of transition, partly because of the passage of time and the coming of age of a new, younger generation, and partly because of the continuing penetration of the revolution into every sector of the Cuban economy. Late in 1968 Fidel Castro launched what he called a new "revolutionary offensive" against the private sector. The Cuban Communist party was intent on moving past the natonalization of public utilities and large corporations to the rest of the economy. Castro was committed to making the Cuban economy the most purely socialist system in the world. When the dust settled, the government had confiscated 55,636 small businesses, and the entire industrial, service, and trade sectors of the economy had passed into the government's hands. Castro had achieved his goal. Of all the socialist countries in the world, including the Soviet Union and the People's Republic of China, Cuba was the most socialistic, with the most property under government ownership. Fidel Castro had pushed his revolutionary vision right to its natural limits. Many people argued that he had pushed past natural limits into the realm of the absurd. The program alienated the last remaining entrepreneurial groups in Cuba, as well as many of their employees, creating a new pool of people ready to emigrate. Many of them exercised their emigration option by becoming part of the Freedom Flights exodus until that program ended in 1973.[7]

With the arrival of the new Cuban immigrants, the social and economic profile of the exile community began to change. For the first time, large numbers of service workers, who had constituted only 7 to 10 percent of the early migration, began coming to the United States. By the early 1970s more than one in four of the Cuban immigrants were cooks, gardeners, domestics, street vendors, shoe shiners, barbers, hairdressers, taxi drivers, and small retail merchants. They were not the well-to-do plantation owners, businessmen, and bankers of the first wave. In 1961 more than 30 percent of the Cuban immigrants had been professionals or company managers in Cuba, but such persons constituted only 12 percent of the 1970 immigrants. Only 36 percent of the 1961 immigrants were working class, while more than 57 percent of the 1970 immigrants came from those backgrounds. That migration did not, of course, completely reverse the social and economic trends established during the early 1960s. By 1980 Cuban immigrants still enjoyed higher incomes and more years of schooling than Mexican and Puerto Rican immigrants, and their median age was substantially higher. But because of the changes in the social and economic backgrounds of the Cuban immigrants between 1968 and 1973, the Cuban-American community had become diverse in its own composition.[8]

The economic composition of the community was not the only change. Because of the newer immigration and the changing political landscape in the United States, the political profile of the Cuban American changed as well. During the 1970s Cuban-American politics became much more diverse. The political extremes, of course, were still there. Among the older Cuban-American residents of South Florida, especially the working-class, Afro-Cubans of Key West, Ybor City, and Tampa, there remained considerable support for Castro. Those *fidelistas*, like so many lower-class workers in Cuba, still believed in the social justice aims of the revolution and still responded to its ideological fervor, even if they were disappointed with its short-term results or disagreed with its implementation. The mass Cuban immigration of the 1960s and 1970s had reduced these left-wingers to a tiny minority. Because the vast majority of the Cuban immigrants were upper- and middle-class whites, the relative size of the Afro-Cuban-American community rapidly diminished. By the early 1970s less than 4 percent of the Cuban-American community was black. But they still represented, as they had for more than a century, a tiny enclave of revolutionary sentiment in the United States.[9]

There were also still a good number of Cuban Americans actively involved in politics at the other extreme. Back in the early 1960s the radical, right-wing extremists enjoyed the complete support of the U.S. government, and with CIA funding they conducted for years the raids, invasions, and sabotage campaigns that were included under the umbrella of the Bay of Pigs and Operation Mongoose. Although the United States disavowed such activities in the late 1960s and the Coast Guard even began patrolling the Straits of Florida to intercept any modern-day filibustering raids, radical activities continued nonetheless from any number of exile groups in Cuba. The group Alpha 66, for example, continued to reject out of hand any discussion of accommodation with Fidel Castro, while a group known as Omega 7 was committed to assassinating Cuban diplomats at the United Nations and at other world capitals. Omega 7 bombed several businesses in Miami in 1983 because they wanted to increase trade with Cuba. Alvin Ross Díaz and Guillermo Novo Sampol of the Cuban Nationalist Movement assassinated Orlando Letelier, former Chilean ambassador to the United Nations, in 1976. Letelier, a leader of Chilean political exiles in the United States, was an outspoken critic of the right-wing government of Augosto Pinochet, which had overthrown Salvador Allende and his leftist regime in 1973. Anti-Castro elements loathed Allende because of his close relationship with Castro, and they interpreted Letelier's anti-Pinochet rhetoric as being pro-Castro.

On 12 October 1971 José Elías de la Torriente, head of a group known as Cuban Forces of Liberation, conducted a raid against the small Cuban port city of Boca de Sama. Castro was able to capture two other exile ships in international waters, and for a few days the entire incident became a diplomatic crisis of sorts, prompting Cuba and the United States to place their forces on a state of military alert. When the tension eased, the United States firmly announced that any exile leaders would be "prosecuted to the fullest extent of the law if they engage in anti-Castro activity from U.S. soil." In May 1972, just before President Richard Nixon's trip to the Soviet Union, more than 5,000 Cuban exiles marched in Washington to protest the visit and to demand that there be no negotiations over Cuba. Antonio Font, a leader of the march, remarked to reporters that "Cuba must be free and Cubans must free her." Other radical groups included Comando Zero, Acción Cubana, and Bloque Revolucionario.[10]

By the late 1960s and early 1970s the political influence of the Cuban-American community was growing. Because of their hatred of Fidel Castro and their intense anticommunism, most Cuban Americans became loyal to the Republican party, and when Richard Nixon entered the White House in 1969, they found a sympathetic ear. If anything, Nixon was the most successful anti-Communist in the world, and Cuban Americans knew he would listen to them. Republican strategists, always interested in penetrating the Democratic South, also saw a chance to win Florida in national elections. Florida was one of the most rapidly growing states in the country, gaining in electoral votes and the size of its congressional delegation, and Cuban Americans gave the Republicans a strong base in South Florida.

Although the frequency of Cuban-American paramilitary activities waned in the 1970s, the CIA nevertheless had a cadre of ideologically pure Cuban exiles to draw on for some of its other enterprises around the world. During the Belgian Congo crisis of the 1960s, Cuban exile pilots flew B-26 aircraft for the CIA bombing campaigns, and during the late 1960s and early 1970s other exile Cuban pilots flew CIA aircraft in support of Portuguese military campaigns against rebel forces in Angola and Mozambique. When in June 1972 Howard Hunt, on behalf of the Committee to Re-Elect the President, broke into the Democratic party's headquarters in the Watergate Hotel, he hired to assist him several Cuban exiles who were former CIA operatives. Bernard Barker and Rolando Martínez were arrested along with Hunt. Martínez had a political résumé that included 324 separate CIA missions on one kind or another against Cuba since 1959. As late as the 1980s, the CIA was still recruiting right-wing Cuban exiles for its Central American activities. The Cuban-American community was a lucrative source of funds for the contras trying to overthrow the leftist Sandinista regime in Nicaragua, and Cuban exiles provided paramilitary training for contra guerrilla leaders and assisted in the CIA mining of Nicaraguan ports in 1983 and 1984.[11]

The decline of the paramilitary radicalism in the Cuban exile community was also a function of assimilation. As time passed and the Cuban immigrants

Anti-Castro protesters demonstrate on 11 October 1979 at the United Nations in New York, where Castro was scheduled to speak the next day. *Courtesy UPI/Bettmann Newsphotos*

became more acclimated to the United States, many of their attitudes began to change. During the 1960s most of the Cuban exiles harbored desires and expectations of an eventual return to Cuba. They were certain that Fidel Castro's fall was imminent. More than 83 percent of Cubans in Miami in 1966 said they would return to Cuba once Castro was overthrown, and the percentage was only modestly lower among those Cubans living in New Jersey's Union City–West New York corridor. But the longer they lived in the United States, the less likely they were to want to return to Cuba. By the mid-1970s less than 25 percent of Cuban immigrants living in the United States expressed any desire to return to Cuba. Increasing numbers of the immigrants were legalizing that commitment by becoming U.S. citizens—a decision that required a statement of intent to live permanently in America. And once they had children born in the United States, the desire of the family to return to Cuba declined dramatically.[12]

Changes were also occurring in the political attitudes of young Cuban Americans. For parents and older teenagers and young adults arriving in the United States in the early 1960s, the revolution in Cuba was the single, formative event in the development of their political philosophies, and for the rest of their lives that event would help shape the way they responded to other political and foreign-policy issues. Life revolved completely around Cuba. But that was not necessarily the case for people who arrived in the United States as young children. Many of them came of age during the civil rights movement and the campaign of young people against the Vietnam War. They did not carry within their psyches, at least to the same degree, the anti-Castro, cold war mentality of their parents, and they were more willing to engage, if not actually to compromise, in an open dialogue about the future. They also were more likely than their parents to debate a broader variety of domestic and foreign-policy issues.

So by the mid-1970s there was an increasingly large political center in the Cuban-American community that was at least willing to talk about new approaches to Fidel Castro and Cuba. They certainly did not represent the Cuban-American majority, and most of them, except for the small group Juventud Cubana Socialista (Cuban Socialist Youth), still maintained an anti-Castro, anti-revolution profile, but they were also willing to abandon the paramilitary vision that had been so influential for so long. To a certain extent, the new mood was part of a modest easing of tensions between the United States and Cuba. Although the movement did not even approach what foreign-policy analysts would consider "normalization," there were a few attempts at solving mutual problems. In 1973, out of mutual necessity in order to guarantee air-passenger security, Fidel Castro and Richard Nixon signed an antihijacking agreement that guaranteed the extradition and criminal prosecution of *all* individuals who hijacked aircraft and flew to Cuba or the United States. The agreement would be enforced even if those individuals claimed political persecution and demanded political asylum.

During 1974 and 1975 secret, high-level meetings took place between Cuban and American representatives to discuss normalization. Those talks were still-born because of Castro's decision to introduce Cuban troops in Africa to assist a variety of insurgent guerrilla groups there and because of immediate protests in the Cuban-American community as soon as word of the talks leaked to the press. In 1977 Cuba and the United States reached an agreement on fishing rights and the maritime boundary in the Florida Straits. But when Castro sent

Cuban troops to Ethiopia in 1978 to assist in the fighting in Somalia, the United States denounced the decision as a form of global aggression. So although little came of the attempts at diplomacy, the mood of the mid-1970s was at least more conducive to dialogue, and it assisted those Cuban Americans who considered themselves in the political mainstream.[13]

As a result of these political and social changes, several new groups appeared that were at least willing to engage in a political dialogue with the Castro government. Among the large, prosperous Cuban-American community in San Juan, Puerto Rico, Alberto Rodríguez Moya emerged as a moderate leader who established political contacts with the Castro regime. Another new community group was the Cuban-American Committee for the Normalization of Relations with Cuba. The Institute of Cuban Studies began holding open seminars about the connections between Cuban Americans and the island, and the Cuban Culture Center wanted to "promote cultural and educational exchange with those living in Cuba," because "the center of our culture is in Cuba." Other new groups with strong but distinct political persuasions appearing in the Cuban-American community were the National Coalition of Cuban Americans, National Union of Cuban Americans, Cuban Christians for Justice and Freedom, Casa de las Américas (House of the Americas), Nueva Generación (New Generation), and Joven Cuba (Young Cuba).[14]

Perhaps the most dramatic of these moderate groups, however, was the Antonio Maceo Brigade, a group of progressive-minded Cuban-American college students who advocated a new relationship between Cubans and Cuban Americans and who were suddenly invited by Castro in December 1977 to tour the island. These *brigadistas* were led by people like Mariana Gastón, Armando García, Rafael Betancourt, and Carlos Muñiz. They consisted of Cuban Americans under the age of 30 who wanted to improve relations with Cuba and search out their own cultural roots. The Antonio Maceo Brigade expressed a basic sympathy for the social justice goals of the Cuban revolution, supported civil rights movements in the United States and Cuba, demanded an end to the American blockade of Cuba, wanted normalization of relations between the United States and Cuba, and called for the independence of Puerto Rico. The *brigadistas* were considered revolutionary themselves by most Cuban Americans. Brigade groups toured Cuba again in 1978 and 1979.[15]

The visit of the Antonio Maceo Brigade to Cuba had a major impact on Fidel Castro. He realized for the first time that the Cuban-American community was not necessarily a homogeneous political bloc committed to his destruction, but that there were Cuban groups in the United States who actually had some sympathy for the revolution or who at least wanted to end the blockade, restore the Cuban economy, and normalize relations between the two countries. On 6 September 1978 Castro held a press conference attended by several exile journalists. There he announced the establishment of "The Dialogue" policy to discuss the future relationship between Cubans and Cuban Americans. In November 1978 Castro convened the Dialogue Conference, at which he presided, and invited 75 Cuban-American exiles to attend and discuss the issues with members of a Cuban commission. There were three items on the conference agenda: the problem and status of approximately 3,600 political prisoners in Cuba, the problem of reuniting Cubans with their Cuban-American relatives in the United States, and the desire of hundreds of thousands of

Cuban nationals and Cuban Americans in the United States to visit the island. At the end of the meeting Castro made a dramatic announcement about his intentions to begin releasing political prisoners and to permit a limited number of family reunifications.

Since the end of the Freedom Flights, the flow of Cuban immigrants to the United States had slowed to a trickle. From 1 July 1973 to 30 September 1979 only 38,000 Cubans arrived in the United States. More than 26,000 of them, except for a few who came to Florida by motorboat or raft, arrived by way of a third country. More often than not, they had to spend some time in Mexico City or Spain before coming to the United States, while a smaller number did so via Jamaica and Venezuela. Fidel Castro's decision to release thousands of political prisoners if they would agree to leave the country increased the migration. Since most of them had relatives in the United States, they headed for Florida. Castro claimed that he was making a humanitarian gesture in the release of the prisoners, but he was also solving a potential problem and making propaganda points. Some of the individuals had been prisoners for nearly 20 years, and in some circles, especially in Florida, they were assuming the aura of martyrs. By getting them out of the country he would neutralize that issue and continue to export all potential sources of counter-revolutionary activity. The fact that the prisoners fled so quickly to the United States also allowed Castro to reinforce his claim that revolution and nationalism were one and the same. Castro also hoped to cement his relationship with members of the moderate Cuban-American community. Cuban exiles formed the Operación Reunificación Cubana (Cuban Reunification Operation), also known as the Committee of Seventy-Five, to organize the charter flights from Havana to Miami. Cuba and the United States cooperated to reestablish regular air traffic, and over the next 17 months a total of more than 12,000 people came to the United States.[16]

Much of the Cuban-American community reacted to the visits of the Antonio Maceo Brigade and the Dialogue Conference with outrage. In fact, the reaction was so intense that the mood of South Florida resembled the early days of the 1960s. Old-line anti-Castro organizations warned that the Communists were two-faced and had no interest in real dialogue, that all they were going to do was infiltrate the Cuban-American community and undermine community solidarity. The Agrupación Abdala, an umbrella organization for Cuban-American student clubs in the United States, campaigned against the Dialogue initiatives, as did the Congress of Dissident Cuban Intellectuals. Some exiles were far more militant. Assassins killed Eulalio Negrín, a prominent Dialogue supporter and member of the Antonio Maceo Brigade, on 25 November 1979 in Union City, New Jersey. Omega 7 assassins murdered Felix García Rodríguez, a member of the Cuban mission at the United Nations, in November 1980.[17]

When the 1970s ended the Cuban-American community had begun the process of assimilation, although that process had by no means completed itself. The 1980 U.S. Census listed 803,226 people of Cuban "origin or descent." More than 52 percent of them lived in the Miami–Ft. Lauderdale corridor, and more than 75 percent of Cuban Americans were living in Miami–Ft. Lauderdale, greater New York, and Los Angeles. And unlike Mexican and Puerto Rican immigrants in the United States, who were becoming more widely dispersed around the country, Cuban Americans were actually more concentrated in 1980 than they had been in 1970. State by state, every section of the country lost

Cuban-American residents in the 1970s, while Florida experienced a dramatic increase. Of course, the Cuban Refugee Resettlement Program had initially tried to disperse the immigrants around the country, whereas Mexican and Puerto Rican immigrants had concentrated originally in the Southwest and New York, respectively. The fact that the Cuban immigrants decided to concentrate as soon as they had the opportunity should not be surprising. Voluntary dispersion out of an ethnic ghetto is the consequence of assimilation, not simply a cause. More recently, Vietnamese, Cambodian, and Hmong immigrants from Indochina have undergone a similar experience of being dispersed around the country in resettlement programs only to concentrate themselves demographically as soon as the opportunity appeared.

The U.S. census revealed that the demographic characteristics of the Cuban-American community were as unique in 1980 as they had been in 1965 and 1975. Cuban Americans tended to be older than the national average and had lower birth rates. Three-generation households were common, and they had more adult women working outside the home than most other ethnic groups. Finally, in terms of income, the Cuban-American median annual family income in 1980 was $18,245, compared with $19,917 for the country as a whole and $14,765 for Mexican immigrants and $10,734 for Puerto Rican immigrants. Only 11.7 percent of Cuban-American families were living below the poverty level, compared with 9.6 percent for the United States as a whole, 20.6 percent for Mexican Americans, and 34.9 percent for Puerto Rican Americans.[18]

Cuban Americans have also exhibited a powerful entrepreneurial instinct, especially for an immigrant group so recently arrived in the United States. They are far more likely than African Americans, Mexican Americans, Filipino Americans, and Puerto Rican Americans to own their own businesses and just as likely as Chinese Americans and Korean Americans to do so—even though the Asian-owned businesses tend to be second- and third-generation concerns. Cuban-American businesses were heavily concentrated in construction, transportation, retail trade, and service industries. Cuban-owned businesses in the United States also enjoyed the highest gross annual receipts when compared with a variety of other recent immigrant groups. In 1970 there were approximately 1,000 Cuban-owned businesses in Miami, but 10 years later that number was up to 10,000. The Cuban presence had penetrated every sector of the Miami economy, and Spanish had become more than a second language: it was virtually the language of communication and the language of commerce in much of Miami.[19]

At the end of the 1970s Cuban Americans still occupied their place as one of the most popular immigrant groups ever to come to the United States. As refugees of a Communist dictatorship, they enjoyed considerable sympathy, and most Americans were impressed with the success Cubans had in adjusting to social and economic life in this country. In fact, some of the rhetoric of success actually disguised much of the discomfort and economic trouble the Cuban immigrants often faced. Although their household income was quite high compared with that of other immigrant groups, it was often a result of the fact that mothers, fathers, grandmothers, and grandfathers all worked, not that they earned higher salaries than other Americans.

seven

The Marielitos

B eginning in 1980, the Cuban-American community was about to under-
go a dramatic change in composition—one that would introduce new
internal political differences among the emigres as well as alter the way
many Americans viewed the Cuban migration. Until 1980 the vast majority of
Cuban immigrants to the United States had come from highly educated, mid-
dle- and upper-class business and professional backgrounds or from small-
business, entrepreneurial groups with high expectations for life. Because they
came from the more well-to-do classes in Cuban society, there were relatively
few Afro-Cubans among them. They were also perceived as political refugees
fleeing the heavy-handedness of a Communist state, and most Americans
viewed the Cuban immigrants as politically conservative, hard-working, and
law-abiding people who would soon become economic assets in the United
States. But the Mariel boatlift, which began in 1980, helped to change that
perception. In fact, the migration of the Marielitos became an extremely controversial issue in the United States because of an inaccurate portrait of the
immigrants that quickly evolved into a stereotype. As late as 1990 a wire-ser-
vice article dealing with the Mariel migration claimed that "'Marielito' became
a dirty word as it became evident that Castro had opened the doors to his prisons and mental institutions."[1]

   The origins of the Mariel migration are rooted in the Caribbean economy, the
political and economic policies of the Castro regime, the foreign policies of the
United States, and the social and economic needs of the Cuban-American community. Historians have long blamed Fidel Castro's mindless socialist maneuver-
ings for ruining the Cuban economy, but larger economic processes were also at
work. Although Castro had tried to reorient the Cuban economy, it remained, as
did so many other Caribbean economies, a peripheral, primary goods–producing,
export-dominated economy. The American boycott put enormous pressures on
the Cuban economy, and the Cuban-Soviet partnership eased some of them, but
in the 1970s Cuba also became a victim of the world sugar market. During the
decade, the average world market price for sugar covered only half of the world
production costs. Sugar production actually fell in Cuba during the early 1970s,
despite annual purchases of sugar at prices above market levels, leaving the
country with an enormous shortage of hard currency. Although production
increased from 4 million tons in 1972 to nearly 8 million tons in 1979, the world
price of sugar fell from nearly 30 cents per pound in 1976 to only 7.8 cents per

pound in 1980. Along with the other sugar economies of the Caribbean, the Cuban economy suffered in the late 1970s.

The economic malaise had a deleterious effect on Cuban economic plans. Ever since 1959 Castro had called on the Cuban people to sacrifice in the short term in order to enjoy the long-term gains socialism would bring. More specifically, he condemned the "bourgeois materialism" of Yankee consumer culture—what he described as "private consumption"—in favor of "collective consumption." He promised that consumer goods would soon become more available. By the mid-1970s consumer goods were more available, but the economic decline of the late 1970s forced him to resurrect the old rhetoric, to speak of the "new socialist man" whose life had meaning independent of the consumer culture. After so many years of sacrifice, most Cubans only saw their standards of living decline.[2]

Desperate for hard currency and aware that there were elements of the Cuban-American community who were not universally hostile to his regime, Castro decided to develop a plan to attract Cuban-American visitors, and their money, to the island. What he did not contemplate, however, was the success they would have in bringing their values with them. The fact that the administration of Jimmy Carter was interested in normalizing relations with Cuba if at all possible also created a positive atmosphere. Castro also saw the possibilities of driving a wedge into the Cuban-American community, alienating more moderate, younger groups from the aging right-wingers. He had an idea for muting much of the criticism of the proposal, or at least enough of it to prevent radical exiles from subverting the moderate elements in the Cuban-American community. One of the main items on the Dialogue Conference agenda had been to provide for a way of permitting Cuban Americans to return to the island for visits with friends and family members. Castro knew that there were hundreds of thousands of Cuban Americans with the time, money, and desire to make the trip. Not only would the visits help strengthen politically the Cuban-American moderates, but they would also bring hard currency into Cuba.

By the late 1970s the Cuban economy was steadily deteriorating, beset with rapid population increases, housing shortages, high unemployment, and severe shortages of consumer goods. The number of 15- to 19-year-olds entering the Cuban labor market increased from 800,000 in 1975 to 1,136,000 in 1980, and the economy could not absorb them. Castro needed development money and hoped visitors to the island would bring it in. He also hoped the step would improve Cuba's human rights image and show the world that he was no longer afraid of the destabilizing influences of the exile community in the United States. The visits would make it clear to the world, and to the Cuban-American community, that a Communist Cuba was a permanent fixture in the Caribbean.[3]

In December 1978 Fidel Castro announced that Cuban Americans would be permitted to make one-week trips to Cuba to visit their families. For many Cuban Americans, it was a dream come true—the opportunity to see people they had been separated from by only 90 miles and a political ideology. The visits began within days, and during December 1979 and early 1980 more than 100,000 Cuban Americans flew to Havana from New York City, Miami, and Los Angeles. The visitors were charged exorbitant rates for airfare and hotel accommodations, and Castro set up special hard-currency stores, known as "dollar stores," where the visitors could buy things for their families. Aware of the chronic shortages of consumer goods, the visitors also brought goods with them to distribute to their families. Collectively they spent more than $100 million in the island and provided a badly needed, if temporary, boost to the economy.

What Castro did not anticipate, however, was the effect of the other things the exiles brought with them. In what some historians and demographers have called the "blue jeans revolution," the Cuban-American visitors brought with them a cornucopia of consumer goods for their deprived relatives: designer jeans, jewelry, televisions, stereos, sports equipment, radios, clothes, toys, liquor, and household items. The consumer goods became living proof of what the relatives had been saying all along—that in the United States they were enjoying the good life. For those Cubans with relatives in the United States, the visits set in motion a revolution of rising expectations. Wayne Smith recalled that at a

> time when most Cubans were asked to tighten their belts and face more years of hard work for little return, relatives from Miami and New Jersey were flooding back into the country with tales of the good life in the U.S. To hear them tell it, everyone had a mansion, three cars, an unlimited number of TV sets, and more food than anyone could eat. Life was easy! More and more Cuban citizens began to yearn for a piece of that vision. Pressure for emigration inexorably increased.[4]

Economists also argued that these gifts "had absolutely no connection to their [Cuban workers] labor productivity." The gifts contrasted sharply with the "collective consumption" goals of Castro's economy and created unrealistic expectations about life in the United States for large numbers of Cuban workers.[5]

It became immediately clear to Castro and other Cuban policymakers that the family visits had created a new kind of discontent among some Cubans. For years they had heard of the abundance of consumer goods in the United States, but they had written much of the news off as Yankee propaganda. But when their relatives landed at Havana airport with their arms loaded with consumer goods, the propaganda suddenly seemed true. The desire to emigrate increased dramatically among those Cubans most interested in the consumer culture. Many of them were Cubans who had been active for years in the Cuban black markets and who had been frequently arrested and fined for profiteering. They were those Cubans who had never accepted socialism over capitalism. For them, the United States had become a mecca of prosperity.

Fidel Castro responded to the situation by announcing on 4 April 1980 that the Peruvian embassy in Havana was open to any Cubans who wished to emigrate. The announcement had been precipitated by José Antonio Rodríguez-Gallegos, who had driven a truck through the gates of the Peruvian embassy in order to get permission to emigrate. The news spread like wildfire throughout the island, and within a few days 11,000 people were ready to leave. Castro decided to let them leave Cuba and head for Costa Rica and Peru before making their way to the United States, but the flight was so rapid, and the images of desperate emigrants so poignant, that the exodus became a public relations disaster for Cuba. Castro tried to exploit the situation politically by organizing public demonstrations against the emigrants, accusing them of being antisocialist, greedy, and materialistic, but the demonstrations had little affect.

Cuban officials decided to regularize the emigration process so it would resemble the previous exile experiences. Castro also hoped to use the emigration as he had used it in the past: to eliminate potential sources of political opposition, validate the revolution in the minds of the Cuban public, and ease the unemployment problem and housing shortages caused by a stagnating economy and a rapidly growing population. Castro also realized that Cuban Americans were a major source of hard currency, and a little more emigration to the United States would augment that capital source. With all this in mind, Castro decided on 21 April 1980 to stop the movement through the Peruvian embassy and authorize the exit through the port of Mariel, Cuba, for any Cubans wanting to go directly to the United States.

Almost immediately, hundreds of Cuban-American motorboats headed across the Florida Straits to Mariel Harbor to pick up relatives. Tens of thousands of Cubans crowded into Mariel, creating a near mob scene of anxious disorder as people tried to get on a boat, any boat. Nobody had anticipated the depth and extent of emigration sentiment. It was embarrassing for Fidel Castro. Between 21 April and 26 September 1980, 124,779 Cubans left the island in what was called the "Freedom Flotilla" or the "Mariel boatlift." Nearly 1 million more Cubans expressed the desire to leave if they could and took the risk of filing the necessary emigration documents with the United States. Once again, Fidel Castro found himself with a pubic relations disaster on his hands, so he decided to get some advantage out of his predicament. Instead of just taking back their relatives on the boats, Castro forced the Cuban Americans to also take back strangers, and Castro selected the strangers: prostitutes, homosexuals, the criminally insane, the mentally retarded, and mental hospital patients. To be sure, such people were only a small minority of the Marielitos, but the decision backfired on Castro when the American press made note of the decision, and the U.S. government began vigorously to protest what he was doing. Castro himself decided to end the flotilla.[6]

Unlike previous waves of Cuban immigrants, the "Marielitos" were not welcomed with open arms by American society in general or even by the Cuban-American community. This time the press coverage of their arrival in the United States and their reasons for immigrating were different. There were a number of reasons for the suspicion and hostility many of them encountered. First, there was a widespread impression, inaccurate though it was, that all of the Marielitos were tainted social misfits, that Castro had emptied the jails and mental hospitals of Cuba.[7] There was, of course, an element of truth in the stereotype. Approximately 26,000 of the Marielitos had prison records, but the vast majority of them were either political prisoners or had been convicted for stealing food or trading on the black market. Most of them were guilty of being capitalists. Nevertheless, 4,000 to 5,000 of the Marielitos had records as hard-core, recidivist criminals, and several thousand Marielitos were suffering from a variety of mental illnesses. So although perhaps 6 percent of the Mariel immigrants brought severe problems with them to the United States, they were only a minority of the migration.[8]

Second, the migration caught both Cuba and the United States off-guard. Between April and October 1980, 124,779 Cubans arrived in the United States requesting political asylum. In the previous eight years combined, not that many Cubans had settled in the United States. There has always been a close correlation between demography and acceptance. Those immigrants who trickle into the country over a long period of time often go relatively unnoticed, while those

Members of South Florida's exile community pilot pleasure boats to pick up Cuban refugees from the Mariel port in Havana, April 1980. *Courtesy UPI/Bettmann Newsphotos*

who flood in during a brief period get a great deal of attention and raise a lot more fears. The Marielito migration was both sudden and large, and the nativist reaction in the United States was hardly surprising.[9]

Third, approximately 70 percent of the Mariel immigrants were male, and a significant proportion of them were single adults. Many of them did not have relatives in Miami, Union City, New York, or Los Angeles who were willing to take care of them. Traditionally, Americans have responded negatively to immigrant groups with a high proportion of males. Also, the vast majority of them decided to stay in Miami, even though the city had nowhere near the necessary housing to take care of them. The Mariel influx was huge and sudden, placing enormous pressures on social-service and government agencies. Those without friends or relatives in the United States had no place to go. Thousands of the immigrants had to be placed in military camps, which often resembled low-security prisons, in Florida, Arkansas, Pennsylvania, and Wisconsin. They often had to stay for extended periods in the camps while social workers tried to locate jobs and housing for them and federal investigators tried to determine if they had criminal records. Government psychiatrists interviewed them to determine which ones suffered from mental illness. The example of East "Little Havana" is a case in point. Before the arrival of the Marielitos, East Little Havana in Miami had a population of 18,000 and the second lowest mean household income of any neighborhood in Miami, but the settlement of 12,000 Marielitos in the neighborhood drove its household income to the bottom of the city. Between 1980 and 1981 Dade County unemployment jumped from 5 to 13 percent and apartment vacancy rates fell to less than 1 percent. One year after their arrival in the United States, most of the Marielitos had not found full-time employment, even though their expectations of success in America were still high.[10]

A fourth reason for the lukewarm reception of the Marielitos was the combination of the general economic malaise in the United States during the 1970s and the increase in immigration from Asia and Latin America. Ever since the Arab oil boycott of 1973, rising oil prices had created the phenomenon of "stagflation"—severe inflation combined with high unemployment. At the same time, the end of the Vietnam War resulted in the immigration of several hundred thousand people from Indochina—Vietnam, Cambodia, and Laos. There was also a high rate of illegal immigration from Mexico and Central America. With large numbers of people already concerned about immigrants taking jobs away from native-born Americans or driving down prevailing wage levels, the arrival of the Marielitos seemed to be adding to an already serious problem. Also, although the Marielitos came from somewhat higher socioeconomic backgrounds than Cuban society in general, they were not the elite that an earlier generation had been.

At least part of that dissatisfaction was due to an increasing sense of frustration in the United States toward the Carter administration. The economic malaise of the 1970s was hardly his doing, but Americans nevertheless held him responsible for the fact that things had not improved at all. They were also frustrated with America's image in world affairs. Carter had been unable to rescue the American hostages in Iran or to negotiate their release. When the Soviet Union invaded Afghanistan in 1979, Carter responded by boycotting the 1980 Olympic Games in Moscow, not exactly a hardline reaction. When news that the

Marielitos might contain a large contingent of criminals and mental misfits became widely known, many Americans thought Castro had hoodwinked a naive Carter.

Finally, and perhaps most important, large numbers of the Marielitos were Afro-Cubans. In 1960 nearly 7 percent of all Cubans living in the United States were Afro-Cubans, but in 1970 that percentage had dropped to only 2.6 percent. More than 98 percent of the Cuban immigrants during the 1960s were white. That was hardly surprising. After the onset of the Castro revolution, most of the immigrants had been upper- and middle-class Cubans, and historically Cuban society had discriminated against black people, confining them to the lower rungs of the socioeconomic ladder. American immigration policy during the 1960s and 1970s was also biased in favor Cubans who had family members in the United States, which also guaranteed a strong priority for whites over blacks. Finally, the Cuban revolution had provided some immediate benefits to Afro-Cubans, eliminating all forms of segregation and opening previously closed employment opportunities to them. But in the deteriorating Cuban economy, more than 40 percent of the Marielitos were Afro-Cubans. At the time of the Marielito migration in 1980, Miami's Little Havana was 99 percent white. Most of those whites carried the traditional white Cuban suspicions of Afro-Cubans. Large numbers of white Cuban Americans were prejudiced against them because of their black skin and their Santería religion.[11] As Benigno Aguirre has written, "Apparently, the ethnic identity of the Cuban Negro cannot neutralize the greater discrimination that all blacks experience. They lack a sense of community that shelters the ethnic individual from the effects of the larger society."[12]

The only real exception for Afro-Cuban immigrants was the Afro-Cuban community in Tampa, Florida. Ever since the 1890s, there had been a distinct, well-organized Afro-Cuban group living in Ybor City and West Tampa, where most of them worked in the cigar industry. Although they experienced discrimination at the hands of Anglo-Americans and Cuban Americans, they did not really amalgamate with the African-American community of South Florida either. They formed groups like La Unión Martí-Maceo, carved out a place for themselves in the labor union movement, and maintained a position of relative social independence between the white and black communities of the region. During the 1950s and 1960s La Unión lost membership and went into a state of decline, especially after urban renewal projects in Ybor City destroyed some of the old housing, but in the 1970s the group underwent a revival. Those Marielitos who ended up living in the Tampa area were more likely to find an ethnic community to nurture and protect them than those Marielitos who stayed in Miami.[13]

Substantial numbers of the Marielitos were Afro-Cubans who brought with them their Santería religion. Santería consisted of several closely related faiths distinguished by the ethnic background of their devotees. The most influential of the Santería cults was the Lucumí, who fused the Yoruba language of West Africa with Spanish. Others included the Arara from Dahomey and *vodún* spiritualism from Haiti, a combination of French and Fon cultures. All of the Santería cults mixed selected Catholic rituals with African mythology, identifying themselves nominally as Catholics, equating Catholic saints with various African deities, and interpreting Catholicism as the Spanish-community version of Santería. The primary figure in Yoruba Afro-Cuban religion is Ifá, an oracle with enormous mythological and cultural significance. As the years passed in Cuba, the African oral religion took on a written dimension in religious texts called *patakin*. The *patakin* became an important means of passing the religion one from generation to another, from the godfather-priests to godson-novices. Eventually the Yoruban images made their way into Cuban religion and culture, mixing with European Catholicism.[14]

Among the Lucumí, Yoruba gods and Catholic saints were treated as replicas of one another, known as *santos* in Spanish and *orishas* in Yoruba. Saint Barbara was the same person as Changó, the god of war, while Saint Francis of Assisi was equated with Orunmila, the god of destiny. Eleguá guarded the gates of heaven for Yorubans and was the same as Saint Peter in Cuban Santería. The most important of the *orishas* was Odudua, identified with the Virgin of Carmen, to whom the Lucumí sacrificed white chickens every month. Each believer also had a patron saint to bring protection and prosperity—Yemayá, the goddess of the sea, for sailors; Ogún, the equivalent of John the Baptist, for blacksmiths and soldiers; or Oshún, the patroness of lovers. Santería rituals combined such Catholic practices as lighting candles and reciting the Lord's Prayer and the rosary with chants, drumming, animal sacrifices, secret oaths, visionary trances, and spiritual possessions.[15]

The believers viewed the world from a unique perspective, uniting all nature into a cosmic whole. Animals, plants, minerals, sun, moon, stars, and the earth were alive, imbued with a measure of knowledge, individual consciousness, and an awareness of the things around them. People gave names to animals, trees, rivers, streams, meadows, caves, mountains, hills, and valleys, as well as to days, weeks, months, and seasons. All of creation had a spiritual essence, and there was a balance and solidarity to nature that people had to carefully respect. Disobedience and lack of respect for those unseen forces could easily ignite vengeance and retaliation. On the other hand, careful observance of those forces could help worshipers predict the future, avoid danger and tragedy, and control the fear, decay, sickness, and misery leading to death. What some people might call superstition was actually a highly complicated, integrated spiritual network linking all natural activities into a holistic unity. The sacred and profane, the spiritual and temporal, were one and the same.

Santería was alive with an unseen world of spirits. The existence of such mythological beings as devils, witches, dwarfs, water spirits, house ghosts, goblins, cloud-beings, vampires, nightmares, and generalized spiritual entities was taken for granted. All these beings functioned actively in the world according to supernatural laws, and when the events of the natural world appeared disruptive or illogical, the people blamed the spirits and appealed to magic for understanding and control. Although heavenly magic and its concourse of living, benevolent spirits and gods were overpowering, the evil magic of Satanic spirits was also very real, a force to be reckoned with through the power of heavenly magic. By seeing life in terms of magical casuality, Santería worshipers learned to deal with their environment, avoiding the fatalistic surrender to outside forces that political oppression and economic exploitation often spawned.

A typical Santería ceremony is the annual pilgrimage at the sacred lagoon of San Joaquín de Ibáñez near Matanzas, Cuba, where Santería worshipers honor Yemayá. The festival lasts for three days, in which there is dancing, feasting, drinking, singing, and worshiping. There are several parts to the ritual. In the morning the shaman, known as a *babalawo*, pours a coconut juice concoction over the railways, which represent the "legs of Ogún," the god of iron and steel. With this refreshment to the god, a metal tool can be used to sacrifice animals. A woman then introduces a lit candle into a hole in the trunk of a sacred tree, known as the *jaguey*, while the priest feeds the tree a mixture of wine, corn, coconut, and tobacco. Singing in the Yoruba language, the people then request, and receive, permission from the tree spirit to begin the animal sacrifice. The woman then opens up the beak of a live rooster and pulls out its tongue and then pulls off its head, passing around the bleeding neck so worshipers can taste the blood and be refreshed. More singing takes place until the worshipers feel that Eleguá, the messenger of the gods, has accepted the sacrifice. The ritualistic sacrifices continue, as does the dancing and singing, with the worshipers convinced that Changó takes over a female body and dances with Ogún. The worshipers then offer a sacrifice to the *ceiba*, a large Cuban tree that they believe possesses a maternal spirit. They then decapitate a turtle as an offering to Osain, the god of herbs and woods. To Changó, they castrate and sacrifice a ram, drinking from its blood as well. They then sacrifice a hen to the goddess Orila and ducks to Yemayá. The formal ceremony ends at noon with the sacrifice of a bird, at which point the congregation receives the blessing of Olorún, whom they believe to be the creator of the universe.[16]

The Santería religious devotions of the Mariel immigrants, which soon became evident in their garden and lawn altars and shrines, scandalized the white Protestants and Cuban-American Roman Catholics of Miami. Even the resident African-American Baptists and Methodists, who shared a racial heritage with the Afro-Cubans in the Mariel migration, took exception to Santería, seeing it as a strange and sometimes even demonic religious aberration. Although the claims about criminal behavior and mental illness among the Marielitos were vastly exaggerated in the American media, the presence of the Santería faith among some of the immigrants tended to confirm the worst fears of many Anglo-Americans and Cuban-Americans.

Not surprisingly, the Marielitos had a more difficult time adjusting to life in the United States than early Cuban immigrants. After five years in the United States, they were far more likely than the earlier generation of immigrants to have suffered from extended periods of unemployment. Large numbers of them had jobs paying less than the minimum wage, and their median incomes were far below those of other Cuban immigrants after similar time periods in the United States. They were more likely to be unemployed and receiving public assistance than the earlier immigrants, and the Afro-Cuban Marielitos were more likely than other Marielitos to be suffering economically. And yet, nearly 80 percent of them, several years after the migration, expressed real satisfaction with life in the United States.[17]

Many other Americans in South Florida, especially African Americans, were not as pleased about life in the United States, and they targeted Cuban Americans as one of the sources of their complaint. Throughout the 1980s, beginning with the Mariel migration, African-Americans became steadily more resentful of the Cuban immigrants. Cuban immigration had come so suddenly beginning in 1959 that the city did not have time really to adjust. The simultaneous arrival of tens of thousands of Haitian and Nicaraguan immigrants in the 1980s only made the situation worse. Job competition between blacks and

Cubans began immediately as the Cubans sought work in the low-paying service-sector jobs traditionally held by blacks. That competition also occurred in the construction, retail trade, and the garment industry. As early as 1963 black groups were complaining about the problem. African-Americans leaders also complained that the emerging "enclave economy" of Cuban Americans effectively froze blacks out of the small-business job market. Cuban immigration also created competition for housing and retail space in Miami, driving up rents and property values. Blacks also resented the billions of dollars the federal government spent resettling the Cuban immigrants.

The presence of the Cuban immigrants also changed forever the political climate in Miami. Ever since Reconstruction, Florida had been part of the "Solid South," consistently Democratic, and in the city of Miami, African Americans were a powerful constituency in the Democratic party and influential in city politics. But the Cuban immigrants tended to vote Republican when they became citizens, and they introduced a new level of political competition to Miami politics that had not been there before. Not only did African Americans find themselves competing for jobs and housing with the Cubans, they saw themselves losing political power in the process.[18]

The competition between the two groups resulted in violent confrontations during the 1960s and 1970s, and became more frequent in the 1980s. The first major race riot over the issue occurred in 1968 when the Republican party held its presidential nominating convention in Miami, and there were smaller "mini riots" during the 1970s. In 1980 several Miami policeman, two of them Hispanics, were charged with beating a black motorcyclist to death. The not-guilty verdict, coupled with the Mariel boatlift and the arrival of 25,000 Haitian immigrants, touched off black rioting in Liberty City and Overtown.[19] In December 1982, when a Hispanic police officer killed a young black male in Overtown, another wave of rioting swept through the black community. On 16 January 1989 Overtown and Liberty City erupted into black rioting again after William Lozano, a Hispanic police officer, shot and killed a black man fleeing a traffic citation on a motorcycle. Another black man riding as a passenger on the motorcycle was killed in the subsequent collision. Those ethnic tensions in Miami would not be easily solved.[20]

The Marielito migration also precipitated an Anglo backlash in Miami that was reflected in the 1980 Dade County elections. In 1973 the Metro Commission, which had no Hispanic members, made a gesture of accommodation to the new Cuban-American community by officially declaring Dade County to be "bilingual." County government agencies aggressively hired Spanish-speaking employees, printed official documents in English and Spanish, introduced bilingual programs into many county schools, and put up information signs in English and Spanish. But when the Marielitos arrived, Anglo citizens in Dade County suddenly reacted negatively to the ordinance. A group known as the Citizens of Dade County forced a countywide referendum on a proposed antibilingualism ordinance that stated that "the expenditure of county funds for the purpose of utilizing any language other than English, or promoting any culture other than that of the United States, is prohibited. All county government meetings, hearings, and publications shall be in the English language only." Spanish-speaking groups mobilized immediately, led by the Spanish American League against Discrimination, but the referendum passed by a substantial majority.[21]

The arrival of the Marielitos created, for the first time, a real generational and ethnic division in the Cuban-American community, a sense of the "old Cubans" versus the "new Cubans." While the "old Cubans" were overwhelmingly white and traditional Catholics or Protestants in background, the "new Cubans" were racially mixed, often black, and frequently practiced the syncretic religions symbolized by Santería. The "new Cubans," without the educational backgrounds of their predecessors, also became a working class in the Cuban-American community, at the bottom of the social and economic system. In that sense, they were not much different from native African Americans in Florida or from their compatriot Afro-Cubans back on the island. Now, in addition to the political factionalism that had always characterized exile politics, a new series of social, racial, religious, and economic divisions appeared.[22]

After the ending of the Mariel boatlift, the number of immigrants arriving in the United States from Cuba declined dramatically. A major reason for the decline had been the controversy in the United States that the Marielito flotilla had precipitated. Also, it was becoming increasingly clear to many American policymakers that the motivation behind the Cuban migration was changing. Throughout the 1960s and 1970s large numbers of the immigrants considered themselves political exiles, driven from Cuba because of the revolution. But with the arrival of the Marielitos, it was clear that most of the immigrants were moving for economic reasons. More and more the Cuban immigrants resembled immigrants from Asia and Latin America who were also coming to the United States for economic reasons. The era of special treatment was over, and most Cuban Americans, because of their own misgivings about the nature of the Marielito migration, were willing to go along with a change in American immigration policy.

Late in 1980 Congress passed the Refugee Act, which imposed severe restrictions on the number of Cubans who could legally enter the United States. After the legislation, prospective Cuban immigrants had to apply for admission like all other nonrefugees, and those seeking refugee status had to prove beyond reasonable doubt that if they were repatriated to Cuba they would suffer political or religious persecution. Still, critics charged that Cuban claims of being persecuted were more readily accepted by immigration officials than those made by other asylum seekers. In 1980, on the eve of the Mariel boatlift, there were 803,226 people of Cuban descent living in the United States. That number climbed to 1,017,000 by mid-1987, an increase of approximately 214,000. Of that number, roughly 125,000 were Marielitos, leaving an increase of 89,000 from other sources. Natural increase accounted for the majority of that total. The great Cuban migration of the twentieth century finally appeared to be over.[23]

The decline in Cuban immigration was accompanied by a decided chilling in Cuban-American relations. During the late 1960s and throughout the 1970s, a growing spirit of détente had characterized the United States' relationship with the Soviet Union and with the People's Republic of China, but relations with Cuba remained stuck in an ideological quagmire. By normalizing diplomatic relations with Cuba, the United States feared sending a message throughout the hemisphere that socialism and communism could be tolerated in Latin America. The fact that Fidel Castro remained in charge of Cuba was even worse, since normalization would have symbolized the triumph of the revolution. The United States was also unable to normalize relations with Cuba because of the power of the Cuban-American lobby. Most Cuban Americans still harbored decidedly anti-Castro sentiments. A number of American economic interest groups, particularly sugar growers in Florida, Louisiana, and Hawaii and the citrus industries of Florida, Texas, and California, opposed normalization because they feared the development of Cuban competition. Finally, the election of Ronald Reagan as president of the United States guaranteed a continuation of the chill in Cuban-American relations. Reagan was the darling of the Republican right-wing and a decided anti-Communist.

The United States also protested several foreign-policy initiatives of the Castro regime during the 1980s. Throughout the 1970s Castro had allowed Cuban troops to be used by communist guerrilla movements in Somalia, Angola, and Mozambique, much to the consternation of the United States, and during the 1980s he worked diligently to export revolution throughout the Caribbean and Central America. The U.S. invasion of Grenada in 1987 was ostensibly done to expel Cuban troops from the island, and President Reagan repeatedly justified the funding of contra guerrilla armies in El Salvador and Nicaragua by citing the presence of Cuban troops there. The Reagan administration decided to punish Cuba for its adventurism abroad. The State Department dramatically increased the number of restrictions on travel to Cuba and suspended tourist travel. By that time there were more than 40,000 Americans traveling to Cuba annually, and Reagan wanted to cut off that source of hard currency to Castro. Only diplomats, journalists, scholars, and individuals on family business could go to Cuba anymore. He limited the amount of money a Cuban American could send to a Cuban relative to no more than $1,200 a year.[24]

The families of those Mariel immigrants, as well as many civil liberties groups in the United States, began to protest the United States' continued detention of so many Cubans in federal prisons. American immigration placed illegal aliens into two categories. People known as "deportable aliens" are those who are captured by immigration authorities after having entered the United States illegally. They can be detained for only six months while their cases are being reviewed before they must be deported or released. The other category consists of "excludable aliens." Excludable aliens are those illegal immigrants taken into custody before actually crossing an American border. The law permits the INS to hold them indefinitely while reviewing their cases. Large numbers of the Marielitos were defined as "excludable aliens," and since Cuba at first refused to repatriate them, several thousand of the Marielitos found themselves in federal detention centers.

Basically, the United States gave the Marielitos what is considered a "parole" status, allowing them to remain in the United States until they commit a crime or are discovered to have committed a crime in Cuba before their immigration. Once either one of those events occurred, they were detained under the status of "excludable alien." More than 2,800 Marielitos were detained indefinitely in federal detention centers. Once they completed their sentence, the INS reviewed their status and decided whether to send them back to Cuba. The INS earned a reputation for conservatism and strictness in reviewing each case, usually deciding to deport the Marielito. Each detainee had the right to a second-level review of his or her case by the Justice Department, and the Justice Department proved to be more liberal, disallowing the deportation orders of 45 percent of those cases they reviewed.[25]

The entire issue became a civil rights controversy in the United States. Groups such as the Commission Pro-Justice of the Mariel Prisoners, the Coalition to Support Cuban Detainees, Facts about Cuban Exiles, and the American Civil Liberties Union argued that of the 125,000 Mariel immigrants, only 300 were mental health patients and only 350 had committed serious felony crimes. They could see no reason for the continued detention of nearly 3,000 people after so many years in the United States. They also argued that the press had given the Mariel immigrants a terrible image. Too many native Americans had wrongly concluded that the Mariel boatlift refugees were a criminally prone people. Actually, they argued, between 1980 and 1987 all of the 125,000 Mariel immigrants committed 2,800 crimes in the United States, of which only 600 were serious felonies. Civil rights advocates called for the release of the detained Marielitos.[26]

The events of the mid-1980s especially demonstrated the classic interrelationship between Cuba, the United States, and the Cuban-American community. Ever since the Marielito migration of 1980, American officials had been concerned about the background of some of the immigrants. Several thousand of the Marielitos were still being held in federal detention centers in 1984, and several thousand more were in state and federal prisons doing time for criminal convictions. The Reagan administration began negotiating for a deportation of these people, and on 14 December 1984 Cuba and the United States signed an agreement providing for their repatriation. In particular, the agreement designated the deportation of 2,746 "excludable aliens" being held in detention centers, and the United States hoped future negotiations would provide for the deportation of the convicted criminals. In February 1985 the first few dozen aliens were returned to Cuba.

In May 1985, however, the U.S. Information Agency, with the express backing of the Reagan administration and much support from the Cuban exile community in Miami, established Radio Martí and began steadily broadcasting anti-Castro programs into Cuba from Florida. Castro bitterly protested the broadcasts, but the Reagan administration refused to stop them, and Castro then suspended the deportation agreement. Recriminations and accusations were exchanged back and forth for the next two years before real negotiations over the issue resumed. On 21 November 1987 the two countries again reached an agreement in which Castro consented to accept the repatriation of the "excludable alien" detainees and the United States agreed to receive 27,000 Cuban immigrants annually.

The agreement precipitated rioting at the federal detention centers in Oakdale, Louisiana, and Atlanta, Georgia, where several thousand Cubans were being held. They did not want to be returned to Cuba, and in protest they took correctional personnel hostage, set fires to the buildings, and demanded their constitutional rights, which they claimed had been denied them by so many years of confinement. The rioting became headlines in the United States and lasted for two weeks until Agustín A. Román, the auxiliary Roman Catholic bishop of Miami, negotiated the release of the hostages and an end to the rioting. The United States then began releasing some of the detainees to their families and returning others to Cuba—a process that took place gradually throughout 1988.

But Cuban-American relations soured again in 1988 when José Mas Canosa, a prominent Miami businessman whom some people accused of having dreams of someday becoming Cuba's president, announced plans for Televisión Martí to broadcast anti-Castro propaganda over the Cuban airwaves. In 1989 the project received the backing of the administration of George Bush, and plans were made for the Voice of America to use a satellite and a balloon tethered 10,000 feet above Florida to conduct the broadcasts. Once again, Castro protested the broadcasts, but by that time his own domestic political and economic problems were taking precedence. Under his dual programs of perestroika and glasnost, Soviet Premier Mikhail Gorbachev began reducing the subsidies that his country had been giving Cuba for the previous quarter-century and stopped selling subsidized petroleum to Castro. Cuba's economy went into a tailspin. At the same time, the Communist governments fell all over Eastern Europe, and throughout the Cuban-American community speculation raged over how long Castro could survive. In 1989 Florida governor Bob Martínez established the Free Cuba Committee to study the impact a collapse of the Castro regime and large-scale Cuban emigration would have on Florida. By the early 1990s the Cuban-American community was praying for redemption.

Despite all the negative publicity, the Marielito immigrants proved to be a hard-working, law-abiding people in the United States. After 10 years in the United States the Marielitos had scattered throughout the country, although 80 percent of them still lived in South Florida. Just more than 400 of them had been deported to Cuba under the 1984 treaty arrangement, and another 2,400 were still being detained. Approximately 100 of the Marielitos were confined in mental institutions and suffering from chronic mental illness. Cuban-American civil rights groups were still protesting the detainment. Siro del Castillo of the Facts about Cuban Exiles group argued in 1990 that "legally, they are telling people who have been here ten years that they have never really been here and can be deported any day. No one should be jailed for an indefinite period. And no one should be deported back to Cuba. It's just hypocritical for the United States to criticize Cuba for human rights violations and then deport people back there."[27] The other 122,000 Marielitos were proving to be as successful in learning English, finding jobs, and building businesses as the earlier generation of Cuban immigrants had been after only 10 years in the United States.

Cuban America in 1995

By the early 1990s the Cuban-American community in the United States had a unique ethnic profile. They were among the most recent immigrants to the United States, but they were also among the most politically visible and the most economically successful, at least considering the relatively short time they had lived here. Since 1901 more than 1 million people had left Cuba for the United States (see Table 1). There had always been an ebb and flow to the migration, rising and declining according to economic conditions in the United States and the political situation in Cuba. And in the early decades of the migration, the net flow of Cubans back to the island was often high, especially if they perceived the resurrection of a political climate consistent with their economic expectations, and their perceived right to rule. Since 1959, however, the number of people returning to the island had slowed to a trickle. Fidel Castro had stamped his own personality and ideology on the political culture and economy of Cuba, and there was no going home again. By 1995 the Cuban-American population of the United States was more than 1.2 million.[1]

Throughout U.S. history, immigrant groups have tended to move in "chain migrations," following paths and settling in areas previously pioneered by earlier arriving family members or compatriots, but more so than any other U.S. ethnic group, Cuban Americans achieved a remarkable degree of demographic concentration. More than 60 percent of Cuban Americans live in Florida, with the great bulk of them in Dade County—what some people call "Little Havana." And within Dade County Cubans exhibited a strong tendency to live near other Cuban Americans. More than 20 percent of Cuban Americans live in New York and New Jersey, with most of them in "Little Havana North" along the west side of the Hudson River in New Jersey's Union City–West New York corridor. Another 7 percent live in California, with smaller concentrations in Illinois, Texas, and elsewhere.[2]

The demographic concentration of the Cuban-American community occurred despite U.S. government attempts to scatter the arriving Cuban immigrants throughout the country. That effort did not really begin until the 1970s, and it occurred most consciously and energetically with the Marielitos. Similar attempts to settle the Vietnamese, Cambodian, and Laotian immigrants throughout the United States also met with failure. The need to congregate with people who shared one's culture was very powerful. The vast majority of Cuban

Table 1.

Number of Cubans Emigrating to the United States

1901–1910	40,159
1911–1920	27,837
1921–1930	15,608
1931–1940	4,122
1941–1950	15,451
1951–1960	149,777
1961–1970	460,214
1971–1980	246,591
1981–1990	122,141
1991–1994	65,000
Total	1,146,900

immigrants had arrived in Miami and were processed there by the Cuban Refugee Resettlement Program. Of that group, approximately half remained in Dade County while the other half were settled in such cities as New York (especially in upper Manhattan and in Queens), Union City–West New York, Chicago, Los Angeles, and New Orleans. But once those immigrants outside of Miami and New Jersey–New York had established a measure of social and economic independence, between 25 and 30 percent of them eventually returned to Florida, attracted by the tropical climate and large Cuban community that reminded them of the island. The appearance of a Cuban-American ghetto in South Florida occurred not because of any legal or political pressure but because the immigrants themselves yearned for the sights and sounds of home.[3]

Despite the arrival of the Mariel boatlift immigrants, the Cuban-American community remained, in terms of racial composition, overwhelmingly white. By the early 1990s more than 80 percent of Cuban Americans were white and only 5 percent were black. The remaining Cubans were of mixed racial heritage. Before the arrival of the Marielitos, only 2 percent of Cuban Americans were black. Although substantial numbers of the Mariel immigrants were of Afro-Cuban descent, they had not dramatically changed the racial profile of the Cuban-American community. For a number of reasons, Afro-Cubans were not usually involved in the emigration from Cuba. The Castro revolution hurt the upper classes in Cuba but helped the lower classes, and most Afro-Cubans were included in the latter group. Also, because so much of Castro's propaganda depicted the United States as a racist society, Afro-Cubans were not anxious to emigrate. Because U.S. immigration policy was geared toward kinship ties, giving preferential treatment to prospective immigrants who already had family in America, the Afro-Cubans who did want to leave, because most of them did not have family members living in the United States, had a difficult time getting exit visas. Those immigrants of Afro-Cuban descent who did make it here, however, were more likely to live in Little Havana North than in Miami or Tampa, probably because of the feeling that racial discrimination in New York and New Jersey would not be as severe as it was in Florida. Also, many Afro-Cubans felt hostility from the white Cuban majority, many of whom felt that Afro-Cubans had supported Castro for too long. In that sense, the racial sensibilities of white Cuban immigrants fit well into the prevailing climate of opinion in the American South.

As far as a social portrait of the Cuban-American community in the early 1990s is concerned, the immigrants were closer to the national averages than any other recent immigrant group, including Mexicans, Central Americans, Puerto Ricans, Vietnamese, Cambodians, Laotians, and Filipinos. While 26 percent of the general population over the age of 14 consisted of single people—and 32 percent for Mexicans, 35 percent for Puerto Ricans, and 33 percent for Central Americans—only 22 percent of Cubans were single. Cuban Americans were more likely to be married than any other ethnic group in the United States. They were also less likely to be living in female-headed households. In terms of educational achievement, Cuban-Americans were twice as likely as other Hispanics to complete four years of college and only slightly less likely than the general American population to do so.[4]

The social and economic background of the immigrants in Cuba, the existence of an enclave economy in Miami and Union City–West New York, the high average age, low fertility rates, family stability, and educational attainment all combined to give Cuban Americans a level of economic success unprecedented among first-generation immigrants to the United States. While 11 percent of all American families lived below the poverty level in 1986, the number was only 13 percent for all Cuban Americans—a surprising number, as it factored in the poverty of the Marielitos. In contrast, although they had been living in the United States much longer, 25 percent of Mexican-American families lived in poverty, as did 38 percent of Puerto Rican Americans. Cuban-American unemployment in 1987 was 5.5 percent, one of the lowest of any ethnic group in the country, compared with 7 percent for the country at large, 11.7 percent for Mexican Americans, and 11 percent for Puerto Rican Americans. The Cuban-American occupational profile was also close to the national average. While 56 percent of Americans worked in managerial, professional, technical, sales, and administrative support capacities, 54 percent of Cuban Americans did so in 1987. That compares with 33 percent for Mexican Americans and 47 percent for Puerto Rican Americans. Although the median annual income for Cuban Americans was below the national average, it was still higher than that of any other Hispanic, African-American, or recent immigrant group in the United States.[5]

To outsiders, ethnic ghettos and enclaves have often appeared to be exotic places full of strange people, strange sounds, strange sights, and strange smells. Those ethnic ghettos have also often been places of poverty, especially for the first generation of arrivals, who struggled to survive economically in a new country. For many Americans, the ghettos have been problems—a social blight on the national landscape. But the ethnic ghettos were neither pathological expressions of fear nor walled, escape-proof communities. Ethnic groups lived there in part because of the emotional security they offered in a different world. Ethnic enclaves were places where culture shock could be contained. Havens rather than prisons, the ghettos eased the adjustment to American life. There the immigrants could hear their own language spoken and live near friends and relatives. The buildings and shops often had the flavor of home; traditional holidays were celebrated; and ethnic institutions existed to assist new immigrants in settling, finding jobs, or seeking assistance of many kinds. In the ghettos were the churches and newspapers that bound the community together and provided them some contact with the Old World. And in the ghettos there were the familiar political discussions and arguments, with Old World passions being played out on a new stage.

The staging area for the Cuban-American success story has been Miami. The heart and soul of Cuban-American life in the United States and in Miami is the area known as "La Sagüesera." By 1965 there were more than 100,000 Cubans living there between Northwest Seventh Street and Southwest Twenty-second Street and between West Twenty-seventh Avenue and Miami Avenue in the center of downtown Miami. As the community expanded in the 1960s and 1970s, the population spread west and northwest of the metropolis, particularly to the Hialeah–Miami Springs districts and to the Edison district. From those points during the late 1970s and 1980s Cuban Americans spread throughout Dade County. By the mid-1990s there were more than 650,000 Cuban Americans living in Dade County. Although most immigration historians now believe that the idea of huge, ethnically homogeneous ethnic ghettos in American cities were not the rule, and that there was much more diversity to settlement patterns even in urban areas, "Little Havana" in Miami defies that characterization. Because of their middle-class origins and high rates of residential concentration and segregation in La Sagüesera, Little Havana is just that—a large Cuban community on the north side of the Florida Straits.[6]

In moving into Miami, Cuban immigrants behaved like earlier generations of immigrants had in other cities. Most immigrants to the United States established ethnic self-help organizations. These associations often offered life insurance, English classes, job placement, government assistance programs, and philanthropic welfare. Often those organizations were based on the region of the Old World from which the immigrant came. The associations were also designed to help the immigrants preserve ethnic identity. They were called *bydelag* societies for the Norwegians, *landsmanschafen* for the Jews, the *kenjinkai* for the Japanese, the *hui kuan* for the Chinese, or the *topikas* for the Greeks. For the Cuban immigrants, they were called *municipios en el exilio* (municipalities in exile). When the migration of the Golden Exiles began in 1959, there were six provinces in Cuba—Pinar del Río, La Habana, Matanzas, Las Villas, Camagüey, and Oriente—and those provinces contained 126 *municipios*, or townships. The early Cuban arrivals in Miami organized *municipios en el exilio* to assist other immigrants from their home township on the island. The *municipios* celebrate traditional Cuban holidays and promote Cuban-American culture. By the early 1990s there were more than 120 *municipios en el exilio* functioning in Miami. An umbrella organization, the Municipios de Cuba en el Exilio, represents them as a group. In addition to providing a variety of social services, most of the *municipios* are highly politicized and consider the promotion of democracy and the destruction of communism, especially in Cuba, to be central missions in their existence.

They also provide citizenship information to new immigrants and conduct voter registration drives.[7]

Because of the *municipios*, as well as the background to the immigration from Cuba, Cuban-American communities have a vibrant, often controversial political life. Ever since Cubans first arrived in the United States, exile politics have been fractious and intense, with most Cuban Americans opposed to the Castro regime but disagreeing over tactics—how best to see that democracy is achieved in Cuba. Traditionally in U.S. history, immigrant groups, especially Roman Catholic immigrant groups, have voted Democratic. The primary reason for that, of course, was economic. Most new immigrants were poor, working-class people who identified more with labor-union interests than with management and who found the Democratic party a more comfortable political home. Cuban Americans have been the great exception. For much of their history in the United States, Cuban workers preferred ethnic solidarity to the class notions of American labor unions and were difficult to recruit. Although many working-class Cuban immigrants, especially after the Mariel boatlift, have been more politically liberal and have voted Democratic, the overwhelming majority of Cuban Americans are conservative Republicans. More than 85 percent of Cuban Americans voted for Ronald Reagan in the elections of 1980 and 1984. They heavily supported George Bush 1988 and 1992. Also, Cuban-American voters tend to be more politically active than the population at large, and they tend to register to vote and to vote in substantially higher numbers. Unlike many Americans, the Cubans see a vitality in politics, an opportunity to exercise real power and effect real change.

That conservative political orientation is a function of a unique interaction between domestic economic interests and foreign-policy concerns. Since their arrival in the United States beginning in the 1960s, Cuban Americans have seen the Democratic presidents exhibit what they consider to be a fatally weak policy toward world communism in general and Cuban communism in particular. John Kennedy's handling of the Bay of Pigs invasion was hopelessly naive and indecisive, while Lyndon Johnson's conduct of the Vietnam War was characterized by vacillation and compromise. Under Jimmy Carter, the United States simply appeared impotent, unable to behave like a world power. Cuban Americans perceived the Republican presidents as much stronger foreign-policy leaders. They celebrated Ronald Reagan's invasion of Grenada in 1984, especially when he expelled the Cuban workers there, and on 26 January 1991 more than 30,000 Cuban Americans demonstrated in Miami in favor of President George Bush's war policy in the Middle East.

By the mid-1980s Cuban Americans had become a formidable political force in South Florida and had changed the region's traditional Democratic orientation. Cuban-American Republicans became extremely influential in Dade County politics, taking control of the mayoral office under Raúl Martínez, sending representatives to the state legislature, and occupying thousands of civil service positions. In 1989 Cuban-born Ileana Ros-Lehtinen was elected to serve in the House of Representatives. Anticommunism was a potent political force in Miami, and Cuban Americans had long memories. When Cuban-born New York playwright Dolores Prida visited Miami in 1989, she received widespread protests because of her earlier stand calling for political accommodation with Fidel Castro. In 1988 Luis Torres, a longtime Castro opponent, received similar condemnation when he visited the island at the invitation of the dictator. Later that year the Dade County Republican party protested a plan by the Justice Department to deport Dr. Orlando Bosch, a Cuban-born pediatrician accused of terrorist activities, and the Reagan administration ordered that Bosch be paroled. When the black South African leader Nelson Mandela visited Miami in June 1990, he refused to denounce Fidel Castro, arguing that Castro had always supported the rights of black people in South Africa. Cuban Americans organized demonstration marches protesting Mandela's comments, and the subsequent controversy pitted Miami's black community against the Cubans. Despite their internal disagreements over political tactics, the conservative, anti-Communist political profile helped knit the immigrant community together.[8]

More so than any other ethnic enclave in American history, Little Havana is a hotbed of entrepreneurial activity in addition to its political profile. By the early 1990s there were more than 20,000 Cuban-American businesses in Miami, most of which were small firms specializing in textiles, construction, finance, retailing, and wholesaling. There were also garment factories, private schools, radio and television stations, compact disk producers, furniture factories, and publication firms. The Cuban-American economy generated nearly $1.5 billion in economic activity by 1990. Cuban Americans controlled 35 percent of the Dade County construction industry and were especially influential in banking. There were also thousands of Cuban-American physicians, dentists, accountants, lawyers, and pharmacists. In the process, Miami has become the major U.S. center for international trade with Latin America.

The ethnic atmosphere in Little Havana is especially tangible along Flagler, Southwest Eighth, Northwest Seventh, Twelfth, Seventeenth, and Twenty-second avenues, or at the Church of San Juan Bosco or at Biscayne Bay Park, known as "El Parque de las Palomas." The whole area is laced with Cuban parks, restaurants, banks, savings and loans, theaters, insurance offices, hardware stores, open-air markets, jewelry stores, flower shops, car dealerships, travel agencies, nightclubs, coffeehouses, bookstores, newsstands, cafeterias, barber shops, cigar factories, clinics, bakeries, funeral homes, and small grocery stores. Peddlers sell fish, poultry, vegetables, and fruits. There are special *botánicas* supplying the roots, herbs, oils, potions, and figurines needed in Santería rituals. Advertisements and billboards are in Spanish, and the stores are called *mercado* or *farmacia* or *zapatería*. Maps of Cuba, posters of José Martí, Cuban flags, and "Cuba libre" signs are in store windows. The smells of Cuban food are everywhere—sautéed butter, green peppers, tomatoes, rice, and garlic; such meat dishes as *lechón asado* (pork roast), *masas de puerco* (fried pork chunks), *pan con lechón* (fried pork sandwich), *palomilla* (thin-sliced sirloin), *falda* (flank steak), *ropa vieja* (shredded beef), *tasajo* (dry shredded beef), *boliche* (pot roast), *picadillo* (spicy beef hash), and *pollo asado* (roast chicken); side dishes like *plátanos maduros fritas* (fried ripe plantains), *plátanos verdes* (green plantains), *mariquitas* (fried green plantain chips), *papas fritas* (fried potatoes); and deserts like *flan* (custard), *natilla* (egg pudding), *arroz con leche* (rice pudding), *pudín de pan* (bread pudding), *boniatillo* (sweet potato pudding), and *empanadas de carne* (meat pies). South Florida was not Havana or Santiago de Cuba, but it was close—close enough to still feel at home.

The sounds of Cuba are also ubiquitous in Little Havana. In the early 1980s Spanish was the language spoken in nearly 93 percent of Cuban-American homes. It was also the language of business and commerce in the Cuban communities of Havana and Union City–West New York. There are 10 AM and FM radio stations that broadcast exclusively in Spanish in Miami, and several more in the New York area. The most well-known of them is WQBA, nicknamed "La Cubanísima," in Miami. Miami also has two Spanish daily newspapers—*El Herald* and *Diario Las Américas*—and more than a dozen weekly newspapers known as *periodiquitos*, including *Patria* (country), *La Verdad* (truth), and *La Nación* (nation). WLTV provides television broadcasts in Spanish, while GALA-TV is a pay-cable station that shows Spanish language films. And coming out of radios, compact disk players, and tape players are the sounds of Cuban music— the infinite variability of the Latin *clave*, an African-derived, off-beat 3/2 rhythmic structure played over a two-bar phrase and treated as one measure. At Antonio Maceo Park at fifteenth Avenue and Calle Ocho (Eighth Street), Cuban men gather to play dominoes, smoke cigars, and talk—about Cuba, the old days, politics, and problems. A few blocks away is the almost reverent atmosphere of the Cuban Memorial Plaza on thirteenth Street, where a monument celebrates Brigade 2506 and the Bay of Pigs invasion.[9]

Cuban-American children even found the public schools to be relatively familiar places, at least when compared with the experiences of earlier immigrants. The Dade County schools became the pioneers in bilingual education. By the early 1960s a new group of political activists, linguists, psychologists, and teachers began to question the consensus that had developed around language teaching. Before the 1960s the public schools had usually followed the path of totally immersing immigrant or bilingual children in English; most states also had statutes requiring English as the language of instruction. Many theorists, however, questioned the validity of the methods for very young children. It seemed to many observers that Hispanic children often withdraw rather than respond, causing them to fall behind in school. And it seemed obvious to most observers that the public schools had not met the needs of children with a primary language other than English. The achievement levels among most non-English-speaking students were well below the national average. Some began to advocate an alternative to total immersion—one more consistent with holistic principles and new cognitive theories. The field of bilingual education was born, albeit in the midst of great controversy.

Bilingual education theorists thought they had a remedy for the situation. Psycholinguists had long recognized that the process of becoming bilingual could involve major conflicts of values and allegiances, and when those conflicts were too great for children to accept and resolve, learning was compromised. Hispanic activists were convinced that public school teachers and curriculum often criticized Hispanic culture, denigrated the Spanish language, and urged children to abandon their own culture in favor of Anglo values. Hispanic children found themselves torn between the values of their parents and families and the values of the public school system and Anglo society. Many children, rather than make a choice, became slow learners or dropped out of school. The scientific literature was clear that children with limited skills in the instructional language of the curriculum and school were going to have achievement problems when compared with children whose primary language was the instructional language.

The bilingualists believed that the problems of educating language minority children could be overcome through a different approach to curriculum and instruction. To overcome the problem of alienation and conflict between two cultures, bilingual education must include ethnic history and ethnic culture as major curriculum components. Children who could be proud of their heritage would be more likely to be comfortable in the school setting than those who feel inferior. Second, the language of instruction in a bilingual program must be the primary language of the minority child. Learning math, science, and social studies in his or her own language would accelerate the learning process compared with being instructed in those subjects in a weaker language. Finally, English must be taught as a second language during the early stages of the bilingual program. Only as the child's competence with English improved could the transition be gradually made to English-language instruction in other subject areas. Although bilingual education was driven by its own concerns, many of which were heavily political, it did offer an early and severe critique of at least one area of language training in the United States.

Cuban immigrants were the first Hispanic immigrants to adopt the notion of bilingual education. In 1963 the Dade County schools undertook a completely bilingual program in grades one, two, and three of the Coral Way School in Miami. At first the program was voluntary, but by the end of the first year it had won almost unanimous approval, and offering an "English-only" option was no longer necessary. Half of the instruction was given in English and half in Spanish. Evaluation of the program showed that it was as effective as the regular program in English. Dr. Mabel Wilson Richardson, a professional evaluator of the bilingual program, wrote that "in addition to performing as well as the control group in the regular curriculum, the English-speaking pupils were learning a second language and the Spanish-speaking pupils were learning to read and write their native language."[10]

The field of bilingual education was born in those Dade County schools when it became clear that when Cuban-American children were able to become literate in their mother tongue as well as learn English, their success rates in school were dramatic. Under the Cuban Refugee Program from 1960 to 1972, the federal government paid more than $130 million to the Dade County public schools for bilingual education programs for Cuban refugees (60 percent of the cost). In October 1965, however, in response to Castro's offer to allow more Cubans to emigrate, President Lyndon B. Johnson announced an open-door policy, and a second wave of Cuban immigrants arrived. Then the federal government paid 100 percent of the cost of the program. In 1961 there were 4,327 Cuban refugee pupils; in 1970, 31,230. These instructional programs became prototypes for current efforts in bilingual education. They also provided Cuban adults with employment as former teachers were hired to coordinate the programs, serve as teacher's aides, and provide a link between the Spanish-speaking community and the school. The results seemed to prove the theorists' point. Cuban-American children were more likely to complete high school and go on to higher education than any other Hispanic immigrant group in the United States.[11]

In the 1980s the issue of bilingual education has been highly politicized, primarily by Anglos in Dade County who fear the Latinization of the community culture. The 1980 referendum outlawing the use of public funds to promote non-English cultural institutions was a blow to bilingualism and multicultural-ism in Dade County, and such activist groups as the Spanish American League against Discrimination continue to lobby for bilingualism in the political and educational life of South Florida, but the proponents of "English-only" and the English-as-a-Second Language curriculum in the schools still have the upper hand and limit the bilingual programs. The continuing immigration of Cubans, Nicaraguans, Puerto Ricans, Mexicans, and other Central Americans to South Florida, however, will continue to make the issue a source of intense political competiton.[12]

In addition to a rich, animated political life, the enclave institutions of Little Havana and Little Havana North, and the bilingual schools, Cuban-American immigrants created a unique religious life in the United States. In the Spanish colonial empire, the Roman Catholic Church had been responsible for the moral and spiritual guidance of the people, and Spain had enjoyed the *Patronato Real*—complete control over the church in the colonies. Highly dependent on the gov-erning classes, the church became a conservative force identified closely with the interests of the elite. Also, because Cuba had long been considered the back-water of the New World empire, it had never attracted high-quality priests, instead often becoming a dumping ground for priests with intellectual and emo-tional problems. Many Cubans became alienated from the parish priests. Because of its upper-class bias, links to the conservative forces of the Spanish crown, and intense opposition to the independence movement, the church had angered large numbers of Cubans, who equated it with corruption, conser-vatism, and authoritarian control. In 1959 there were only 700 priests working in only 200 parishes on the whole island.

The Roman Catholic diocese of Miami had been established in 1958 with Coleman F. Carroll, a priest of Irish-American descent, serving as bishop. At the time there were 65 parishes in the diocese serving 305,000 Roman Catholics. Those parishes were staffed by priests who were overwhelmingly Irish and Irish American. By the early 1980s there were more than 900,000 people in Miami, and the diocese had been raised to an archdiocese, with Edward A. McCarthy, also an Irish American, serving as archbishop. There were 134 parishes then, with more than 600 priests, most of whom were Irish American, but also 118 who had Spanish surnames and 25 who were Cuban-born. Although the arch-diocese was overwhelmingly Hispanic in its ethnic composition—Cuban and Puerto Rican—its administrative culture was overwhelmingly Irish. The Cuban immigrants, many of whom were only nominal Catholics, were confronting a Roman Catholic Church in the United States that was quite different from what they had been accustomed to in Cuba. Irish Catholicism had traditionally been known for its strict piety, its spiritual activism, and its puritanical culture. Many Cuban immigrants found the Irish-American church to be uptight, fanatical, and intolerant of their Hispanic values.[13]

In the past the Roman Catholic Church had reacted to the challenge of new immigrants by allowing them to establish nationality parishes manned by their own ethnic priests, named after their own patron saints, and imbued with their Old World culture, liturgies, language, and symbols. For several generations those nationality parishes served as comfortable spiritual homes and social enclaves for the immigrants and their children. Only as time passed and the descendants of the immigrants scattered out into the territorial parishes of the suburbs did the national parishes decline in membership. By the time the Cubans exiles began arriving in the 1960s, however, the U.S. Roman Catholic Church had decided to abandon the nationality parish in the name of assimilation. By bringing the new immigrants directly into territorial parishes where Roman Catholics of all ethnic persuasions worshiped, the church hoped to accelerate the incorporation of the immigrants into American society.

Although the Miami archdiocese did not make the transition to formal ethnic parishes, the regular parishes were only technically territorial because the Cuban-American population was so residentially concentrated. After Vatican II allowed the Mass to be performed in the vernacular language, Spanish became the language of the services. There were not enough Spanish-speaking priests to serve all of the parishes, and the Cubans were not always enamored of the Irish-American priests, but the appointment of Father Agustín Román, a Cuban-born priest, as the auxiliary bishop of the archdiocese helped many of the immigrants identify more closely with the church. Román had arrived in the United States in 1966 and came to the attention of church leaders when he was selected to raise money for construction of a shrine to Our Lady of Charity (the patron saint of Cuba) on Biscayne Bay. Román organized the whole project around the *municipios* groups, drawing up yearly schedules of pilgrimages to the shrines, with three *municipios* visiting each week. He scheduled Masses to coincide with the pilgrimages and organized the Confraternity of Our Lady of Charity. In 1968 more than 500,000 visited the site of the shrine, and in 1973 a new chapel was dedicated. By the 1980s there were Roman Catholic yard shrines—dedicated usually to Our Lady of Charity, Saint Barbara, and Saint Lazarus—all over the city. The shrines consisted of glass-paneled alcoves with a statue inside surrounded by candles, crucifixes, beads, stones, miniature figurines, and other paraphernalia. Little Havana had a distinctly Roman Catholic flavor.

With each increasing wave of immigration from Cuba, however, the religious profile of the exiles changed. During the early 1960s, among the upper-class exiles, religious loyalty to the Catholic Church was quite high, with more than 80 percent of the immigrants being regular worshipers at Sunday Mass and fairly consistent in attending confession. As the economic profile of the immigrants changed in the later 1960s and 1970s, however, there was steadily less loyalty to the institutional church and an increasing number of inactive Roman Catholics and active Santería worshipers entering the United States. Back on the island, Santería had been making steady inroads over the years, with increasing numbers of more educated Cubans adopting some of its rituals and beliefs, and this change was reflected in the religious life of Little Havana. By the early 1980s, especially after the Marielito migration, there were more and more Santería yard shrines in the front yards of Little Havana, most of them dedicated to Changó (Saint Barbara), Eleguá (Holy Guardian Angel), Obatalá (Our Lady of Mercy), Ogún (Saint Peter), Orúnmila (Saint Francis of Assisi), Oshún (Our Lady of Charity), or Yemayá (Our Lady of Regla).[14] In the familiar world of Little Havana, Cuban Americans found a safe haven for adjusting to American society.[15]

The Cuban-American identity was also shaped by demographic change in Dade County. During the 1980s the flight of Anglo-Americans to the suburbs accelerated, as did the influx of more than 70,000 Haitians—desperately poor and frequently suffering from tuberculosis and AIDS—into the county. The vast majority of the Haitian immigrants were African in their ancestry and they, along with native African Americans, became increasingly resentful of the power exercised by Cuban Americans in Miami. Within two decades Hispanics in general and Cubans in particular had become the dominant, majority ethnic group in Miami, and they brought with them from the island a tradition of anti-African racism. By the mid-1970s African-American groups like the National Association for the Advancement of Colored People and the National Urban League were complaining that job discrimination by Cubans against blacks was widespread. Disc jockeys in Miami radio stations appealing primarily to the African-American community began regularly chanting "Go away José" on their broadcasts. In 1980, when four white policemen were exonerated after killing a black insurance salesman, the African-American ghetto of Liberty City in Miami erupted in an enormous race rebellion in which whites were targeted for random violence. Many blacks blamed Cuban Americans for their economic plight. And because of the black hostility, the Cuban-American ethnic identity became sharper still.[16]

But Little Havana in particular and the Cuban-American community in general is not a static, unchanging place but a mobile one, changing all the time. For several generations historians and sociologists have debated the nature of ethnicity in American life and how and to what extent the processes of assimilation have worked their magic in such a diverse society. Although ethnic loyalties created stability within individual groups, they often generated competition, fear, and instability for the society as a whole. Americans have been preoccupied with their diversity, worried about whether the centrifugal forces of race, religion, language, and national origins would eventually tear the country apart.

In recent years Americans have flirted with the "ethnic revival," seeing in the civil rights and ethnic power movements proof positive that diversity survives, that older patterns of race, religion, language, and national origins continue to govern social life in the United States. At any given point in American history the society seems quite diverse, apparently confirming the opinions of cultural pluralists about the continuing vitality of racial, religious, nationality, and linguistic differences. Despite appearances, however, the processes of modernization, acculturation, and assimilation have been inexorable, constantly working to transform minority values and loyalties and bring them in line with those of the larger society. Each immigrant group has had to adjust Old World values and associate itself with larger groups. The speed and extent of assimilation have varied from group to group, but no group has remained immune. While American society has remained culturally diverse from generation to generation, the nature of that diversity has changed at each stage, with older groups slowly mixing in with the larger society and new groups appearing isolated and distinct. Cuban immigrants, no less than any of their immigrant predecessors, have faced the forces of acculturation and assimilation, and although they are still in an early stage, those social, political, and economic forces are working their "melting pot" magic.[17]

For many Cuban Americans, the acculturation process—the tendency of immigrants to adopt the material culture and language of their new society—had already started before they arrived in the United States. The historically close economic and social relationship between the Cuban upper class and their counterparts in the United States helped limit the ravages of culture shock when they first arrived in Miami. Many of them spoke at least some English, had shopped and vacationed in the United States, and had attended American universities. In the process they had acquired a taste for the consumer culture and the products of the American market. The enclave institutions of Little Havana served to blunt the culture shock even more. So unlike many immigrants to the United States, the first waves of Cuban exiles were in an excellent position to begin the acculturation process.

The initial stage in that process, of course, was the individual decision to remain permanently in the United States. Those first immigrants in the early 1960s firmly believed that their sojourn in the United States would be a temporary one, that once again American troops would intervene in Cuban politics to restore the elite to power and expel Fidel Castro and the rebels. But as time passed two things happened. First, the Cuban exiles slowly came to realize that Castro was well entrenched and that the United States, deeply absorbed in the Vietnam War, was not about to undertake a military assault on the Castro regime. Castro was likely to be in power for a long time. Second, life in the United States, economically at least, was infinitely superior to what was going on in Cuba. As the Cuban economy slowly declined in the 1960s and 1970s and then imploded in the 1980s and early 1990s, Cuban Americans realized that to go back to Cuba, even if Castro was gone, would mean a tremendous economic sacrifice. A few were willing to make that sacrifice, but for the vast majority home was going to be on the north side of the Florida Straits. More so than other Hispanic immigrants, the Cubans were anxious to apply for citizenship in their new homeland.

Although the enclave institutions helped the immigrants preserve elements of the Old World culture, Little Havana was hardly immune from external cultural intrusions. Cuban-American children attended public schools and inevitably mixed with Mexican, Haitian, Puerto Rican, African-American, and Anglo-American children. Even though many of the schools were bilingual and worked hard at preserving the Spanish language, the children learned English. Like most second-generation immigrants in the United States, Cuban-American children preferred English over Spanish. By the early 1990s, although Spanish was the primary language language of more than 90 percent of Cuban-American homes, English was the preferred language of more than 65 percent of Cuban Americans born in the United States. Among the third-generation Cuban Americans, who are children or teenagers, English is their only language. By the 1980s Little Havana was also home to movie theaters showing English-language films, radio stations broadcasting American music, and fast-food places like McDonald's, Burger King, Jack-in-the-Box, and Wendy's. In fact, a new syncretic language, nicknamed "Spanglish," appeared in Miami as the immigrants mixed thousands of English words and phrases into Spanish grammatical structures.[18]

As the Cuban-American economy matured in the United States, the occupational diversity of the community became more complex. By 1990 the number of Cuban-owned businesses in Dade County was approaching 30,000, and social commentators continued to praise the entrepreneurial instincts of the Cuban American community. But businessmen nevertheless constituted only a small segment of the Cuban-American work force. There were more than 350,000 other Cuban workers in Dade County, and they were employed as laborers, craftsmen, and service workers. Between 1966 and 1980 the percentage of Cuban workers employed as unskilled laborers dropped from 32 percent to only 16 percent, while the percentage employed as skilled workers increased from 17 percent to 37 percent. The numbers of technical, managerial, and professional workers jumped from just under 13 percent to nearly 18 percent. Those trends continued into the 1990s, and those Cuban workers also became much more likely to join a labor union—something Cubans had been loathe to do ever since the nineteenth century. The Amalgamated Clothing Workers Union and the Textile Workers were especially successful at recruiting Cuban workers, as have many of the construction trades. A leading force behind the movement has been the Labor Council for Latin American Advancement of Dade County.[19]

Occupational diversity and growing labor union membership has introduced a new level of political awareness and political division in the Cuban-American community. Traditionally, Cuban workers saw their security in terms of ethnic solidarity; they felt they had more in common with a Cuban-American businessman than with another non-Cuban worker. As time passed, however, many Cuban-American workers began to acquire a blue-collar perspective. Economic solidarity became less ethnic in scope and more class-oriented. Cuban-American workers also became more likely to vote Democratic, even though the traditional leaders of the Cuban-American community were Republicans. Domestic, bread-and-butter issues moved to the forefront of their concerns, and foreign-policy issues gradually became less compelling.

By the 1980s the residential concentration that had characterized the Cuban-American community began to change. In places like Los Angeles and Chicago, where the critical mass of immigrants did not exist to sustain an enclave life, the residential dispersion had been almost immediate. It occurred more slowly in the Union City–West New York area, although by the 1970s many Cuban families were relocating to more distant suburbs where they mixed with a more diversely American population. More and more Cuban Americans were scattering out from Little Havana to other areas of Dade County, and in the suburbs they were less likely to be residentially concentrated than they had been before. From that residential dispersal came more and more social relationships with non-Cubans.

The ultimate form of assimilation, of course, is intermarriage. The results of being a white, English-speaking, upwardly mobile ethnic group are obvious. As time passed the frequency of personal social relationships with non-Cubans steadily increased, even in Miami and New Jersey. By the 1980s more and more Cubans were joining non-Cuban organizations whose primary focuses were economic, political, and religious. From those memberships and social relationships, as well as friendships and acquaintances at work and school, came marriage partners. Cubans are far more likely than Mexican Americans or Puerto Rican Americans to marry non-Cubans. By the 1980s more than half of American-born Cubans were marrying non-Cubans. That was most likely to occur in areas outside of New Jersey and Florida, primarily because in Little Havana and Little Havana North most social relationships were with other Cuban Americans. So although the ethnic fabric of the Cuban-American community is still intact, the forces of assimilation are doing to them what they have done to most other immigrant groups in United States—incorporating them into the larger society. This is not to say, of course, that Little Havana is about to disappear. As long as there continues to be a flow of new Cuban immigrants into Miami, there will be a distinctly visible Cuban-American community. Still, for every new immigrant coming into the city there is a second- or third-generation Cuban American marrying and disappearing into the larger society.[20]

From Exiles to Ethnics

Although the forces of assimilation have been working to absorb Cuban Americans into the larger American community, they are proceeding very slowly and gradually. The Cuban-American identity is still intact, highly visible, and politically active. The cold war continued to survive in South Florida. In fact, by the early 1990s the only place on earth where the cold war against communism continued unabated was in the homes of Cuban Americans in Miami, Tampa, West Miami, Hialeah, West New York, and Union City. The symbolic politics of anticommunism and ethnicity were as healthy as ever. During the 1960s and early 1970s, political activism in South Florida was oriented toward the overthrow of Fidel Castro, the planting of democracy in Cuba, and the return of the exiles to the island. U.S. foreign policy toward Cuba during those years reinforced that emphasis on foreign politics in the Cuban-American community. The cultural currency of the Cuban community in South Florida was the exile experience, a hatred for Fidel Castro, and intense opposition to communism anywhere in the world.

That political climate continued to exist in the 1980s and 1990s. In 1982, for example, the Miami City Commission sponsored a nonbinding, straw vote referendum over whether city funds should be used for any multinational or cultural conference where representatives from Communist countries would participate. Commissioner Joe Carollo sponsored the measure when a controversy had erupted over whether delegations from Eastern European countries should be allowed to participate in a city-sponsored conventon of international travel agents. The referendum passed, and another controversy erupted in 1983 when the city helped sponsor the Miss Universe Pageant and allowed Communist-bloc contestants to participate. Critics charged city officials with disobeying the spirit of the referendum. In 1982 and 1983 the Miami City Commission passed 28 resolutions dealing with foreign policy. In 1984 Hialeah severed its sister-city relationship with Managua, Nicaragua, and West Miami ended its sister-city relationship with León, Nicaragua, after the Sandanistas came to power there. Dade County's representatives in the Florida state legislature regularly sponsored anti-Castro and anti-Communist measures. One commentator observed that "Miami is likely the only city in the United States where anti-Communism is a municipal issue."[1]

At the national level, the political clout of Cuban Americans with the Florida congressional delegation, and South Florida's significance to Republican presidential politics, allowed Cuban Americans to influence national policy. The decisions of the Reagan and Bush administrations to sponsor Radio Martí and TV Martí, to appoint Armando Valladares, a former Cuban political prisoner, to represent the United States at the United Nations Conference on Human Rights, and to continue the economic embargo on Cuba, and the decision by the INS to accept Cuban immigrants from "third countries" all reflected the substance of Cuban-American political power.

In 1990, just a few months after his release from a quarter-century of imprisonment in South Africa, Nelson Mandela made a triumphant tour of the United States, pleading for the support of the black African majorities struggling for liberation in his homeland. He was received as a hero in the black communities of the United States and was widely respected by most Americans, black or white. Miami, Florida, was one of his stops, and the people of Dade County—Hispanic, African-American, Anglo-American, and Jewish-American—welcomed him with open arms, scheduling speeches and fancy luncheons where he could talk about freedom. To the approximately 1,100,000 Cuban Americans, "freedom" was a powerful word, symbolizing all the reasons they had left Cuba, all the reasons they had come to the United States, and all the reasons they wanted to see communism destroyed on the island. Nelson Mandela was the country's latest icon of civil rights and social equality. It seemed the perfect opportunity to bring the diverse ethnic communities of Miami—Anglo, Jew, Puerto Rican, Haitian, African, and Cuban—together in a great celebration of the universal human struggle for freedom.

But the party did not last in Miami. In response to a journalist's question about Fidel Castro, Mandela praised the Cuban leader for the consistent support he had given to the black people of South Africa. A dumbfounded silence settled over the room. When he would not back away from that support in face of outraged protests from Cuban-American leaders, Nelson Mandela practically became a persona non grata in Miami, at least in Little Havana. Protest demonstrations took place against him. Cuban Americans took their politics seriously, and they had long memories. For most of them, Fidel Castro was the embodiment of evil, a symbol of oppression, not freedom, and they could not abide anyone praising him, even Nelson Mandela. The African-American community in Miami was outraged at the anti-Mandela protests that immediately emerged from Cuban Americans. It was bad enough, they firmly believed, that Cuban Americans had a stranglehold on the Miami economy and regularly discriminated against African Americans, but to protest against an international symbol of black pride and human freedom was unthinkable. Miami was riddled with demonstrations and counter-demonstrations, both groups becoming angrier and angrier with each other, all in the name of human freedom.

Cuban Americans were still fighting the same battles in 1990. Groups like the Cuban American National Foundation worked for the overthrow of Fidel Castro, while the Cuban American Political Action Committee has poured money into the coffers of Republican and Democratic politicians, demanding in return only the continuation of the cold war against Cuba. Radio Martí and Television Martí were still broadcasting anti-Castro and pro-American messages over Cuban airwaves. Jorge Mas Canosa, the Cuban-American millionaire who arrived in the United States in 1960 and fought at the Bay of Pigs invasion in 1961, served as chairman of the powerful Cuban American National Foundation and refused to deny rumors that he was contemplating a run for the presidency of Cuba once Fidel Castro's regime had fallen. José Rodríguez, another tough anti-Castro Cuban American, repeatedly led flotillas of American-based yachts and motorboats in expeditions to the edge of Cuban territorial waters to protest the Castro regime.

By 1992 militant Cuban-American leaders were hoping that the end of the Castro regime would come naturally, not requiring any real external military initiatives. During the late 1980s, as the economy of the Soviet Union declined so dramatically, Mikhail Gorbachev began making cuts in the country's annual subsidy payments to Cuba. The Soviet Union simply could not afford to send billions each year only to watch it disappear into a Cuban economy that was at least as weak its own. Castro openly denounced the compromises Gorbachev was making with private enterprise inside the Soviet Union. In August 1991, when Communist hardliners attempted their coup d'état and imprisoned Gorbachev, Fidel Castro openly praised their actions, condemning Gorbachev as a traitor to world socialism and calling on the new Soviet leaders to redouble their efforts to restore Marxism-Leninism to its ideological pedestal.

But the coup failed in just a few days. Boris Yeltsin, president of the Russian Republic, refused to yield to the conspirators, and millions of Moscow residents and soldiers in the Soviet Army supported him. In supporting the misguided and poorly planned coup so impetuously, Fidel Castro had made a monumental political miscalculation. Within a matter of weeks the Soviet Union outlawed the Communist party and began its own dissolution. Gorbachev's political star was setting, and Boris Yeltsin's was rising. The centrifugal forces of ethnic nationalism broke the Soviet Union apart during the fall of 1991, and at the end of the year the country ceased to exist. As head of the Russian Republic, Boris Yeltsin became a world leader, and he despised Fidel Castro, ending whatever economic benefits Cuba was still enjoying from its relationship with Russia.

The Cuban economy went into a tailspin. Consumer goods, which had always been in short supply, completely disappeared from the shelves of state stores, and it became impossible to get gasoline of any kind. People walked or took bicycles to work and school, and mules and oxen replaced tractors on state farms. Castro's foreign-policy adventures in Africa, Central America, and South America came to a stop; he simply could not afford to maintain troops abroad. To earn some hard currency, the Castro regime tried to boost the island's tourist industry, but at the same time the Bush administration made the travel of Americans to the island even more restrictive. Not in the entire history of the revolution had economic times been more difficult in Cuba. And while the dictator continued to preach the virtues of socialism, to hold the line, Cuban suffering increased. Desperate people tried to cross the Straits of Florida in small boats and inner tubes, fleeing an economy that was in a state of absolute collapse. Castro's own daughter illustrates the state of affairs on the island. Alina Fernandez Revuelta, a longtime critic of her father's regime, defected to the United States in December 1993. On 20 December she disguised herself as a Spanish tourist, purchased a fake Spanish passport, and fled to Madrid. The U.S. embassy there granted her asylum, and she arrived in New York the next day.

Although the foreign-policy issue will continue to play a very prominent role in Cuban-American ethnicity, it is only a matter of time before the Castro regime collapses because of its own internal problems or with the death of Fidel Castro. In either case, communism is probably doomed in Cuba, and anticommunism cannot indefinitely continue to be the issue that binds the Cuban-American community together. The exile politics of the previous 30 years, which emphasized foreign-policy issues, are going to be transformed into ethnic group politics emphasizing a more diverse series of issues. The Cuban identity has already given way to a Cuban-American identity among the vast majority of people of Cuban descent living in the United States. They have no intention of returning to the island once communism is destroyed there. The United States is their home, not Cuba, and that tendency will only become more pronounced the longer Castro remains in power. At the turn of the century, most of the first-wave Cuban immigrants will be elderly people, and by 2010 most of them will be dead. Unless there is a massive new influx of Cuban immigrants into South Florida who bring anti-Communist feeings with them, the politics of South Florida are certain to change.

Some of those issues will continue to revolve around ethnic symbolism, but they will not have the same foreign-policy focus. Domestic questions will come to the forefront. The question of bilingualism is certain to be long-term. Groups like the Cuban American National Foundation and the Spanish American League against Discrimination will continue to demand repeal of the 1980 antibilingual ordinance in Dade County. The Cuban American National Foundation unsuccessfully tried to push a bill through the state legislature establishing a Cuban Studies Institute at Florida International University. The foundation also launched a boycott of the *Miami Herald*, which they considered pro-Anglo and anti-Cuban in its editorial policies.

But even these symbolic ethnic issues will become sources of political conflict in the Cuban-American community. The community has a number of internal divisions that exile politics traditionally were able to obscure. The interests of a first-generation exile are different from those of a third-generation Cuban American. Afro-Cubans and Marielitos perceived themselves as being distinct from the larger community. An upper-class Cuban-American businessman has economic interests that are quite different from a Cuban-American construction worker. A 20-year-old Cuban-American college student who does not speak Spanish is different from his or her grandparent who arrived in Miami 35 years ago with the first-wave exiles.

Those divisions find political expression in a variety of ways that illustrate increasing Cuban-American diversity. In 1987, for example, the interest group Unidos, composed of Cuban-American business and civil leaders, actually opposed a new attempt to repeal the 1980 antibilingual referendum ordinance. Although most of them actually favored repeal, they felt the political campaign would, in the long run, be too damaging to Cuban Americans because of the hostility it would generate among Anglos and African Americans in Dade County. Late in the 1980s the Cuban American National Foundation and the Latin Builders Association worked to remove Miami city commissioner Joe Carolla because they felt his anti-Communist rhetoric and zealotry were too extreme. A number of Cuban-American scholars at Florida International University actually opposed the attempt to establish a state-funded Cuban Studies Institute on the campus.

Economic issues will also help to restructure Cuban-American politics. Although the Cuban-American community is still overwhelmingly Republican, the number of Cuban-American Democrats is on the rise, and that increase will

In December 1988 Fidel Castro visited Tuxpan, the Mexican town from which he had set sail to launch the Cuban revolution 32 years earlier. *Courtesy Reuters/Bettmann*

continue. Blue-collar Cuban Americans will increasingly see their own economic well-being in terms of a working-class mentality instead of ethnic solidarity. The transition from ethnic to economic issues will be slow and tortuous, but it will certainly occur over the next 20 years, and in the process the two-party system will take root in the Cuban-American community.

Cuban-American ethnicity will also continue to revolve around relations with neighboring ethnic communities. The growing power of Cuban Americans in South Florida has created resentments among Anglos and African Americans. The congressional election of 1988 demonstrated just how well-defined those ethnic lines had been drawn. The Democrats ran Gerald Richman against Republican Ileana Ros-Lehtinen, a Cuban American, to fill the seat vacated by Claude Pepper. Richman had a simple strategy—to stir up Anglo and African-American fears of the "Cuban takeover of Florida" and secure enough non-Hispanic votes to win. In its ethnic composition, the district was 38 percent Cuban, 20 percent Jewish, 19 percent African American, 16 percent Anglo, and 7 percent non-Cuban Hispanic. Ros-Lehtinen focused on bread-and-butter domestic issues and voter turnout, emphasizing the importance of Hispanics voting. Richman managed to secure 88 percent of the Anglo and Jewish vote and 96 percent of the African-American vote. Ros-Lehtinen got 94 percent of the Hispanic vote. Because Hispanics were far more likely to vote than either Anglos or African Americans, Ros-Lehtinen won the election with 53 percent of the vote. Similar ethnic struggles for power in South Florida are guaranteed in the 1990s.

In August 1994 Cuban-American relations were again strained and a major political controversy erupted. Economic conditions had become so dismal in

Cuba that hundreds of thousands of people wanted to leave the island. During the summer several ferries operating out of Havana were highjacked, and by early August thousands of Cubans gathered each morning near the ferries at the Malacon seafront in Havana, hoping to hitch a ride if another highjacking occurred. When police tried to disperse the crowd on 5 August an anti-Castro riot developed, with hundreds of young Cubans attacking the police, shouting anti-Fidel epithets, and praising America. The riot astonished longtime residents of Havana, who had never seen such visceral resentment of the Castro regime.

The riot caught Castro off-guard. Still a true believer in Marxism, Castro was convinced that the 34-year-old American embargo on the island, not the inherent contradictions of communism, had ruined the Cuban economy. Castro wanted to force the United States to lift the embargo. He also wanted to defuse some of the internal political hostility to the regime. The administration of President Bill Clinton was already dealing with a difficult situation in Haiti, forcibly capturing Haitian refugees on the high seas and returning them to Port-au-Prince. Many black leaders in the United States protested the policy as racist, since Cuban refugees still enjoyed ready access to permanent residency and citizenship. Castro saw a political opportunity in Clinton's political difficulties.

Hoping to force Clinton into lifting the embargo, Castro let it be known that he would not oppose the emigration of any Cuban wanting to leave for America. The announcement of 8 August 1994 opened the floodgates. By the tens of thousands, Cubans headed for the island's north-shore beaches, assembled makeshift boats and rafts, and started across the Florida Straits. The exodus had the potential of becoming another Mariel, when 125,000 Cubans arrived in the United States in 1980. Florida's governor, Lawton Chiles, demanded that the federal government deal with the situation by either stopping the exodus or providing the funds to feed, house, and educate the Cubans. Clinton faced a dilemma. He could not let the Cubans enter unopposed while still keeping the Haitians out. At the same, he could not let both groups enter the United States without incurring the wrath of millions of Americans who were concerned about the costs of caring for the new immigrants.

To buy some political time, the Clinton administration built a huge refugee camp at the U.S. naval base at Guantanamo Bay and resettled Cuban and Haitian refugees there. The State Department also negotiated with several Caribbean and Central American governments to take some of the Cubans. Clinton suspended the easy access all Cuban refugees had enjoyed under the Cuban Adjustment Act of 1966, when the very act of reaching American soil guaranteed permanent residency and citizenship. Attorney General Janet Reno solemnly declared early in September that the new wave of Cuban refugees would not be admitted to the United States.

But they kept coming. By mid-September more than 35,000 Cuban refugees, now known as *balseros* because of the homemade boats and rafts in which they floated, had been picked up in the Florida Straits and transferred to the holding centers. Untold thousands more had drowned at sea. The United States and Cuba opened negotiations to end the crisis. Castro demanded lifting of the embargo, but President Clinton flatly refused. The issue was non-negotiable. Most Cuban Americans backed the president in his decisions to maintain the embargo and to suspend the Cuban Adjustment Act. They did not want Fidel Castro dictating policy to the United States. For more than three decades Castro had solved his political problems by letting disaffected Cubans emigrate. When Castro realized that Clinton was not facing the political wrath of the Cuban-American community, he backed away from his demands for an end to the embargo. The United States agreed late in September 1994 to allow up to 20,000 Cubans to enter the United States annually. Castro agreed to put a stop to the exodus. He no doubt intended to see that the most dissident Cubans would be in that group. The crisis then ceased.

In the meantime, however, Fidel Castro still wears the khaki-green and delivers his four- and five-hour tirades against "Yanquí imperialism" and the virtues of socialism. Political prisoners still languish in Cuban jails and hundreds of thousands of Cuban Americans worry about fathers and mothers, brothers and sisters, and aunts, uncles, and cousins on the island. Right now, somewhere on the north shore of the island, a desperate Cuban has a couple of inner tubes and rope hidden in the brush. Early in the morning he is going to lash the tubes together and launch himself out into the Straits of Florida, hoping to float his way to America. As long as there are Cubans like him risking their lives for the chance of freedom in the United States, identity in the Cuban-American community will continue to revolve around foreign policy as well as domestic ethnic issues.

Notes and References

one

1. James S. Olson, *Catholic Immigrants in America* (Chicago: Nelson Hall, 1987), 148.

2. Quoted in Jaime Suchlicki, *Cuba: From Columbus to Castro* (New York: Charles Scribner's Sons, 1986), 5.

3. Quoted in Samuel Eliot Morison, *Admiral of the Ocean Sea: The Life of Christopher Columbus* (Boston: Houghton Mifflin, 1942), 253.

4. Morison, *Admiral of the Ocean Sea*, 251.

5. Quoted in Morison, *Admiral of the Ocean Sea*, 259–60.

6. Irene A. Plunket, *Isabel of Castile* (New York: Alfred A. Knopf, 1973).

7. For a survey history and anthropological analysis of the Arawakan people, see Fred Olsen, *On the Trail of the Arawaks* (Norman: University of Oklahoma Press, 1971).

8. Jesse Walter Fewkes, *The Aborigines of Porto Rico and Neighboring Islands* (New York: Johnson Reprint Co., 1907), and Cornelius Osgood, *The Ciboney Culture of Ceyo Redondo, Cuba* (New Haven, Conn.: Yale University Press, 1942).

9. For an excellent analysis of the political power wielded by the Columbus family in Hispaniola, see Troy S. Floyd, *The Colombus Dynasty in the Caribbean, 1492–1526* (Albuquerque: University of New Mexico Press, 1973).

10. Two excellent accounts of the early explorations of Cuba in particular and the Caribbean in general are Carl Ortwin Sauer, *The Early Spanish Main* (Berkeley: University of California Press, 1966), and Timothy Severin, *The Golden Antilles* (New York: Alfred A. Knopf, 1970).

11. The best English-language description of the conquest of Cuba is Irene A. Wright's *The Early History of Cuba, 1492–1586* (New York: Macmillan, 1916).

12. Henry Raup Wagner and Helen Rand Parish, *The Life and Writings of Bartolomé de las Casas* (Albuquerque: University of New Mexico Press, 1967); Francisco Morales Padrón, "Las Leyes nuevas de 1542–1543: Ordenanzas para la gobernación de las Indias y buen tratamiento y conservación de los indios," *Anuario de Estudios Americanos* 16 (1959): 561–619.

13. Although most scholars have concluded that the Indians of Cuba were completely extinct by the end of the sixteenth century, there are some surviving Cubans living in the southwestern tip of the island who, although thoroughly

detribalized, still view themselves as an indigenous people. See José Barreiro, "Indians in Cuba," *Cultural Survival Quarterly* 13 (1989): 56–60.

14. Henry R. Wagner, *The Discovery of Yucatán by Francisco Hernández de Córdoba* (Berkeley: Cortez Society, 1942).

15. Saturnino Ullivarri, *Piratas y corsarios en Cuba* (Havana, 1931); Irene A. Wright, "'Rescates': With Special Reference to Cuba, 1599–1610," *Hispanic American Historical Review* 3 (August 1920): 333–61.

16. See the early chapters of Leland Jenks, *Our Cuban Colony: A Study of Sugar* (New York: Macmillan, 1928).

17. Charles Gibson, *Spain in America* (New York: Vanguard Press, 1966), 80. See also W. E. Shiels, *The Rise and Fall of the Patronato Real* (New York, 1961).

18. Margaret E. Crahan, "Catholicism in Cuba," *Cuban Studies* 19 (1989): 3–4.

19. Marianne Masferrer and Carmelo Mesa Lago, "The Gradual Integration of the Black in Cuba: Under the Colony, the Republic, and the Revolution," in Robert Brent Toplin, ed., *Slavery and Race in Latin America* (Westport, Conn.: Greenwood Press, 1974), 348–60.

20. Isabel Macías Domínguez, *Cuba en la primer mitad del siglo XVII* (Seville: Beltiere, 1978).

21. Louis A. Pérez, Jr., *Cuba: Between Reform and Revolution* (New York: Oxford University Press, 1988), 63. For an early history of slaves and free blacks in colonial Cuba, see Fernando Ortiz Fernández, *Los Esclavos negros* (Havana: Editorial de Ciencias Sociale, 1975). See also H. H. S. Aimes, "Coartación: A Spanish Institution for the Advancement of Slaves into Freedmen," *Yale Review* 17 (1909): 412–31.

22. For an outstanding description of how Spanish policies served to raise the *criollo* consciousness, see Allan J. Keuthe, *Cuba, 1753–1815: Crown, Military, and Society* (Knoxville: University of Tennessee Press, 1986). See also Francis Russell Hart, *The Siege of Havana* (Boston: Houghton Mifflin, 1931).

23. For an outstanding biography of Charles III, see Anthony H. Hull, *Charles III and the Revival of Spain* (Washington, D.C.: University Press of America, 1981).

24. See John Fisher, *Commercial Relations between Spain and Spanish America in the Era of Free Trade, 1778–1796* (Liverpool, England: Centre for Latin-American Studies, 1985).

25. Pérez, *Cuba*, 62–63.

26. For a description of the slave uprising in St. Domingue in the 1790s, see Stephen Alexis, *Black Liberator: The Life of Toussaint Louverture* (London: E. Benn, 1949).

27. Pérez, *Cuba*, 73, 77; Manuel Moreno Fraginals, *El ingenio: complejo económico social cubano del azúcar (*Havana: Editorial de Ciencias Sociale, 1978*), 3: 43–45.

28. Suchlicki, *Cuba*, 45–49. See also Edward Boorstein, *The Economic Transformation of Cuba* (New York: 1968).

29. The best work on the demographics of slavery and the slave trade in Cuba is Kenneth F. Kiple, *Blacks in Colonial Cuba, 1774–1899* (Gainesville: University Presses of Florida, 1976).

30. Robert L. Paquette, *Sugar Is Made with Blood: The Conspiracy of La Escalera and the Conflict between Empires over Slavery in Cuba* (Middletown, Conn.: Wesleyan University Press, 1988), 35–41; Verena Martínez-Alier, *Marriage, Class, and Colour in Nineteenth-Century Cuba: A Study of Racial Attitudes and Sexual Values in a Slave Society* (London: Cambridge University Press, 1974), 1–99.

31. Kiple, *Blacks in Colonial Cuba*, 84–91.

32. Paquette, *Sugar Is Made with Blood*, 40–45.

33. Franklin W. Knight, "Slavery, Race, and Social Structure in Cuba During the Nineteenth Century," in Toplin, ed., *Slavery and Race in Latin America*, 204–27.

two

1. Eugene Lyon, *The Enterprise of Florida: Pedro Menéndez Avilés and the Spanish Conquest of 1565–1568* (Gainesville: University Presses of Florida, 1976).

2. For the early history of Florida, see Michael J. Curley, *Church and State in the Spanish Floridas (1783–1822)* (Washington, D.C.: Catholic University of America Press, 1940), and the first two chapters of Gloria Jahoda, *Florida: A History* (Gainesville: University Presses of Florida, 1984).

3. Charlton W. Tebeau, *A History of Florida* (Coral Cables, Fla.: University of Miami Press, 1971), 133–35.

4. P. Justo Zaragoza, *Las Insurrecciones en Cuba* (Madrid: Simón, 1872).

5. For the life of Felix Varela, see J. I. Rodríguez, *Vida del presbitero don Felix Varela* (Havana: Editorial de Ciencias Sociales, 1944).

6. Herminio Portell Vilá, *Narciso López y su época*, 3 vols. (Havana: Cultural, 1930–58); Gerald E. Poyo, *"With All, and for the Good of All": The Emergence of Popular Natonalism in the Cuban Communities of the United States, 1848–1898* (Gainesville: University Presses of Florida, 1990), 3–7.

7. Amos A. Ettinger, *The Mission to Spain of Pierre Soulé, 1853–1855* (New Haven, Conn.: Yale University Press, 1932), 391–93; C. Stanley Urban, "The Africanization of Cuba Scare, 1853–1855," *Hispanic American Historical Review* 37 (1957): 27–45.

8. Pérez, *Cuba*, 112.

9. Mary Turner, "Chinese Contract Labour in Cuba, 1847–1874," *Caribbean Studies* 14 (1974): 66–81; Mats Lundahl, "A Note on Haitian Migration to Cuba, 1890–1934," *Cuban Studies* 12 (1982): 21–36; Franklin W. Knight, "Jamaican Migrants and the Cuban Sugar Industry, 1900–1934," in *Between Slavery and Free Labor: The Spanish-Speaking Caribbean in the Nineteenth Century*, ed. Manuel Moreno Fraginals, Frank Moya Pons, and Stanley L. Engerman (Baltimore: Johns Hopkins University Press, 1985), 84–114.

10. For a biography of Céspedes, see Herminio Portell Vila, *Céspedes, el Padre de la Patria Cubana* (Madrid: Espasa-Calpe, 1931); Poyo, *"With All, and for the Good of All,"* 20–34.

11. Philip Foner, *Antonio Maceo* (New York: Monthly Review Press, 1977); Grover Flint, *Marching with Gómez* (New York: Lawson, Wolff & Co., 1898).

12. Richard B. Gray, *José Martí, Cuban Patriot* (Gainesville: University Presses of Florida, 1962); John M. Kirk, *José Martí: Mentor of the Cuban Nation* (Tampa: University Presses of Florida, 1983).

13. Ramiro Guerra y Sánchez, *Guerra de los diez años, 1868–1878* (Havana: Cultural, 1972); Enrique Collazo, *Desde Yara hasta el Zanjón* (Havana: Instituto del Libro, 1967); Poyo, *"With All, and for the Good of All,"* 35–51.

14. A. J. Jaffe, Ruth M. Cullen, and Thomas D. Boswell, *The Changing Demography of Spanish Americans* (New York: Academic Press, 1980), 247; Gerald E. Poyo, "Key West and the Cuban Ten Years' War," *Florida Historical Quarterly* 57 (1979): 289–307; Louis A. Pérez, Jr., "Cubans in Tampa: From Exiles to Immigrants, 1892–1901," *Florida Historical Quarterly* 56 (1978): 129–40.

15. Luis Rodolfo Miranda, *Calixto García Iñiguez: Estratega* (Havana: Cultural, 1951).

16. Gerald E. Poyo, "Cuban Patriots in Key West, 1878–1996: Guardians at the Separatist Ideal," *Florida Historical Quarterly* 61 (1982): 20–36.

17. Gary R. Mormino and George E. Pozzetta, *The Immigrant World of Ybor City: Italians and Their Latin Neighbors in Tampa, 1885–1985* (Urbana: University of Illinois Press, 1987), 77–78.

18. Gerald E. Poyo, "The Impact of Cuban and Spanish Workers on Labor Organizing in Florida, 1870–1900," *Journal of American Ethnic History* 5 (1986): 46–63. See also Durward Long, "Labor Relations in the Tampa Cigar Industry, 1885–1911," *Labor History* 12 (1971): 551–59.

19. Rebecca J. Scott, "Class Relations in Sugar and Political Mobilization in Cuba, 1868–1899," *Cuban Studies/Estudios Cubanos* 15 (1985): 15–28.

20. Gerald E. Poyo, "The Anarchist Challenge to the Cuban Independence Movement, 1885–1890," *Cuban Studies/Estudios Cubanos* 15 (1985): 29–42.

21. Fernando Ortiz Fernández, "Martí y las razas de librería," *Cuadernos Americanos* 21 (1945): 79–101.

22. For a brilliant analysis of the history of Cuban-American social and political thought during the last half of the nineteenth century, see Gerald E. Poyo, "Evolution of Cuban Separatist Thought in the Emigré Communities of the United States, 1848–1895," *Hispanic American Historical Review* 66 (1986): 485–507. See also Juan J. E. Casasús, *La Emigración cubana y la independencia de la patria* (Havana: Instituto del Libro, 1953).

three

1. Jaffe, Cullen, and Boswell, *The Changing Demography of Spanish Americans*, 247.

2. The best study in English of the Cuban rebellion against Spanish imperialism is Louis A. Pérez, Jr., *Cuba between Empires, 1878–1902* (Pittsburgh: University of Pittsburgh Press, 1983).

3. Earl R. Beck, "The Martínez Campos Government of 1879: Spain's Last Chance in Cuba," *Hispanic American Historical Review* 56 (1976): 268–89.

4. José Ibáñez Marín and Marqués de Cabriñana, *El General Martínez Campos y su monumento* (Madrid: Espana-Calpe, 1905).

5. Patricia Weiss Fagen, "Antonio Maceo: Heroes, History, and Historiography," *Latin American Research Review* 11 (1976): 69–94.

6. Rebecca J. Scott, "Class Relations in Sugar and Political Mobilization in Cuba, 1868–1899," *Cuban Studies/Estudios Cubanos* 15 (1985): 15–28. For the argument that American intervention was more directed at preventing Cuban independence than ending Spanish imperialism, see Ramón de Armas, *La Revolución pospuesta* (Havana: Editorial de Ciencias Sociales, 1975).

7. For the role of the American press in the Cuban conflict, see Joseph E. Wisan, *The Cuban Crisis as Reflected in the New York Press, 1895–1898* (New York, 1934).

8. On the events leading up to the American intervention in Cuba, see Walter Millis, *The Martial Spirit* (New York: Literary Guild of America, 1931), and the first volume of Philip S. Foner's *The Spanish-Cuban-American War and the Birth of American Imperialism* (New York: Monthly Review Press, 1972). See also H. G. Rickover, *How the Battleship Maine Was Destroyed* (Annapolis: Naval Institute Press, 1976).

9. David F. Trask, *The War with Spain in 1898* (New York: Macmillan, 1981).

10. Pérez, *Between Reform and Revolution*, 182.

11. All quoted in Pérez, *Between Reform and Revolution*, 180–84.

12. For the history of the American military occupation of Cuba, see David

F. Healy, *The United States in Cuba, 1898–1902* (Madison: University of Wisconsin Press, 1963).

13. *New York Times*, 19 December 1898.

14. Quoted in Jaime Suchlicki, *Cuba: From Columbus to Castro* (New York: Charles Scribner's Sons, 1986), 83.

15. Louis A. Pérez, Jr., "The Pursuit of Pacification: Banditry and the United States' Occupation of Cuba, 1889–1902," *Journal of Latin American Studies* 18 (1987): 313–32.

16. Erwin H. Epstein, "Social Structure, Race Relations, and Political Stability under U.S. Administration," *Revista/Review Interamericana* 8 (Summer 1978): 192–208.

17. Louis A. Pérez, Jr., "Insurrection, Intervention, and the Transformation of Land Tenure Systems in Cuba, 1895–1902," *Hispanic American Historical Review* 65 (1985): 229–54.

18. For a description of the American economic colonization of Cuba, see Jules R. Benjamin, *The United States and Cuba: Hegemony and Dependent Development, 1880–1934* (Pittsburgh: University of Pittsburgh Press, 1974), and Leland H. Jencks, *Our Cuban Colony* (New York: Macmillan, 1928).

19. Louis A. Pérez, Jr., *Cuba and the United States: Ties of Singular Intimacy* (Athens: University of Georgia Press, 1991), 136–43.

20. Louis A. Pérez, Jr., "Politics, Peasants, and People of Color: The 1912 'Race War' in Cuba Reconsidered," *Hispanic American Historical Review* 66 (1986): 509–39.

21. Jules R. Benjamin, "The Machadato and Cuban Nationalism, 1928–1932," *Hispanic American Historical Review* 55 (1975): 66–91.

22. For an account of the rise to power of Fulgencio Batista, see José A. Tabares del Real, *La Revolución del 30: sus dos ultimos años* (Havana: Editorial de Ciencias Sociales, 1975).

23. Pérez, *Cuba and the United States*, 219–23.

24. Charles Page, "The Development of Organized Labor in Cuba," Ph.D. diss., University of California, Berkeley, 1952, 13–23.

25. Charles D. Ameringer, "The Auténtico Party and the Political Opposition in Cuba, 1952–1957," *Hispanic American Historical Review* 65 (1985): 327–51.

26. See Mario Llerena, *The Unsuspected Revolution: The Birth and Rise of Castroism* (Ithaca, N.Y.: Cornell University Press, 1978), and Alfred L. Padula, Jr., "Financing Castro's Revolution, 1956–1958," *Revista/Review Interamericana* 8 (1978): 234–46.

four

1. Lisandro Pérez, "Cubans in the United States," *Annals of the American Academy of Political and Social Science* 487 (1986): 128, 131; James S. Olson, *The Ethnic Dimension in American History* (New York: St. Martin's Press, 1979), 206.

2. Gerald E. Poyo, "The Cuban Experience in the United States, 1865–1940: Migration, Community, and Identity," *Cuban Studies* 21 (1991): 27.

3. Poyo, "The Cuban Experience," 30–32.

4. Raymond Mohl, "Cubans in Miami: A Preliminary Bibliography," *Immigration History Newsletter* 16 (1984): 1–4.

5. Elmore J. Seraile, "Persons of Spanish Origin in the United States: March 1972 and 1971: Population Characteristics," *Current Population Reports* (Washington, D.C.: U.S. Government Printing Office, 1973).

6. Olson, *Ethnic Dimension in American History*, 221.

7. Desi Arnaz, Jr., *A Book* (New York: Morrow, 1976).

8. John S. Roberts, *The Latin Tinge: The Impact of Latin American Music on the United States* (New York: Oxford University Press, 1978); James R. Curtis and Richard F. Rose, "'The Miami Sound': A Contemporary Latin Form of Place-Specific Music," *Journal of Cultural Geography* 4 (1983): 110–18.

9. Eric A. Wagner, "Baseball in Cuba," *Journal of Popular Culture* 18 (1984): 113–20.

10. Randy Roberts and James S. Olson, *Winning Is the Only Thing: Sports in America since 1945* (Baltimore: Johns Hopkins University Press, 1990), 25–46.

11. Angel Torres, *La Historia del béisbol cubano, 1878–1976* (Los Angeles: Murray, 1976), 143.

12. José Yglesias, "The Radical Latino Island in the Deep South," *Nuestro* 1 (1977): 1–10.

13. Robert Ingalls, *Urban Vigilantes in the New South: Tampa, 1882–1936* (Knoxville: University of Tennessee Press, 1988); Gene Burnett, "Death and Terror Scar Tampa's Past," *Florida Trend* 18 (1975): 76–80.

14. Margaret E. Crahan, "Catholicism in Cuba," *Cuban Studies/Estudios Cubanos* 19 (1989): 3–4; John M. Kirk, "Toward an Understanding of the Church-State Rapprochement in Revolutionary Cuba," *Cuban Studies/Estudios Cubanos* 19 (1989): 25–26.

15. Eric Williams, *From Columbus to Castro: The History of the Caribbean, 1492–1969* (London: André Deutsch, 1970); Frank Knight, *Slave Society in Cuba during the Nineteenth Century* (Madison: University of Wisconsin Press, 1970), 106–12; Fred Ward, *Inside Cuba Today* (New York: Crown, 1978), 51–54.

16. Leslie Dewart, *Christianity and Revolution: The Lesson of Cuba* (New York: Herder & Herder, 1963), 95; Wyatt MacGaffey and Clifford R. Barnett, *Cuba: Its People, Its Society, Its Culture* (New Haven, Conn.: Yale University Press, 1962), 51–54.

17. Quoted in Michael J. McNally, *Catholicism in South Florida, 1868–1968* (Gainesville: University Presses of Florida, 1982), 33.

18. George Simpson Easton, *Religious Cults of the Caribbean* (San Juan, 1960), 11–111, 157–200; MacGaffey and Barnett, *Cuba*, 205–10.

19. Susan D. Greenbaum, "Afro-Cubans in Exile: Tampa, Florida, 1886–1984," *Cuban Studies/Estudios Cubanos* 15 (Winter 1985): 59–72; Fabio Grobart, "The Cuban Working Class Movement from 1925 to 1933," *Science and Society* 39 (Spring 1975): 73–102; Durward Long, "'La Resistencia': Tampa's Immigrant Labor Union," *Labor History* 6 (1965): 193–210.

20. Quoted in Pérez, *Cuba and the United States*, 217.

21. Eustasio Fernández and Hector Beltrán, *The Ybor City Story, 1885–1954* (Tampa: University Presses of Florida, 1976); Durward Long, "The Historical Beginnings of Ybor City and Modern Tampa," *Florida Historical Quarterly* 45 (1966): 31–44; James W. Covington, "Ybor City: A Cuban Enclave in Tampa," *Florida Anthropologist* 19 (1966): 85–90.

22. Louis A. Pérez, Jr., "The Imperial Design: Politics and Pedagogy in Occupied Cuba, 1899–1902," *Cuban Studies/Estudios Cubanos* 12 (Summer 1982): 1–19; Severin K. Turosienski, *Education in Cuba* (Washington, D.C.: U.S. Government Printing Office, 1943).

23. Margaret E. Crahan, "Religious Penetration and Nationalism in Cuba: U.S. Methodist Activities, 1898–1958," *Revista/Review Interamericana* 8 (Summer 1978): 204–24; Crahan, "Catholicism in Cuba," 3–5, 21.

five

1. Bert Useem, "Peasant Involvement in the Cuban Revolution," *Journal of Peasant Studies* 5 (1977): 99–111; Jaime Suchlicki, *University Students and Revolution in Cuba, 1920–1968* (Coral Gables, Fla.: University of Miami Press, 1969).

2. For biographies of Fidel Castro, see Peter G. Bourne, *Fidel: A Biography of Fidel Castro* (New York: Dodd Mead, 1986), and Tad Szulc, *Fidel: A Critical Portrait* (New York: Morrow, 1986).

3. Alfred Padula, "Financing Castro's Revolution, 1956–1958," *Revista/Review Interamericana* 8 (1978): 234–46.

4. Morris H. Morley, "The U.S. Imperial State in Cuba, 1952–1958: Policymaking and Capitalist Interests," *Journal of Latin American Studies* 14 (1982): 143–70.

5. Ameringer, "The Auténtico Party and the Political Opposition in Cuba," 327–51; Andrés Suárez, "The Cuban Revolution: The Road to Power," *Latin American Research Review* 7 (Autumn 1972): 5–29.

6. Leo Huberman and Paul M. Sweezy, *Cuba: Anatomy of a Revolution* (New York: Monthly Review Press, 1960), 3–96.

7. Edward González, "Castro's Revolution, Cuban Communist Appeals, and the Soviet Response," *World Politics* 21 (October 1968): 39–68; see also the early chapters of Andrés Suárez, *Cuba: Castroism and Communism, 1959–1966* (Cambridge, Mass.: MIT Press, 1967). See also Samuel Farber, "The Cuban Communists in the Early Stages of the Revolution: Revolutionaries or Reformists?" *Latin American Research Review* 18 (1983): 59–83.

8. Quoted in Margaret E. Crahan, "Catholicism in Cuba," *Cuban Studies/Estudios Cubanos* 19 (1989): 9.

9. Sergio Díaz Briquets and Lisandro Pérez, *Cuba: The Demography of Revolution* (Washington, D.C.: U.S. Government Printing Office, 1981), 26; Jules R. Benjamin, "Interpreting the U.S. Reaction to the Cuban Revolution, 1959–1960," *Cuban Studies/Estudios Cubanos* 19 (1989): 145–65.

10. Pérez, *Cuba and the United States*, 247.

11. J. P. Morray, *The Second Revolution in Cuba* (New York: Monthly Review Press, 1962); Arthur MacEwan, "Ideology, Socialist Development, and Power in Cuba," *Politics and Society* 5 (1975): 67–81.

12. John Prados, *Presidents' Secret Wars: CIA and Pentagon Covert Operations since World War II* (New York: Morrow, 1986), 171–81.

13. See Haynes P. Johnson, *The Bay of Pigs* (New York: Norton, 1964), and Peter Wyden, *Bay of Pigs: The Untold Story* (New York: Simon & Schuster, 1979).

14. Margaret E. Crahan, "Cuba: Religion and Revolutionary Institutionalization," *Journal of Latin American Studies* 17 (1985): 319–40.

15. Prados, *Presidents' Secret Wars*, 210–13. See also Bradley Earl Ayers, *The War That Never Was: An Insider's Account of CIA Covert Operations against Cuba* (Indianapolis: Bobbs-Merrill, 1976).

16. U.S. Department of State, *Department of State Bulletin*, 21 January 1963, 89.

17. Abram Chayes, *The Cuban Missile Crisis: International Crisis and the Role of Law* (New York: Oxford University Press, 1974); Graham Allison, *Essence of Decision: Explaining the Cuban Missile Crisis* (Boston: Little, Brown, 1971); and Herbert Dinnerstein, *The Making of a Missile Crisis* (New York: Alfred A. Knopf, 1976).

18. Quoted in Prados, *Presidents' Secret Wars*, 216.

19. Max Azicri, "The Politics of Exile: Trends and Dynamics of Political Change among Cuban-Americans," *Cuban Studies/Estudios Cubanos* 11 (July 1981): 55–74.

20. Barent Landstreet, "Cuba," in Aaron Lee Segal, ed., *Population Policies in the Caribbean* (Lexington, Mass.: Lexington Books, 1975), 140–41; Silvia Pedraza-Bailey, "Cuba's Exiles: Portrait of a Refugee Migration," *International Migration Review* 19 (1985): 16–17.

21. Jorge Duany, "Hispanics in the United States: Cultural Diversity and Identity," *Caribbean Studies* 22 (1989): 9.

22. Richard R. Fagen, Richard A. Brody, and Thomas J. O'Leary, *Cubans in Exile: Disaffection and the Revolution* (Stanford, Calif.: Stanford University Press, 1968).

23. Alejandro Portes, Juan M. Clark, and Robert L. Bach, "The New Wave: A Statistical Profile of Recent Cuban Exiles to the U.S.," *Cuban Studies* 7 (January 1977): 17.

24. Eleanor Meyer Rogg, *The Assimilation of Cuban Exiles: The Role of Community and Class* (New York: Aberdeen Press, 1974), 135–37.

25. Jaffe, Cullen, and Boswell, *The Changing Demography of Spanish Americans*, 248.

26. Silvia Pedraza-Bailey, "Cubans and Mexicans in the United States: The Functions of Political and Economic Migration," *Cuban Studies/Estudios Cubanos* 11 (July 1981): 87–89.

27. Tom Alexander, "Those Amazing Cubans," *Fortune*, October 1966, 144–49; "Cuba's New Refugees Get Jobs Fast," *Business Week*, 12 March 1966, 69; "Cuban Success Story in the United States," *U.S. News and World Report*, 20 March 1967, 104–106.

28. Alejandro Portes and Robert L. Bach, "Immigrant Earnings: Cuban and Mexican Immigrants in the United States," *International Migration Review* 14 (1980): 315–37; Lisandro Pérez, "Immigrant Economic Adjustment and Family Organization: The Cuban Success Story Reexamined," *International Migration Review* 20 (1986): 4–20; Jimmy M. Sanders and Victor Nee, "Limits of Ethnic Solidarity in the Enclave Economy," *American Sociological Review* 52 (December 1987): 745–73.

SIX

1. Pérez, *Cuba and the United States*, 250–52.

2. Juan M. Clark, "The Exodus from Revolutionary Cuba (1959–1974): A Sociological Analysis," Ph.D. diss., University of Florida, 1975, 85–98.

3. Barent Landstreet, "Cuba," in *Population Policies in the Caribbean*, ed. Segal, 141.

4. *Washington Post*, 1 September 1971.

5. Lynn Darrell, "U.S. Cuban Policy under the Nixon Administration: Subtle Modifications," *Revista/Review Intermaericana* 2 (1972): 330–41.

6. Lynn Darrell Bender, "The Cuban Exiles: An Analytical Sketch," *Journal of Latin American Studies* 5 (1973): 271–78.

7. Silvia Pedraza-Bailey, "Cuba's Exiles: Portrait of a Refugee Migration," *International Migration Review* 19 (1986): 4–34.

8. Barry R. Chiswick, "The Labor Market Status of Hispanic Men," *Journal of American Ethnic History* 7 (1987): 30–31.

9. Bengino Aguirre, "Differential Migration of Cuban Social Races," *Latin*

American Research Review 11 (1976): 103–24; James W. Covington, "Ybor City: A Cuban Enclave in Tampa," *Florida Anthropologist* 19 (1966): 85–90.

10. Prados, *Presidents' Secret Wars*, 216–17; Bender, "The Cuban Exiles," 276–77; Jeff Stein, "An Army in Exile," *New York*, 10 September 1979, 42–49.

11. Prados, *Presidents' Secret Wars*, 216–17.

12. Rogg, *The Assimilation of Cuban Exiles*, 93–95; Laureano F. Batista, "Political Sociology of the Cuban Exile, 1959–1986," M.A. thesis, University of Miami, 1969, 147; Eleanor Meyer Rogg, "Comment—Six Years Later: The Process of Incorporation of Cuban Exiles in the United States," *Cuban Studies/Estudios Cubanos* 11 (January 1982): 25–28.

13. Pérez, *Cuba and the United States*, 259–60.

14. Azicri, "The Politics of Exile," 55–74.

15. Yolanda Durán and Miriam Múñiz Varela, "Brigada Antonio Maceo II, Contigente Carlos Muñiz Varela," *Areito* (1979): 34–38.

16. Thomas D. Boswell and James R. Curtis, *The Cuban-American Experience: Culture, Images, and Perspectives* (Totowa, N.J.: Rowman & Littlefield, 1984), 50.

17. Azicri, "The Politics of Exile," 63–65.

18. Lisandro Pérez, "The Cuban Population of the United States: The Results of the 1980 U.S. Census of Population," *Cuban Studies/Estudios Cubanos* 15 (Summer 1985): 1–17.

19. Sergio Díaz Briquets, "Cuban-Owned Businesses in the United States," *Cuban Studios/Estudios Cubanos* 14 (Summer 1984): 57–64

seven

1. *Houston Chronicle*, 2 June 1991.

2. Robert L. Bach, "Socialist Construction and Cuban Emigration: Explorations into Mariel," *Cuban Studies/Estudios Cubanos* 15 (Summer 1985): 19–35.

3. Sergio Díaz Briquets, "Demographic and Related Determinants of Recent Cuban Emigration," *International Migration Review* 17 (1983): 98–99.

4. Quoted in Pérez, *Cuba and the United States*, 257.

5. Bach, "Socialist Construction," 31.

6. Juan M. Clark, José L. Lasaga, and Rose S. Reque, *The 1980 Mariel Exodus: An Assessment and Prospect* (Washington, D.C.: Council for Inter-American Security, 1981); Guy Gugliotta, "How a Trickle Became a Flood: Origins of the Freedom Flotilla," in *The Cuban Exodus* (Miami, 1980).

7. *Miami Herald*, 19 April and 13 December 1981.

8. Mark F. Peterson, "The Flotilla Entrants: Social Psychological Perspectives on Their Employment," *Cuban Studies/Estudios Cubanos* 12 (July 1982): 81–86.

9. Alejandro Portes, Juan M. Clark, and Robert D. Manning, "After Mariel: A Survey of the Resettlement Experiences of 1980 Cuban Refugees in Miami," *Cuban Studies/Estudios Cubanos* 15 (Summer 1985): 37.

10. Charles A. Frankenhoff, "Cuban, Haitian Refugees in Miami: Public Policy Needs for Growth from Welfare to Mainstream," *Migration Today* 13, no. 3 (1985): 6–13; Mark F. Peterson, "Work Attitudes of Mariel Boatlift Refugees," *Cuban Studies/Estudios Cubanos* 14 (Summer 1984): 1–13.

11. Robert L. Bach, "The New Cuban Immigrants: Their Background and Prospects," *Monthly Labor Review* 103, no. 4 (1980): 39–46.

12. Benigno Aguirre, "Differential Migration of Cuban Social Races: A Review and Interpretation of the Problem," *Latin American Research Review* 11 (1976): 115.

13. Susan D. Greenbaum, "Afro-Cubans in Exile: Tampa, Florida, 1886–1984," *Cuban Studies/Estudios Cubanos* 15 (Winter 1985): 59–60.

14. Julia Cuervo Hewitt, "Ifá: Oraculo Yoruba y Lucumí," *Cuban Studies/Estudios Cubanos* 13 (1983): 25–43.

15. William R. Bascom, "The Focus of Cuban Santería," in Michael M. Horowitz, ed., *Peoples and Cultures of the Caribbean* (Garden City, N.Y.: Doubleday, 1971), 522–28.

16. Jorge Duany, "Stones, Trees, and Blood: An Analysis of a Cuban Santería Ritual," *Cuban Studies/Estudios Cubanos* 12 (July 1982): 37–54.

17. Portes, Clark, and Manning, "After Mariel," 37–57.

18. Raymond A. Mohl, "On the Edge: Blacks and Hispanics in Metropolitan Miami since 1959," *Florida Historical Quarterly* 69 (July 1990): 37–56.

19. Bruce Porter and Marvin Dunn, *The Miami Riot of 1980* (Lexington, Mass.: Lexington Books, 1984).

20. Mohl, "On the Edge," 37.

21. Raymond A. Mohl, "Miami's Metropolitan Government: Retrospect and Prospect," *Florida Historical Quarterly* 63 (July 1984): 24–50.

22. R. L. Bach, J. B. Bach, and T. L. Triplett, "The Flotilla 'Entrants': Latest and Most Controversial," *Cuban Studies/Estudios Cubanos* 11–12 (July 1981–January 1982): 29–48; Gaston A. Fernandez, "Comment—the Flotilla Entrants: Are They Really Different?" *Cuban Studies/Estudios Cubanos* 11 (July 1981): 49–54.

23. "Hispanic Americans: An Emerging Group," *Statistical Bulletin* (October–December 1988): 2–12.

24. Azicri, "The Politics of Exile," 67–71.

25. *New York Times* 14 April 1990.

26. Commission Pro-Justice Mariel Prisoners, *The Mariel Injustice* (Coral Gables, Fla.: CPJMP, 1987).

27. *New York Times*, 14 April 1990.

eight

1. Pérez, "Cubans in the United States," 128, 131.

2. "Hispanic Americans: An Emerging Group," *Statistical Bulletin* (October–December 1988): 6; Jorge Duany, "Hispanics in the United States: Cultural Diversity and Identity," *Caribbean Studies* 22 (1989): 6.

3. Thomas D. Boswell, Guarione M. Díaz, and Lisandro Pérez, "Socioeconomic Context of Cuban-Americans," *Journal of Cultural Geography* 3 (Fall–Winter 1982): 32–33.

4. Ibid., 35–37.

5. "Hispanic Americans: An Emerging Group," 9.

6. B. E. Aguirre, Kent P. Schwirian, and Anthony J. La Greca, "The Residential Patterning of Latin American and Other Ethnic Populations in Metropolitan Miami," *Latin American Research Review* 15, no. 2 (1980): 35–63.

7. Boswell and Curtis, *The Cuban-American Experience*, 175–77.

8. Alejandro Portes and Rafael Mozo, "The Political Adaptation Process of Cubans and Other Ethnic Minorities in the United States: A Preliminary Analysis," *Immigration Migration Review* 19 (1986): 35–63.

9. Bernard Harding, *Key to the Jazz World* (Miami: Serrano, 1978), 108–109.

10. Quoted in Theodore Andersson and Mildred Boyer, *Bilingual Schooling in the United States*, vol. 1 (Austin, Texas: Southwest Educational Development Laboratory, 1970), 18.

11. Silvia Pedraza-Bailey, "Cubans and Mexicans in the United States: The Functions of Political and Economic Migration," *Cuban Studies/Estudios Cubanos* 11 (July 1981): 86.

12. Mohl, "Miami's Metropolitan Government," 49.

13. McNally, *Catholicism in South Florida*, 127–66.

14. James R. Curtis, "Miami's Little Havana: Yard Shrines, Cult Religion, and Landscape," *Journal of Cultural Geography* 1 (Fall–Winter 1980): 1–15.

15. Olson, *Catholic Immigrants in America*, 155–57.

16. Robert Sherrill, "Can Miami Save Itself? A City Beset by Drugs and Violence," *New York Times Magazine*, 19 July 1987, 18–26, 44–48.

17. Duany, "Hispanics in the United States: Cultural Diversity and Identity," 3–4.

18. Jaffe, Cullen, and Boswell, *The Changing Demography of Hispanic America*, 63–68; Isabel Castellanos, "The Use of English and Spanish among Cubans in Miami," *Cuban Studies* 20 (1990): 49–63.

19. Guillermo J. Grenier, "Ethnic Solidarity and the Cuban-American Labor Movement in Dade County," *Cuban Studies* 21 (1990): 29–45.

20. Alejandro Portes and Robert L. Bach, *Latin Journey: Cuban and Mexican Immigrants in the United States* (Berkeley: University of California Press, 1985); Joseph P. Fitzpatrick and Douglas T. Gurak, *Hispanic Intermarriage in New York City* (New York: Fordham University Press, 1979), 23–25.

Epilogue

1. Quoted in John F. Stack, Jr., and Christopher L. Warren, "Ethnicity and the Politics of Symbolism in Miami's Cuban Community," *Cuban Studies* 20 (1990): 18.

Selected Bibliography

Abel, Christopher, and Nissa Torrents, eds. *José Martí, Revolutionary Democrat.* Durham, N.C.: Duke University Press, 1986.

Aguilar, Luis E. *Cuba 1933: Prologue to Revolution.* Ithaca, N.Y.: Cornell University Press, 1972.

Aguirre, Benigno. "Differential Migration of Cuban Social Races." *Latin American Research Review* 11, no. 1 (1976): 103–24.

———. "Ethnic Newspapers and Politics: Diario Las Americas and the Watergate Affair." *Ethnic Groups* 2 (1979): 155–65.

Aguirre, Benigno, et al. "The Marital Stability of Cubans in the United States." *Ethnicity* 8 (1981): 387–405.

———. "The Residential Patterning of Latin American and Other Ethnic Populations in Metropolitan Miami." *Latin American Research Review* 15 (1980): 35–63.

Aimes, Hubert H. S. *A History of Slavery in Cuba, 1511–1868.* London: Frank Cass & Co., 1972.

Allahar, Anton L. "Slaves, Slave Merchants, and Slaveowners in 19th-Century Cuba." *Caribbean Studies* 21 (1988): 159–91.

Allison, Graham T. *Essence of Decision: Exploring the Cuban Missile Crisis.* Boston: Little, Brown, 1971.

Ameringer, Charles D. "The Auténtico Party and the Political Opposition in Cuba, 1952–1957." *Hispanic American Historical Review* 65 (May 1985): 327–51.

Andrews, Kenneth R. *The Spanish Caribbean: Trade and Plunder, 1536–1630.* New Haven: Yale University Press, 1978.

Ayers, Bradley Earl. *The War That Never Was: An Insider's Account of CIA Covert Operations against Cuba.* Indianapolis: Bobbs-Merrill, 1976.

Azicri, Max. "The Politics of Exile: Trends and Dynamics of Political Change among Cuban-Americans." *Cuban Studies/Estudios Cubanos* 11–12 (July 1981–January 1982): 55–73.

Bach, Robert L. "The New Cuban Exodus: Political and Economic Motivations." *Caribbean Review* 11 (Winter 1982): 22–25, 58–60.

———. "The New Cuban Immigrants: Their Background and Prospects." *Monthly Labor Review* 103 (October 1980): 39–46.

Bach, Robert L., Jennifer Bach, and Timothy Triplett. "The Flotilla 'Entrants': Latest and Most Controversial." *Cuban Studies/Estudios Cubanos* 11/12 (July 1981–January 1982): 29–48.

Balseiro, J. A., ed. *The Hispanic Presence in Florida: Yesterday and Today, 1513–1976.* Miami: E. A. Seaman, 1977.

Beck, Earl R. "The Martinez Campos Government of 1879: Spain's Last Chance in Cuba." *Hispanic American Historical Review* 56 (May 1976): 268–89.

Bender, Lynn Darrell. "The Cuban Exiles: An Analytical Study." *Journal of Latin American Studies* 5 (November 1973): 271–78.

———. "The Cuban Exiles: Gusanos or Mariposas? *Revista/Review Interamericana* 9 (1979): 331–34.

———. "Cuba, the United States, and Sugar." *Caribbean Studies* 14 (1981): 155–60.

———. "U.S. Cuban Policy under the Nixon Administration: Subtle Modifications." *Revista/Review Interamericana* 2 (Autumn 1972): 330–41.

Benjamin, Jules R. "The 'Machadato' and Cuban Nationalism, 1928–1932." *Hispanic American Historical Review* 55 (February 1975): 66–91.

———. "Interpreting the U.S. Reaction to the Cuban Revolution, 1959–1960." *Cuban Studies/Estudios Cubanos* 19 (1989): 145–65.

———. *The United States and Cuba: Hegemony and Dependent Development, 1880–1934.* Pittsburgh: University of Pittsburgh Press, 1977.

Bequer, Marta M. "A Look at Bilingual Programs in Dade County." *Educational Leadership* 35 (May 1978): 644–48.

Bergad, Laird W. "The Economic Viability of Sugar Production Based on Slave Labor in Cuba, 1859–1878." *Latin American Research Review* 24 (1989): 95–113.

———. "Slave Prices in Cuba, 1840–1875." *Hispanic American Historical Review* 67 (1987): 631–55.

Bonachea, Ramón L., and Marta San Martín. *The Cuban Insurrection, 1952–1959.* New Brunswick, N.J.: Transaction Books, 1973.

Bonsal, Philip W. *Cuba, Castro, and the United States.* Pittsburgh: University of Pittsburgh Press, 1971.

Boswell, Thomas D., Guarione M. Díaz, and Lisandro Pérez. "Socioeconomic Context of Cuban Americans." *Journal of Cultural Geography* 3 (Fall–Winter 1982): 29–41.

Boswell, Thomas D., and James R. Curtis. *The Cuban-American Experience: Culture, Images and Perspectives.* Montclair, N.J.: Rowman & Allanheld, 1983.

Bourne, Peter G. *Fidel: A Biography of Fidel Castro.* New York: Dodd, Mead & Co., 1986.

Briquets, Sergio Díaz. "Demographic and Related Determinants of Recent Cuba Emigration." *International Migration Review* 17 (Spring 1983): 59–119.

Browne, Jefferson B. *Key West: The Old and the New.* Gainesville: University Presses of Florida, 1973.

Bryce-La Porte, Roy S., and Dolores M. Mortimer, eds. *Caribbean Immigration to the United States.* Washington, D.C.: Research Institute on Immigration and Ethnic Studies, Smithsonian Institution, 1976.

Castellanos, Isabel. "The Use of English and Spanish among Cubans in Miami." *Cuban Studies* 20 (1990): 49–63.

Chayes, Abram. *The Cuban Missile Crisis: International Crises and the Role of Law.* New York: Oxford University Press, 1974.

Clark, Juan M. "The Cuban Escapees." *Latinamericanist* 6 (1 November 1970): 1–4.

Clark, Juan M., et al. *The 1980 Mariel Exodus: An Assessment and Prospect*. Washington, D.C.: Council for Inter-American Security, 1981.

Clytus, John. *Black Man in Red Cuba*. Miami: University of Miami Press, 1970.

Cooney, Rosemary Santana, and Maria Alina Contreras. "Residence Patterns of Social Register Cubans: A Study of Miami, San Juan, and New York SMSAs." *Cuban Studies/Estudios Cubanos* 8 (July 1978): 33–49.

Copeland, Ronald. "The Cuban Boatlift of 1980: Strategies in Federal Crisis Management." *Annals of the American Academy of Political and Social Science* 467 (May 1983): 138–50.

Corbitt, Duvon C. *A Study of the Chinese in Cuba, 1847–1947*. Wilmore: Asbury College Press, 1971.

———. "Immigration in Cuba." *Hispanic American Historical Review* 22 (May 1942): 280–308.

Cortada, James W. "Florida's Relations with Cuba during the Civil War." *Florida Historical Quarterly* 59 (July 1980): 42–52.

Cortés, Carlos E., ed. *The Cuban Exiles in the United States*. New York: Arno Press, 1980.

———. *Cuban Refugee Programs*. New York: Arno Press, 1980.

———. *The Cuban Experience in the United States*. New York: Arno Press, 1980.

———. *The Latin American Brain Drain to the United States*. New York: Arno Press, 1980.

Corwin, Arthur F. *Spain and the Abolition of Slavery in Cuba, 1817–1886*. Austin: University of Texas, 1967.

Crahan, Margaret E. "Catholicism in Cuba." *Cuban Studies/Estudios Cubanos* 19 (1989): 3–24.

———. "Cuba: Religion and Revolutionary Institutionalization." *Journal of Latin American Studies* 17 (1985): 319–40.

———. "Religious Penetration and Nationalism in Cuba: U.S. Methodist Activities, 1898–1958." *Revista/Review Interamericana* 8 (Summer 1978): 204–24.

Crahan, Margaret E., and Franklin W. Knight, eds. *Africa and the Caribbean: The Legacies of a Link*. Baltimore: Johns Hopkins University Press, 1979.

Cripps, Louise L. *The Spanish Caribbean, from Columbus to Castro*. Boston: G. K. Hall, 1979.

Curtis, James R. "Miami's Little Havana: Yard Shrines, Cult Religion, and Landscape." *Journal of Cultural Geography* 1 (Fall–Winter 1980): 1–15.

Curtis, James R., and Richard F. Rose. "'The Miami Sound': A Contemporary Latin Form of Place-Specific Music." *Journal of Cultural Geography* 4 (Fall–Winter 1983): 110–18.

Dana, Richard Henry. *To Cuba and Back*. Boston: Ticknor & Fields, 1859.

Dauer, Manning J., ed. *Florida's Politics and Government*. Gainesville, Florida: University Presses of Florida, 1980.

Díaz Briquets, Sergio. "Demographic and Related Determinants of Recent Cuban Emigration." *International Migration Review* 17 (Spring 1983): 95–119.

Díaz Briquets, Sergio, and Lisandro Pérez. "Cuba: The Demography of Revolution." *Population Bulletin* 36 (April 1981): 2–42.

Domínguez, Jorge I. *Cuba: Order and Revolution*. Cambridge: Harvard University Press, 1978.

———. "International and National Aspects of the Catholic Church in Cuba." *Cuban Studies/Estudios Cubanos* 19 (1989): 43–60.

Domínguez, Virginia R. *From Neighbor to Stranger: The Dilemma of Caribbean Peoples in the United States.* New Haven: Antilles Research Program, Yale University, 1970.

———. "Show Your Colors: Ethnic Divisiveness among Hispanic Caribbean Migrants." *Migration Today* 6 (February 1978): 5–9.

Duany, Jorge. "Hispanics in the United States: Cultural Diversity and Identity." *Caribbean Studies* 22 (1989): 1–25.

———. "Stones, Trees, and Blood: An Analysis of a Cuban Santería Ritual." *Cuban Studies/Estudios Cubanos* 12 (July 1982): 37–54.

Egerton, John. *Cubans in Miami: A Third Dimension in Racial and Cultural Relations.* Nashville: Race Relations Information Center, 1969.

Epstein, Erwin H. "Social Structure, Race Relations, and Political Stability under U.S. Administration." *Revista/Review Interamericana* 8 (Summer 1978): 192–203.

Fagan, Richard R., Richard M. Brody, and Thomas J. O'Leary. *Cubans in Exile: Disaffection and Revolution.* Stanford: Stanford University Press, 1968.

Fagen, Patricia Weiss. "Antonio Maceo: Heroes, History, and Historiography." *Latin America Research Review* 11 (1976): 69–94.

Fagg, John Edwin. *Cuba, Haiti, and the Dominican Republic.* Englewood Cliffs, N.J.: Prentice-Hall, 1965.

Farber, Samuel. "The Cuban Communists in the Early Stages of the Cuban Revolution." *Latin America Research Review* 18, no. 1 (1983): 59–84.

———. *Revolution and Reaction in Cuba, 1933–1960.* Middletown, Conn.: Wesleyan University Press, 1976.

Fernández, Fernando Ortiz. *Cuban Counterpoint: Tobacco and Sugar.* New York: Alfred A. Knopf, 1947.

Fernández, Gastón A. "Comment—the Flotilla Entrants: Are They Different?" *Cuban Studies/Estudios Cubanos* 11 (July 1981): 49–54.

———. "The Freedom Flotilla: A Legitimacy Crisis of Cuban Socialism?" *Journal of Interamerican Studies and World Affairs* 24 (May 1982): 183–209.

Fernández, Susan. "The Sanctity of Property: American Responses to Cuban Expropriations, 1959–1984." *Cuban Studies/Estudios Cubanos* 14 (Summer 1984): 21–34.

Ferree, Myra Marx. "Employment without Liberation—Cuban Women in the United States." *Social Science Quarterly* 60 (June 1979): 35–50.

Finnan, Christine Robertson. "Occupational Assimilation of Refugees." *International Migration Review* 15 (Spring–Summer 1981): 292–309.

Fitchen, Edward D. "The United States Military Government: Alexis E. Frye and Cuban Education, 1898–1902." *Revista/Review Interamericana* 2, no. 2 (Summer 1972): 123–49.

Fitzgibbon, Russell H. *Cuba and the United States, 1900–1935.* New York: Russell & Russell, 1964.

Fitzpatrick, Joseph P., and Lourdes Travieso Parker. "Hispanic-Americans in the Eastern United States." *Annals of the American Academy of Political and Social Science* 454 (March 1981): 98–110.

Foner, Philip S. *Antonio Maceo: The "Bronze Titan" of Cuba's Struggle forIndependence.* New York: Monthly Review Press, 1977.

Fox, Geoffrey E. "Working-Class Emigrés from Cuba: A Study of Counter-Revolutionary Consciousness." Ph.D. diss. Northwestern University, 1975.

Frankenhoff, Charles A. "Cuban, Haitian Refugees in Miami: Public Policy Needs for Growth from Welfare to Mainstream." *Migration Today* 13, no. 3 (1985): 7–13.

Gallagher, Patrick Lee. *The Cuban Exile: A Socio-Political Analysis*. New York: Arno Press, 1980.

Gellman, Irwin F. *Roosevelt and Batista: Good Neighbor Diplomacy in Cuba, 1933–1945*. Albuquerque: University of New Mexico Press, 1973.

Gernard, Renée. *The Cuban Americans*. Boston: Chelsea House, 1988.

Gonzales, Edward. *Cuba under Castro: The Limits of Charisma*. New York: Houghton Mifflin, 1974.

Gould, Lewis. *The Spanish-American War and President McKinley*. Lawrence: University of Kansas Press, 1980.

Gray, Richard Butler. *José Martí, Cuban Patriot*. Gainesville: University Presses of Florida, 1962.

Greenbaum, Susan D. "Afro-Cubans in Exile: Tampa, Florida, 1886–1984." *Cuban Studies/Estudios Cubanos* 15 (Winter 1985): 59–72.

Grenier, Guillermo J. "Ethnic Solidarity and the Cuban-American Labor Movement in Dade County." *Cuban Studies* 21 (1990): 28–42.

Grobart, Fabio. "The Cuban Working Class Movement from 1925 to 1933." *Science and Society* 39 (Spring 1975): 73–102.

Guggenheim, Harry F. *The United States and Cuba*. New York: Arno Press, 1969.

Hall, Gwendolyn Midlo. *Social Control in Slave Plantation Societies: A Comparison of St. Domingue and Cuba*. Baltimore: Johns Hopkins University Press, 1971.

Halperin, Maurice. *The Rise and Decline of Fidel Castro: An Essay in Contemporary History*. Berkeley: University of California Press, 1972.

Harrington, Mark Raymond. *Cuba before Columbus*. New York: Museum of the American Indian, 1921.

Hart, Francis Russell. *The Siege of Havana, 1762*. Boston: Houghton Mifflin, 1931.

Healy, David F. *The United States in Cuba, 1898–1902*. Madison: University of Wisconsin Press, 1963.

Hewitt, Julia Cuervo. "Ifá: Oraculo Yoruba y Lucumi." *Cuban Studies/Estudios Cubanos* 13 (Winter 1983): 25–40.

Hinckle, Warren, and William W. Turner. *The Fish Is Red: The Story of the Secret War against Castro*. New York: Harper & Row, 1981.

"Hispanic Americans: An Emerging Group." *Statistical Bulletin* (October–December 1988): 2–12.

Hitchman, James H. *Leonard Wood and Cuban Independence, 1898–1902*. The Hague: Marinus Nijhoff, 1971.

Hitchman, James H. "U.S. Control over Cuban Sugar Production, 1898–1902." *Journal of Inter-American Studies and World Affairs* 12 (January 1970): 90–106.

Hoernel, Robert B. "Sugar and Social Change in Oriente, Cuba, 1898–1946." *Journal of Latin American Studies* 8 (November 1976): 215–49.

Hoffman, Paul E. *The Spanish Crown and the Defense of the Caribbean, 1535–1585*. Baton Rouge: Louisiana University Press, 1980.

Humboldt, Alexander von. *The Island of Cuba*. New York: Derby & Jackson, 1856.

Hyman, J. Patton. "Immigration: The Status of Cuban Refugees in the United States." *University of Florida Law Review* 21 (Summer 1968): 73–84.

Jenks, Leland Hamilton. *Our Cuban Colony*. New York: Vanguard Press, 1928.

Jenna, William W. *Metropolitan Miami: A Demographic Overview*. Coral Gables, Fla.: University of Miami Press, 1972.

Johnson, Haynes B. *The Bay of Pigs*. New York: Dell, 1964.

Judson, C. Fred. *Cuba and the Revolutionary Myth: The Political Education of the Cuban Rebel Army, 1953–63*. Boulder, Colo.: Westview Press, 1984.

Karol, K. S. *Guerrillas in Power: The Course of the Cuban Revolution*. New York: Hill & Wang, 1970.

Kennedy, Edward F. "The Refugee Act of 1980." *International Migration Review* 15 (Spring–Summer 1981): 141–56.

Kiple, Kenneth F. *Blacks in Colonial Cuba, 1774–1899*. Gainesville: University Presses of Florida, 1976.

Kirk, John M. *José Martí, Mentor of the Cuban Nation*. Gainesville: University Presses of Florida, 1983.

———. "Toward an Understanding of the Church-State Rapprochement in Revolutionary Cuba." *Cuban Studies/Estudios Cubanos* 19 (1989): 25–42.

Knight, Franklin W. "Jamaican Migrants and the Cuban Sugar Industry, 1900–1934." In *Between Slavery and Free Labor: The Spanish-Speaking Caribbean in the Nineteenth Century*, edited by Manuel Moreno Fraginals, Frank Moya Pons, and Stanley L. Engerman. Baltimore: Johns Hopkins University Press, 1985.

———. "Origins of Wealth and the Sugar Revolution in Cuba, 1750–1850." *Hispanic American Historical Review* 57 (May 1977): 231–53.

———. "Slavery, Race, and Social Structure in Cuba during the Nineteenth Century." In *Slavery and Race in Latin America*, edited by Robert Brent Toplin. Westport, Conn.: Greenwood Press, 1974.

Klein, Herbert S. *Slavery in the Americas: A Comparative Study of Cuba and Virginia*. Chicago: University of Chicago Press, 1967.

Kuethe, Allan J. *Cuba, 1753–1815: Crown, Military, and Society*. Knoxville: University of Tennessee Press, 1986.

Langley, Lester P. *The Cuban Policy of the United States*. New York: John Wiley & Sons, 1968.

Legrande, William. "Continuity and Change in the Cuban Political Elite." *Cuban Studies/Estudios Cubanos* 8 (July 1978): 1–32.

———. "Cuba Policy Recycled." *Foreign Policy* 46 (Spring 1982): 105–17.

Liss, Sheldon B. *Roots of Revolution: Radical Thought in Cuba*. Lincoln: University of Nebraska Press. 1987.

Llanas, José. *Cuban Americans: Masters of Survival*. Cambridge, Mass.: Abt Books, 1982.

Llerena, Mario. *The Unsuspected Revolution: The Birth and Rise of Castroism*. Ithaca, N.Y.: Cornell University Press, 1978.

Loescher, Gilburt, and John Scanlan. "U.S. Foreign Policy, 1959–1980: Impact on Refugee Flow from Cuba." *Annals of the American Academy of Political and Social Science* 467 (May 1983): 116–37.

Long, Durward. "'La Resistencia': Tampa's Immigrant Labor Union." *Labor History* 6 (Autumn 1965): 193–210.

———. "Labor Relations in the Tampa Cigar Industry, 1885–1911." *Labor History* 12 (Autumn 1971): 551–59.

Losman, Donald. "The Embargo of Cuba: An Economic Appraisal." *Caribbean Studies* 14 (October 1974): 95–119.

Lundahl, Matt. "A Note on Haitian Migration to Cuba, 1890–1934." *Cuban Studies/Estudios Cubanos* 12 (July 1982): 21–36.

Lyon, Eugene. "Pedro Menéndez's Strategic Plan for the Florida Peninsula." *Florida Historical Quarterly* 67 (July 1988): 1–14.

MacGaffey, Wyatt. "Social Structure and Mobility in Cuba." *Anthropological Quarterly* 34 (January 1961): 94–109.

MacGaffey, Wyatt, and Clifford R. Barnett. *Twentieth-Century Cuba*. Garden City, N.Y.: Anchor Books, 1965.

Mackey, William F., and Von Nieda Beebe. *Bilingual Schools for a Bicultural Community: Miami's Adaptation to the Cuban Refugees*. Rowley, Mass.: Newbury House, 1977.

MacNamara, Mark. "Santería." *Miami Magazine*, November 1982, 98–101, 109–10, 169–70.

Madden, Richard Robert. *The Island of Cuba*. London: C. Gilpin, 1849.

Mankiewicz, Frank, and Kirby Jones. *With Fidel: A Portrait of Castro and Cuba*. New York: Playboy Press, 1975.

Marable, Manning. "The Fire This Time—the Miami Rebellion." *Black Scholar* 11 (July–August 1980): 2–18.

Martin, Lionel. *The Early Fidel: Roots of Castro's Communism*. Secaucus, N.J.: Lyle Stuart, 1978.

Masferrer, Marianne, and Carmelo Mesa Lago. "The Gradual Integration of the Black in Cuba: Under the Colony, the Republic, and the Revolution." In *Slavery and Race in Latin America*, edited by Robert Brent Toplin, 348–84. Westport, Conn.: Greenwood Press, 1974.

Massey, Douglas, and Kathleen M. Schnabel. "Recent Trends in Hispanic Immigration to the United States." *International Migration Review* 17 (Summer 1983): 212–43.

Masud-Piloto, Felix Roberto. *With Open Arms: Cuban Migration to the United States*. Totowa, N.J.: Rowman & Littlefield, 1988.

May, Robert. *The Southern Dream of a Caribbean Empire, 1859–1861*. Baton Rouge: Louisiana State University Press, 1973.

Mesa-Lago, Carmelo. *Cuba in the 1970s: Pragmaticism and Institutionalization*. Albuquerque: University of New Mexico Press, 1974.

———. *Revolutionary Change in Cuba*. Pittsburgh: University of Pittsburgh Press, 1971.

Millett, Allan Reed. *The Politics of Intervention: The Military Occupation of Cuba, 1906–1909*. Columbus: Ohio State University Press, 1968.

Mohl, Raymond A. "Miami's Metropolitan Government: Retrospect and Prospect." *Florida Historical Quarterly* 63 (July 1984): 24–50.

———. "Race, Ethnicity, and Urban Politics in the Miami Metropolitan Area." *Florida Environmental and Urban Issues* 9 (April 1982): 2–6, 23–25.

Moncarz, Raul. "Effects of Professional Restrictions on Cuban Refugees in Selected Health Professions in the United States, 1959–1969." *International Migration Review* 8 (1970): 22–30.

———. "The Golden Cage—Cubans in Miami." *International Migration Review* 16 (1978): 160–73.

———. "A Model of Professional Adaptation of Refugees: The Cuban Case in the U.S., 1959–1970." *International Migration* 11 (1973): 171–83.

———. "Professional Adaptation of Cuban Physicians in the United States, 1959–1969." *International Migration Review* 4 (Spring 1970): 80–86.

Montaner, Carlos Alberto. "The Roots of Anti-Americanism in Cuba." *Caribbean Review* 13 (Spring 1984): 13–16, 42–46.

Morley, Morris H. "The U.S. Imperial State in Cuba, 1952–1958: Policymaking and Capitalist Interests." *Journal of Latin America Studies* 14 (May 1982): 143–70.

Mormino, Gary R. "Tampa and the New Urban South: The Weight Strike of 1899." *Florida Historical Quarterly* 60 (January 1982): 337–55.

Mormino, Gary R., and George E. Pozzetta. *The Immigrant World of Ybor City: Italians and Their Latin Neighbors in Tampa, 1885–1985*. Urbana: University of Illinois Press, 1987.

Morray, J. P. *The Second Revolution in Cuba*. New York: Monthly Review Press, 1962.

Neil, Andrew. "America's Latin Beat: A Survey of South Florida." *Economist* 285 (16 October 1982): 1–26.

O'Connor, James. "Agrarian Reform in Cuba, 1959–1963." *Science and Society* 32 (Spring 1968): 169–217.

Oglesby, J. C. M. "Faltering Revolution Sparks Mass Exodus from Cuba." *International Perspective* (May–June 1980): 33–36.

Orum, Thomas Tondee. "The Politics of Color: The Racial Dimension of Cuban Politics during the Early Republican Years, 1900–1912." Ph.D. diss. New York University, 1975.

Osgood, Cornelius. *The Ciboney Culture of Cayo Redondo, Cuba*. New Haven, Conn.: Yale University Press. 1942.

Padula, Alfred L. "The Fall of the Bourgeoisie in Cuba, 1959–1961." Ph.D. diss. University of New Mexico, 1975.

Page, John Bryan, et al. *The Ethnography of Cuban Drug Use*. Miami: University of Miami Center for Social Research on Drug Abuse, 1981.

Paterson, Thomas G. *Contesting Castro: The United States and the Triumph of the Cuban Revolution*. New York: Oxford University Press, 1994.

Pedraza-Bailey, Silvia. "Cubans and Mexicans in the United States: The Function of Political and Economic Migration." *Cuban Studies/Estudios Cubanos* 11 (July 1981) and 12 (January 1982): 79–97.

———. "Cuba's Exiles: Portrait of a Refugee Migration." *International Migration Review* 19 (1985): 4–34.

———. "Political and Economic Migrants in America: Cubans and Mexicans." Ph.D. diss. University of Chicago, 1980.

Pérez, Lisandro. "Immigrant Economic Adjustment and Family Organization: The Cuban Success Story Reexamined." *International Migration Review* 20 (1986): 4–20.

Pérez, Louis A., Jr. *Army Politics in Cuba, 1898–1958*. Pittsburgh: University of Pittsburgh Press, 1976.

———. "Army Politics in Socialist Cuba." *Journal of Latin American Studies* 8 (November 1976): 251–71.

———. *Cuba and the United States: Ties of Singular Intimacy*. Athens: University of Georgia Press, 1991.

———. *Cuba between Empires, 1878–1902*. Pittsburgh: University of Pittsburgh Press, 1983.

———. *Cuba: Between Reform and Revolution*. New York: Oxford University Press, 1988.

————. Cuba under the Platt Amendment, 1902–1934. Pittsburgh: University of Pittsburgh Press, 1986.

————. "Cubans in Tampa: From Exiles to Immigrants, 1892–1901." *Florida Histoical Quarterly* 57 (October 1978): 129–40.

————. "The Imperial Design: Politics and Pedagogy in Occupied Cuba, 1899– 1902." *Cuban Studies/Estudios Cubanos* 12 (Summer 1982): 1–19.

————. "Insurrection, Intervention, and the Transformation of Land Tenure Systems in Cuba, 1895–1902." *Hispanic American Historical Review* 65 (May 1985): 229–54.

————. *Intervention, Revolution, and Politics in Cuba, 1913–1921.* Pittsburgh: University of Pittsburgh Press, 1978.

————. "Politics, Peasants, and People of Color: The 1912 'Race War' in Cuba Reconsidered." *Hispanic American Historical Review* 66 (1986): 509–39.

————. "Supervision of a Protectorate: The United States and the Cuban Army, 1898–1908." *Hispanic American Historical Review* 52 (May 1972): 250–71.

————. "The Pursuit of Pacification: Banditry and the United States Occupation of Cuba, 1889–1902." *Journal of Latin American Studies* 18 (1986): 313–32.

————. "Reminiscences of a 'Lector': Cuban Cigarworkers in Tampa." *Florida Historical Quarterly* 53 (April 1975): 443–49.

Pérez-López, Jorge F. "Cuban Industrial Production, 1930–1958." *Caribbean Studies* 14 (1981): 161–68.

Peterson, Mark F. "The Flotilla Entrants: Social Psychological Perspectives on Their Employment." *Cuban Studies/Estudios Cubanos* 11–12 (July 1981–January 1982): 79–98.

Philipson, Lorrin, and Rafael Llerena. *Freedom Flights: Cuban Refugees Talk about Life under Castro and How They Fled His Regime.* New York: Random House, 1980.

Phillips, R. Hart. *Cuba, Island of Paradox.* New York: McDowell, Obolensky, 1959.

Pierson, William Whatley, Jr. "Francisco de Arango y Parreño." *Hispanic American Historical Review* 16 (November 1936): 451–78.

Plank, John, ed. *Cuba and the United States: Long-Range Perspectives.* Washington, D.C.: Brookings Institution, 1967.

Portes, Alejandro. "Dilemmas of a Golden Exile: Integration of Cuban Refugee Families in Milwaukee." *American Sociological Review* 34 (August 1969): 505–18.

————. "Assimilation or Consciousness: Perceptions of U.S. Society among Recent Latin American Immigrants to the United States." *Social Forces* 59 (September 1980): 200–24.

————. "Immigrant Aspirations." *Sociology of Education* 51 (October 1978): 241–60.

Portes, Alejandro, et al. "The New Wave: A Statistical Profile of Recent Cuban Exiles to the United States." *Cuban Studies/Estudios Cubanos* 7 (January 1977): 1–32.

————. "Six Years Later: The Process of Incorporation of Cuban Exiles in the United States, 1973–1979." *Cuban Studies/Estudios Cubanos* 11–12 (July 1981–January 1982): 1–24.

Portes, Alejandro, and Rafael Mozo. "The Political Adaptation Process of Cubans and Other Ethnic Minorities in the United States: A Preliminary Analysis." *International Migration Review* 19, no. 1 (1985): 35–63.

Portes, Alejandro, and Robert L. Bach. "Immigrant Earnings: Cuban and Mexican Immigrants in the United States." *International Migration Review* 14 (Fall 1980): 315–41.

Poyo, Gerald E. "The Anarchist Challenge to the Cuban Independence Movement, 1885–1890." *Cuban Studies/Estudios Cubanos* 15 (Winter 1985): 29–42.

———. "Cuban Patriots in Key West, 1878–1886: Guardians at the Separatist Ideal." *Florida Historical Quarterly* 61 (July 1982): 20–36.

———. "Cuban Revolutionaries and Monroe County Reconstruction Politics, 1868–1876." *Florida Historical Quarterly* 55 (April 1977): 407–23.

———. "Evolution of Cuban Separatist Thought in the Emigré Communities of the United States, 1848–1895." *Hispanic American Historical Review* 66 (1986): 485–507.

———. *"With All, and for the Good of All": The Emergence of Popular Natonalism in the Cuban Communities of the United States, 1848–1898*. Gainesville: University Presses of Florida, 1990.

Prieto, Yolanda. "Cuban Women in the U.S. Labor Force: Perspectives on the Nature of Change." *Cuban Studies* 17 (1987): 73–90.

Prohías, Rafael J., and Lourdes Casal. *The Cuban Minority in the U.S. Preliminary Report*. Boca Raton: Florida Atlantic University Press, 1974.

Provenzo, Eugene. "Exiled Teachers and the Cuban Revolution." *Cuban Studies/Estudios Cubanos* 13 (Winter 1983): 1–16.

Richmond, Marie LaLiberte. *Immigrant Adaptation and Family Structure among Cubans in Miami, Florida*. New York, 1980.

Rogg, Eleanor M. *The Assimilation of Cuban Exiles: The Role of Community and Class*. New York: Aberdeen Press, 1974.

———. "Comment—Six Years Later: The Process of Incorporation of Cuban Exiles in the United States." *Cuban Studies/Estudios Cubanos* 11 (January 1982): 25–28.

———. "The Influence of a Strong Refugee Community on the Economic Adjustment of Its Members." *International Migration Review* 5 (Winter 1971): 474–81.

Ropka, Gerald William. *The Evolving Residential Pattern of the Mexican, Puerto Rican, and Cuban Population of the City of Chicago*. New York: Arno Press, 1980.

Ruiz, Ramón Eduardo. *Cuba: The Making of a Revolution*. Amherst: University of Massachusetts Press, 1968.

Salas, Luis P. "The Traumas of Exile." *Caribbean Review* 9 (Winter 1980): 42–43.

Salter, Paul S., and Robert C. Mings. "The Projected Impact of Cuban Settlement on Voting Patterns in Metropolitan Miami, Florida." *Professional Geographer* 24 (May 1972): 123–31.

Sanders, Jimmy M., and Victor Nee. "Limits of Ethnic Solidarity in the Enclave Economy." *American Sociological Review* 52 (December 1987): 745–73.

Sauer, Carl Ortwin. *The Early Spanish Main*. Berkeley: University of California Press, 1966.

Scanlan, John, and Gilburt Loescher. "U.S. Foreign Policy, 1959–1980: Impact on Reguee Flow from Cuba." *Annals of the American Academy of Political and Social Sciences* 467 (May 1983): 116–37.

Scott, Rebecca J. "Class Relations in Sugar and Political Mobilization in Cuba, 1868–1899." *Cuban Studies/Estudios Cubanos* 15 (Winter 1985): 15–28.

————. "Explaining Abolition: Contradiction, Adaptation, and Challenge in Cuban Slave Society, 1860–1886." *Comparative Studies in Society and History* 26 (January 1984): 83–111.

————. "Gradual Abolition and the Dynamics of Slave Emancipation in Cuba, 1868–1886." *Hispanic American Historical Review* 63 (August 1983): 449–77.

————. *Slave Emancipation in Cuba: The Transition to Free Labor, 1860–1899.* Princeton, N.J.: Princeton University Press, 1985.

Severin, Timothy. *The Golden Antilles.* New York: Alfred A. Knopf, 1970.

Sims, Harold D. "Cuban Labor and the Communist Party, 1937–1958: An Interpretation." *Cuban Studies/Estudios Cubanos* 15 (Winter 1985): 43–58.

Simpson, George Eaton. "Afro-American Religions and Religious Behavior." *Caribbean Studies* 12 (1979): 5–30.

Smallwood, Lawrence. "African Cultural Dimensions in Cuba." *Journal of Black Studies* 6 (December 1975): 191–99.

Smith, Robert Freeman. *The United States and Cuba: Business and Diplomacy, 1917–1960.* New Haven, Conn.: College and University Press, 1960.

Spalding, Hobart A., Jr. "The Workers' Struggle: 1850–1961." *Cuba Review* 4 (July 1974): 3–10.

Stack, John F., Jr., and Christopher L. Warren. "Ethnicity and the Politics of Symbolism in Miami's Cuban Community." *Cuban Studies* 20 (1990): 11–28.

Stevenson, James. "Cuban Americans: New Urban Class." Ph.D. diss. Wayne State University, 1973.

Stubbs, Jean. *Tobacco in the Periphery: A Case Study in Cuban Labour History, 1860–1958.* London: Cambridge University Press, 1985.

Suárez, Andrés. "The Cuban Revolution: The Road to Power." *Latin American Research Review* 7 (Autumn 1972): 5–29.

Suchlicki, Jaime. *Cuba, from Columbus to Castro.* New York: Charles Scribner's Sons, 1974.

————. *University Students and Revolution in Cuba, 1920–1968.* Coral Gables, Fla.: University of Miami Press, 1969.

Szapocznik, José, ed. *Cuban-Americans: Acculturation, Adjustment, and the Family.* Washington, D.C.: National Coalition of Hispanic Mental Health, 1978.

Szulc, Tad. *Fidel: A Critical Portrait.* New York: Morrow, 1986.

Thomas, Hugh. "Middle-Class Politics and the Cuban Revolution." In *The Politics of Conformity in Latin America*, edited by Claudio Veliz. New York: Oxford University Press, 1967.

Thomas, John. "Cuban Refugee Program." *Welfare in Review* 1 (September 1963): 1–20.

————. "Cuban Refugees in the United States." *International Migration Review* 1 (Spring 1967): 46–57.

————. "U.S.A. as a Country of First Choice." *International Migration* 3 (1965): 5–16.

Turner, Mary. "Chinese Contract Labour in Cuba, 1847–1874." *Caribbean Studies* 14 (July 1974): 66–81.

Turton, Peter. *José Martí, Architect of Cuba's Freedom.* London: Zed Books, 1986.

Urban, C. Stanley. "The Africanization of Cuba Scare, 1853–1855." *Hispanic American Historical Review* 37 (February 1957): 27–45.

Useem, Bert. "Peasant Involvement in the Cuban Revolution." *Journal of Peasant Studies* 5 (October 1977): 99–111.

Valdes-Cruz, Rosa. "The Black Man's Contribution to Cuban Culture." *The Americas* 34 (October 1977): 244–51.

Verril, A. Hyatt. *Cuba, Past and Present*. New York: Dodd, Mead & Co., 1920.

Victoria, Nelson Amaro. "Mass and Class in the Origins of the Cuban Revolution." In *Masses in Latin America*, edited by Irving Louis Horowitz. New York: Oxford University Press, 1970.

Wallich, Henry Christopher. *Monetary Problems of an Export Economy: The Cuban Experience, 1917–1947*. New York: Arno Press, 1978.

Walsh, Bryan O. "Cuban Refugee Children." *Journal of Inter-American Studies and World Affairs* 13 (July–October 1971): 378–414.

Welch, Richard E., Jr. *Response to Revolution: The United States and the Cuban Revolution, 1959–1961*. Chapel Hill: University of North Carolina Press, 1985.

Wenk, Michael J. "Adjustment and Assimilation: The Cuban Refugee Experience." *International Migration Review* 3 (Fall 1968): 38–49.

Williams, Eric. *From Columbus to Castro: The History of the Caribbean, 1492–1969*. London: André Deutsch, 1970.

Williams, William Appleman. *The United States, Cuba, and Castro*. New York: Monthly Review Press, 1962.

Wiliamson, David. "Adaptation of Socio-Cultural Change: Working Class Cubans in New Orleans." *Caribbean Studies* 16 (1977): 217–27.

Wilson, Kenneth L., and W. Allen Martin. "Ethnic Enclaves: A Comparison of the Cuban and Black Economies in Miami." *American Journal of Sociology* 88 (July 1982): 135–60.

Wilson, Kenneth L., and Alejandro Portes. "Immigrant Enclaves: An Analysis of the Labor Market Experience of Cubans in Miami." *American Journal of Sociology* 86 (September 1980): 295–319.

Winsberg, Morton D. "Ethnic Competition for Residential Space in Miami, Florida, 1979–80." *American Journal of Economics and Sociology* 38 (October 1979): 403–18.

———. "The Latin Melting Pot Is Boiling Over." *American Journal of Economics and Sociology* 40 (October 1981): 349–52.

Wisan, Joseph E. *The Cuban Crisis as Reflected in the New York Press, 1895–1898*. New York: Octagon Press, 1965.

Wolf, Donna M. "The Cuban People of Color and the Independence Movement: 1879–1895." *Revista/Review Interamericana* 5 (Autumn 1975): 403–21.

Wright, Irene A. "'Rescates': With Special Reference to Cuba, 1599–1610." *Hispanic American Historical Review* 3 (August 1920): 333–61.

———. *The Early History of Cuba, 1492–1586*. New York: Macmillan, 1916.

Wyden, Peter. *Bay of Pigs: The Untold Story*. New York: Simon & Schuster, 1979.

Zimbalist, Andrew. "Incentives and Planning in Cuba." *Latin America Research Review* 24, no. 1 (1989): 65–93.

Index

The Authors

James S. Olson holds a Ph.D. from the State University of New York at Stony Brook and is currently Distinguished Professor of History at Sam Houston State University in Huntsville, Texas. He is the author of many books, including *The Ethnic Dimension in American History* (1979), *Native Americans in the Twentieth Century* (1984), *Catholic Immigrants in America* (1987), and *Where the Domino Fell* (1991).

Judy Olson holds a Ph.D. from Texas A&M University and is currently director of the Learning Assistance Center and assistant professor of bilingual education at Sam Houston State University.

The Editor

Thomas J. Archdeacon is professor of history at the University of Wisconsin-Madison, where he has been a member of the faculty since 1972. A native of New York City, he earned his doctorate from Columbia University under the direction of Richard B. Morris. His first book, *New York City, 1664–1710: Conquest and Change* (1976), examines relations between Dutch and English residents of that community during the late seventeenth and early eighteenth centuries. Building on that work, he has increasingly concentrated his research and teaching on topics related to immigration and ethnic-group relations. In 1983 he published *Becoming American: An Ethnic History.*